36.95

Presbyterian Missions
and Cultural Interaction
in the Far Southwest,
1850–1950

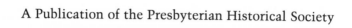

A Publication of the Presbyterian Historical Society

Presbyterian Missions and Cultural Interaction in the Far Southwest, 1850–1950

MARK T. BANKER

University of Illinois Press
Urbana and Chicago

© 1993 by the Board of Trustees of the University of Illinois
Manufactured in the United States of America
C 5 4 3 2 1

This book is printed on acid-free paper.

Library of Congress Cataloging-in-Publication Data

Banker, Mark T., 1951–
    Presbyterian missions and cultural interaction in the far
Southwest, 1850–1950 / Mark T. Banker.
        p.   cm.
    Includes bibliographical references and index.
    ISBN 0-252-01929-6 (alk. paper)
    1. Presbyterian Church — Missions — Southwest, New —
History.
    I. Title.
    BV2800.B36   1992   91-44767
    266'.5179 — dc20   CIP

Contents

Maps

Tables

Preface

In anticipation of the June 1990 meeting of the General Assembly of the Presbyterian Church (U.S.A.) in Salt Lake City, a special task force of the Presbytery of Utah prepared a brief report entitled *A Present Day Look at the Latter-day Saints*. While commenting frankly on many significant differences between Mormonism and Reformed Christianity, this report recognizes many admirable Mormon traits and calls for Presbyterians to relate to Mormons with "love," "openness," "empathy," and "respect." The spirit of this report is very much in accord with the general Presbyterian stance on cultural and religious pluralism as stated time and again over the past twenty-five years. Nevertheless, it would most certainly surprise the missionary pioneers who more than 120 years ago carried Presbyterianism to Utah and the adjacent territories of New Mexico and Arizona.

When the 1848 Treaty of Guadalupe-Hidalgo first brought the Far Southwest under United States control, these territories were hardly an empty frontier. In addition to Mormons, who had settled in Utah only a few years earlier, westward-moving Anglo Americans encountered a deeply entrenched Hispanic Catholic population in the upper Rio Grande valley of northern New Mexico and southern Colorado, and an array of Native American peoples scattered through the region. The Presbyterian response to the "native" southwesterners was simultaneously typical of and quite different from that of other Anglo Americans who arrived in the region in the post–Civil War era.

Like most of the newcomers, the missionaries saw many shortcomings in the peoples they encountered. An array of pejorative adjectives such as "degraded," "benighted," "superstitious," and "ignorant" colored early missionary letters and official reports from the Southwest. While Presbyterians no doubt recognized many obvious differences in the three southwestern peoples, mission promoters emphasized with alarm that the Southwest's

Native Americans, New Mexicans (the name this study will use for the region's Hispanic Catholic people), and Mormons all shared a common flaw. They were all exceptions to the prevailing cultural standards of mainstream American society. Like many other prominent members of that society, Presbyterians identified closely with its most basic cultural institutions and considered it their duty to share these superior ways with those who were less fortunate. The typical nineteenth-century view that cultural heterogeneity would bring only misfortune to their own nation and society strengthened this impulse and heightened the urgency of the Presbyterian response to southwestern pluralism.

In contrast to many of their fellow Anglo-American newcomers to the Southwest, early Presbyterian missionaries were confident that the native southwesterners could *and* should be incorporated into the national mainstream. Missionaries observed that all three southwestern peoples were capable of civilization and that Christian charity and the grace of God would inevitably achieve this end. Buoying this optimism was the Presbyterian conviction that they had a panacea that would cure the ills of the native southwesterners. Mindful of their Calvinist heritage, of the absence of public education in the region, and of the strategies of their fellow missionaries among foreign peoples overseas, Presbyterians instinctively turned to mission schools to reach and regenerate southwestern Indians, New Mexicans, and Mormons. In the Presbyterian scheme Christian education would produce nothing less than a radical cultural transformation. By exposing southwestern children to Anglo-American cultural institutions and converting as many of them as possible to Protestant Christianity, mission schools would save the southwesterners — and in turn the nation — from their degenerate ways.

Thanks to the promotional efforts of the energetic Sheldon Jackson and financial support from Presbyterian women, the mission school became by 1880 *the* key in the Presbyterian strategy for the Southwest. A decade later Presbyterians operated seventy-six schools in the region that served 4,300 students and employed 183 teachers. From the mid-1880s until the end of the century, between four and five thousand southwestern youths annually enrolled in Presbyterian schools. Presbyterians, however, never intended for the mission schools to be permanent. As the Southwest slowly became incorporated into the national mainstream and as new developments in the broader American society and their church attracted Presbyterian attention to other causes, retrenchment of the mission school effort occurred. By 1920 fewer than 1,500 southwestern youths attended Presbyterian schools. While remnants of the once far-flung missionary effort remain even to this day, in the 1950s Presbyterians abandoned their once ambitious crusade to transform the Southwest.

Accounts of missionary work traditionally focus on the impact of that work on the target populations. For example, in writing about their own endeavors, missionaries invariably cite numbers of converts and graphic improvements in the lives of the people among whom they labor. Other observers who view mission endeavors favorably generally share this concern with end results. Indeed, even critics who conclude that uplift efforts are arrogant and self-serving also point to the effects of those efforts on the supposed beneficiaries to prove their case.

Thus it is hardly surprising that commentators on the Presbyterian experience in the Southwest have concentrated almost entirely on the impact of that work on the native southwesterners. That impact was indeed significant and undoubtedly greater than generally recognized. Presbyterian mission schools filled an educational void in the Southwest until well into the twentieth century; moreover, missionaries provided medical care and other services to many isolated communities throughout the region long before government agencies assumed these duties. These endeavors improved the quality of life for many southwesterners and helped them adapt to the new society that had assumed control of their homeland.

The Presbyterian impact on the Southwest, however, was more varied and complex than most observers who have written about it have suggested. Presbyterian influence also helped erode traditional ways and thus contributed to traumatic tensions and fissures within the three southwestern societies. What is most clear, however, is that the southwestern mission schools did *not* produce the radical cultural transformation Presbyterians initially anticipated. More often than not, native southwesterners who came into contact with Presbyterian missionaries selectively adopted some aspects of Anglo-Protestant culture and rejected others, often including the missionaries' own faith. In short, the evidence in this study suggests that the targets of the Presbyterian missionary effort were *neither* passive beneficiaries of the newcomers' superior ways *nor* innocent victims of a Presbyterian brand of cultural imperialism. Additional studies, which more fully utilize anthropological methodology and resources from the native perspective, are needed to test and refine these hypotheses and to shed further light on the direct effects of the Presbyterian schools.

The primary concern of this study, however, is not the Presbyterian impact on the Southwest but instead the impact of the Southwest on the Presbyterians. Previous studies of the Presbyterian missions in the Southwest almost completely overlook this dimension of the missionary experience. Indeed, until recently studies of the American Protestant missionary effort in general have ignored this aspect of mission work, in spite of its obviously significant implications for the broader scope of American social history. By considering how service in the Southwest affected individual missionaries and how their experiences, in turn, influenced their church's mission perspective, this investigation hopes to contribute to a more balanced under-standing of the Anglo-Protestant encounter with cultural and religious diversity. Secondly, it hopes to shed light on the important and controversial response of altruistic-minded individuals and groups to the needs of those they consider less fortunate.

Like its findings about the impact of the Presbyterian missionary crusade on the native southwesterners, evidence from this study also challenges many widely held notions about the missionaries themselves. Some Presbyterians who labored in the Southwest undeniably fulfilled the stereotype of the inflexible, self-righteous, and not so charitable missionary. However, the typical missionary was neither deceitful do-gooder nor saint, but instead a complex and flexible historical actor. Like many well-intentioned people, Presbyterian missionaries in the Southwest were both terribly human and wonderfully humane. Most interestingly, it is clear that extended tours of duty in the Southwest often humbled and changed missionaries. Unexpected hardships, repeated disappointments, and the vitality and tenacity of the southwestern cultures led some veteran missionaries to question (albeit usually very quietly) the assumptions that undergirded the missionary cause in which they were engaged. Paradoxically, schools that were initiated to eradicate traditional ways and transform the native southwesterners more often became arenas for ethnocultural interaction, where mutually held stereotypes and distrust eroded and natives and newcomers sometimes learned to accept and appreciate one another. By the mid-twentieth century Presbyterians in the Southwest and beyond began to embrace a stance on cultural and religious pluralism that differed radically from that of their nineteenth-century predecessors. The mission schools in the Southwest contributed in a small way to this cultural transformation.

As I contemplate this endeavor now completed, I find especially appropriate the metaphor of a journey. Like many journeys this one took longer than expected and often led me in directions that I hardly anticipated when I began. All along the way, however, I have benefited from the co-operation and kindness of numerous friends and fellow travelers.

I first seriously considered this topic more than ten years ago, when I was a part-time graduate student at the University of New Mexico. At the time, Ferenc Szasz and Richard N. Ellis provided invaluable encouragement and guidance. When the effort evolved into a dissertation, Richard Etulain and Patrick McNamara joined them in assisting me. Each of these men provided unique perspectives and talents that greatly strengthened this work. Their support and friendship made the completion of the dissertation a pleasurable experience; moreover, their example and enthusiasm encouraged me these past five years as I have refined that earlier effort into a publishable manuscript.

Like all investigators, I accumulated innumerable debts in completing the research that undergirds this study. My most extensive, fruitful, and enjoyable research was completed at the Presbyterian Historical Society in Philadelphia and the Menaul Historical Library of the Southwest in Albuquerque. Gerald Gillette, Frederick Heuser, and the staff of the Presbyterian archives were always helpful and gracious. Carolyn Atkins, founder and former director of the Menaul Historical Library, deserves special accolade. She first stirred my interest in this topic and has provided invaluable assistance and support as that interest evolved into its present form. Dorothy Stevenson and Esther McEntyre, also of the Menaul Historical Library, made valuable contributions to this effort, as did many other archivists and librarians. These include Mark Thomas, librarian of the Cook Theological School in Tempe, Arizona; Richard Wunder, librarian and archivist at Westminster College in Salt Lake City; Howard Den Hertog of the Pierce Historical Hall at Wasatch Academy in Mt. Pleasant, Utah; Richard Crawford of the National Archives; and the cooperative personnel of the Arizona Historical Society, the Arizona Room of the general library of Arizona State University, and the Coronado Room of Zimmerman Library at the University of New Mexico. The Sandia Foundation, trustees of the estate of Dorothy Woodward (late professor of history at the University of New Mexico), provided funds that enabled me to travel extensively to complete much of the research at these archives in the summer of 1985.

As I have revised and refined this project for publication, Norman Bender, Douglas Brackenridge, and James Smylie have kindly reviewed the several drafts and made numerous suggestions that have improved this final version. Liz Dulany, Cynthia Mitchell, and the staff of the University of Illinois Press have been extremely patient and cooperative throughout this project.

Several other special contributions must be noted. My brother Tim Banker, cartographer extraordinaire, prepared the maps that accompany this volume. The red pen of my mother (and former English teacher), Katy Banker, tidied up this manuscript and improved my prose; in addition her interest and support for this effort have been constant. Numerous others contributed to this effort without even knowing it. My coworkers and students at Menaul School in Albuquerque from 1976 to 1983 taught this "back-East Anglo" a great deal and awakened me to many of the issues dealt with in this study. Throughout the years I was a student at the University of New Mexico, many fellow graduate students offered invaluable suggestions and advice to "the fellow preoccupied with missionaries." Finally, my colleagues and especially my students at Albuquerque Academy (1986–87) and the Webb School of Knoxville (since 1987) contributed more to this study than they will ever know. I owe special thanks to two Webb colleagues, Shirley Dumont for assistance with the illustrations and Janet Colbert for proofreading the final manuscript.

My wife, Kathy, and our daughter, Tollie, have been my best friends and companions throughout this journey. Their patience, encouragement, and love have been constant and inexhaustible. For this I will always be grateful.

Finally, I must mention my father, L. Eugene Banker, and father-in-law, Luther S. Forbes. Their deaths during the time I was writing the dissertation were certainly the most trying and unanticipated disruptions of this effort. Long before this journey began, however, each of them made what I now know was a fundamental contribution to it. Dad through personal example showed me the creative power of charity and altruism, even as he taught me that goodwill often becomes misguided and self-serving. Luther, as we spent countless hours together fishing, taught me not to become overly dismayed with this basic human paradox. With fond recollections and deep appreciation, I dedicate this book to the memory of these two fellow travelers.

Presbyterian Missions
and Cultural Interaction
in the Far Southwest,
1850–1950

Prologue

Exceptional Populations

Over the countless millennia since Amer-Indian hunters wandered into the rugged country drained by the Rio Grande and the Colorado River, this region has been a crossroads for migrating peoples. Repeated encounters between newcomers and native peoples have shaped the region's rich and colorful past. Like many other Anglo Americans who arrived in the half-century after the region became "the American Southwest," the Presbyterian missionaries, who are the focus of this study, responded in a mixed fashion.[1] They found the southwestern landscape — with its vast distances, arid plains and deserts, rugged mountains and mesas — both enchanting and threatening. Even more intriguing and bewildering to the Presbyterians was the rich mosaic of cultures that repeated migrations into the region had forged. While Presbyterians did not fail to distinguish obvious differences among the Southwestern natives, they were even more aware how much the people they encountered differed from the prevailing cultural standards of their own nation. As prominent members of that society who proudly identified with its values and institutions, Presbyterians viewed southwestern pluralism as a challenge — and an opportunity.

The American acquisition of the Southwest brought Anglo Americans into contact with a vast and diverse Native American population. Among these "Indians," three groups in particular attracted Presbyterian attention: the Pueblos of the valley of the Rio Grande and its tributaries; the Pima-Papago peoples of the northern Sonora Desert; and the Navajos of the San Juan and Chama river valley of present-day northwestern New Mexico (see map 1). The white man's generic label *Indian* fails to capture the richness and diversity of these Native American peoples. The Pueblos and Pima-Papagos were remnants of two of the most highly advanced pre-Columbian peoples north of Mexico, the Anasazi and Hohokam. In the years after the mid-fourteenth-century decline of their more advanced ancestors, both the

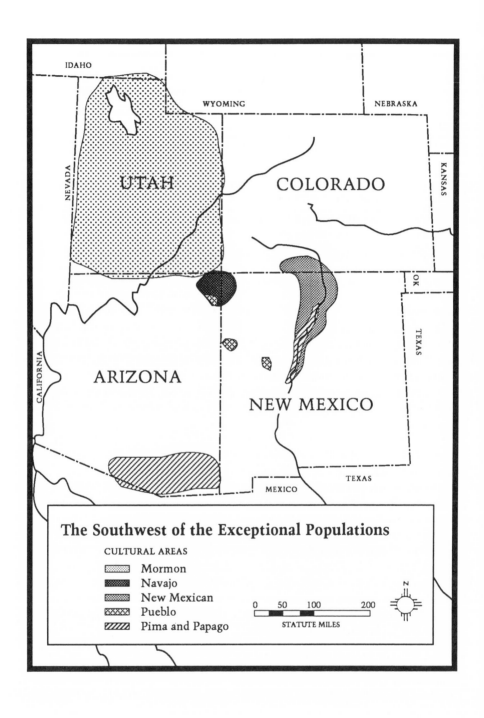

The Southwest of the Exceptional Populations

CULTURAL AREAS

- Mormon
- Navajo
- New Mexican
- Pueblo
- Pima and Papago

0   50   100   200
STATUTE MILES

Pueblos and some of the Pima-Papagos developed stable, sedentary societies centered around subsistence agriculture. In contrast, the Navajos were descendants of a relatively late group of newcomers to the Southwest. Their nomadic and warlike ancestors arrived from the North at about the same time the Anasazi and Hohokam cultures began to decline. By the nineteenth century Navajos were semi-nomads who supplemented their traditional hunting economy with some agriculture and the herding of sheep and goats, skills they had learned from Pueblo and later Spanish neighbors.[2]

The great diversity among these three Indian peoples is particularly obvious in their dwellings, languages, and their interaction with subsequent new arrivals to their homeland. The Pueblos earned their name from the multistoried communal dwellings of stone and adobe brick that sixteenth-century Spaniards described as "towns" (pueblos). Bands of the Pimas, who lived along rivers, lived in similar, though not so elaborate, structures. In contrast, the brush huts of other Pima-Papago peoples and the Navajo hogans — octagonal huts made of logs and mud — were temporary dwellings better suited to less sedentary lifestyles. The languages of the three southwestern Indians were mutually unintelligible; indeed, the scattered Pueblos alone spoke four distinct tongues, each of which had several dialects. With the notable exception of the Pueblo revolt against the Spaniards in 1680, the Pueblos and Pima-Papagos lived in relative peace with the Spaniards, Mexicans, and Anglo Americans who followed them into the Southwest. In contrast, warfare was a significant part of Navajo life, as they raided, and engaged in hostilities with, Indian neighbors as well as the various European groups.

Despite these and many other obvious differences, the three indigenous southwestern peoples shared common traits that made them Indians in Anglo-American eyes. All three groups engaged in simple subsistence economies in which the welfare of the community was paramount. Politically and socially each group was loosely organized into villages, clans, and bands. Finally, complex, animistic religious traditions permeated and made meaningful the lives of all three peoples. These traits, of course, contrasted greatly with the cultural baggage of the American newcomers, few of whom doubted that these discrepancies were evidence of their own superiority.

The southwestern Indians were not alone in viewing the nineteenth-century American arrival as an invasion. For more than three hundred years, the upper Rio Grande Valley and surrounding Sangre de Cristo mountains had been the home of a small, but deeply entrenched, Hispanic population. In the mid-sixteenth century Spanish conquistadors had marched north from New Spain to acquire wealth, save souls, and share the glory of their mother country. The demands of the difficult southwestern envi-

ronment and a sobering defeat at the hand of the Pueblos in the 1680s led
subsequent Spanish colonials to assume a less hostile and more humble
outlook. From Pueblo neighbors the Spaniards borrowed and shared food-
stuffs, architectural knowledge, and folk traditions. Most notably the two
peoples intermingled blood lines to produce a *meztizo*—New Mexican—
population.[3]

Paradoxically the same geographical isolation that encouraged cultural
blending with Pueblos simultaneously led colonial New Mexicans to preserve other aspects of their Spanish legacy. At the very time that consti-
tutionalism, capitalism, and Protestant reform were transforming Western
civilization, provincial New Mexicans clung to the feudal political and
economic patterns, mores and values, and Catholic faith of their medieval
forebears. Over the years a uniquely New Mexican culture took root in
scattered *plazas* (villages) in present-day northern New Mexico and southern
Colorado (see map, page 4). Together the villagers built adobe homes and
farmed and grazed livestock on communally owned lands. The arrival of
trade caravans from Chihuahua or Mexico City (and much later Missouri)
only occasionally interrupted their simple subsistence economies and lifestyles. At the center of each *plaza* stood a Roman Catholic church or chapel
where the villagers gathered for baptisms, weddings, holy days, fiestas, and
funerals. And when priests failed to visit the distant New Mexican parishes
for extended periods of time (as became increasingly common in the late
eighteenth century), local lay brotherhoods, most notably a group known
as *Los Penitentes,* maintained church buildings, assisted needy community
members, and conducted services and performed rituals that clearly reflected
the persistent legacy of medieval Catholicism. Not surprisingly, the New
Mexicans, no less than the Indians, appeared strange to the Anglo-American
newcomers of the mid-nineteenth century.

Westward-moving Americans encountered a third entrenched group of
peoples on the northern rim of the territory acquired from Mexico. Mormons, a self-proclaimed "peculiar people," had arrived in Utah only a few
years before the United States assumed control of the region. Because they
were in many respects similar to the newcomers yet in other ways shock-
ingly different, the Mormons bewildered the Anglo Americans even more
than Indians and New Mexicans did. Mormonism had its origins in upstate
New York in the 1820s, when young Joseph Smith reported a series of visits
from an angel. These miraculous happenings culminated in his discovery
of golden plates that contained an account of God's dealings with ancient
Semitic peoples who had settled in the New World during the Old Testament
period. Published as the *Book of Mormon* in 1830, this and other revelations

to Smith became the basis for the theology, ritual, and polity of what was officially named the Church of Jesus Christ of Latter-day Saints.

Mormonism grew rapidly, thanks to Smith's charismatic and pragmatic leadership and the general ferment of the antebellum era. Missionaries won converts from throughout the United States and Western Europe, and Smith's increasingly persecuted band migrated from Ohio to Missouri to Illinois. Many factors fostered anti-Mormon sentiment: Smith's claim to divine revelation, the secrecy that surrounded Mormon ritual, the movement's rapid growth, and finally Smith's 1843 revelation to "restore plural marriage" (polygamy). The hostilities culminated with Smith's assassination in 1844. Thereafter, the highly capable Brigham Young assumed leadership of the movement. In 1846 Young led the first wave of the Mormon exodus to the shores of Utah's Great Salt Lake, where he hoped his people would escape the hostility and persecution they had experienced in the United States.[4]

Thanks largely to Young's organizational genius, Utah did become Mormondom's "Great Basin Kingdom." By 1865 more than 65,000 pilgrims had crossed the Great Plains and Rockies on foot and horseback and in caravans of wagons and handcarts; they settled in Salt Lake City and a network of villages scattered throughout the inter-mountain west (see map 1). Most remarkably, Mormons succeeded in winning a stable livelihood from an environment that was 95 percent desert and mountain. By Young's decree Mormon pioneers were friendly with Indians and shared communal rights to water, minerals, timber, and grasslands; they developed vast irrigation systems and perfected the practice of dry farming. When large numbers of forty-niners passed through Salt Lake City en route to California gold fields, Mormon merchants and farmers made quick profits that provided capital for their currency-poor economy. Of course the arrival of the prospectors meant an early end to the isolation that Young had sought. Not long thereafter other Gentiles (non-Mormons) began arriving in Mormon Utah in ever-greater numbers.[5]

The cultures and traditions of the southwestern Indians, New Mexicans, and Mormons were each unique and distinct. Nevertheless, in the eyes of the Anglo-Protestant majority who dominated the nation that assumed control of the Southwest in 1848, the southwestern natives shared a common flaw: they did not conform to the cultural norms of the American mainstream. The Anglo-American newcomers commented often and critically on the simple lifestyles, communitarian traditions, and subsistence economies of the southwestern peoples. Aggressive, capitalistic Anglo Americans would make no such concessions to the harsh molding forces of isolation and the rugged southwestern environment, and they had little respect for peoples who had done so. Although the political structures of the three peoples differed markedly, in the eyes of the newcomers they all lacked the balance between freedom and order that nineteenth-century Americans confidently believed had assured the triumph of their nation's republican experiment. Finally, all three southwestern peoples were deeply religious. But in the eyes of Protestant Americans, these beliefs—whether Indian paganism, the peculiarly New Mexican brand of Catholicism, or the new Mormon faith—were hopeless, potentially dangerous delusions.

Included in the disparate cultural baggage of the natives and newcomers were sharply contrasting attitudes toward cultural diversity itself. The southwesterners had not always lived in peace, but the presence of many culturally diverse peoples in the region and the demands of a rugged environment fostered a tradition of cultural borrowing and sharing. This, in turn, led to a relatively benign (albeit fortuitous) acceptance of cultural differences. Even when southwestern peoples fought among themselves (as in the mutual raiding between Navajos and Pueblo–New Mexican allies), the relationship appears to have been symbiotic. Consequently total destruction of one's foes was never an option.[6]

Conversely, the relatively homogeneous Anglo Americans tended to view cultural variety with suspicion, if not alarm. Since colonial times Anglo-American frontiersmen pressed westward rapidly with little regard for Indians. Antebellum Americans were so adverse to living in an ethnically diverse society that many of them preferred spending large sums of money to remove Indians and colonize free Blacks on distant lands. At the very time the Southwest came under U.S. control, Anglo-Protestant nativists clamored about the corrupting impacts of foreign immigrants, Catholics, and Mormons on their republic.

American acquisition of the Southwest did produce considerable tensions and occasional violence, such as the Taos Rebellion of 1848, the "Mormon War" of the 1850s, and United States–Navajo hostilities in the 1850s and 1860s. Nevertheless, there was no immediate cultural showdown between the southwestern peoples and Americans. Land-hungry Americans in the 1850s still found more geographically familiar and accessible land in Texas and the Mississippi Valley. And adventuresome individuals who aspired to make the Overland Trek usually found Oregon's fertile valleys or California and Colorado gold fields more enticing than the arid, isolated Southwest. Furthermore, sectional hostilities that grew increasingly heated through the 1850s and boiled over from 1861 to 1865 distracted American attention from the newly acquired lands.

Much like their fellow Anglo-American newcomers to the Southwest, early Presbyterian visitors commented on the anomalous ways of the southwestern natives. Indeed, Presbyterians were so mindful of the differences between their own cultural traditions and those of the southwesterners that they eventually would lump Indians, New Mexicans, and Mormons together under the label "exceptional populations of the Southwest." Initially, however, Presbyterians, like their fellow Anglo Americans, were too preoccupied with more immediate concerns and less distant lands and peoples to show more than casual interest in the Southwest. To be sure, individual Presbyterians migrated there, but prior to the 1860s only one missionary was officially assigned to the region. And close scrutiny of the scant records of William J. Kephart's work in Santa Fe in the early 1850s suggests that abolitionism, not uplifting Pueblos or New Mexicans, was his major priority.[7] Moreover, a half century of disputes over theology, polity, and slavery left American Presbyterians fragmented into four weakened and feuding factions.[8] Only when these divisions healed after the Civil War did Presbyterians begin to seriously consider the exceptional ways of the Southwest's peoples and of the need for missions among them.

Notes

1. As used in this study, *Southwest* refers to the area commonly known as the four corners region; this includes parts of the present states of Colorado, Utah, Arizona, and New Mexico. Historian Howard Lamar call this "the far southwest." These lands came under U.S. control as a result of the Treaty of Guadalupe-Hidalgo that ended war between Mexico and the United States in 1848.

2. A great deal has been written about the southwestern Indians. See the chapters on the three groups in *The Handbook of North American Indians*, edited by Alfonso Ortiz, vols. 9 and 10 (Washington, D.C.: Smithsonian Institution Press, 1979). Edward Spicer's *Cycles of Conquest: The Impact of Spain, Mexico, and the United States on the Indians of the Southwest, 1533–1960* (Tucson: University of Arizona Press, 1981) is particularly useful for the issues raised in this study. There are also a number of tribal histories of the three groups, including Joe Sando, *The Pueblo Indians* (San Francisco: Indian Historical Press, 1976); Edward Dozier, *The Pueblo Indians of New Mexico* (New York: Holt, Rinehart and Winston, 1970); Anna Shaw, *The Pima Past* (Tucson: University of Arizona Press, 1974); James Downs, *The Navajos* (New York: Holt, Rinehart and Winston, 1972).

3. A great deal has also been written about the New Mexicans. Two useful sociological studies are George Sanchez, *Forgotten People: A Study of New Mexicans* (Albuquerque: Calvin Horn Publishers, 1967), and Nancie L. Gonzalez, *The Spanish Americans of New Mexico: A Heritage of Pride* (Albuquerque: University of New Mexico Press, 1969). Among the many important historical studies are David J. Weber, ed., *New Spain's Far Northern Frontier: Essays on Spain in the American West* (Albuquerque: University of New Mexico Press, 1979); idem, *The Mexican Frontier, 1821–1846: The American Southwest under Mexico* (Albuquerque: University of New Mexico Press, 1982); Howard R. Lamar, *The Far*

Southwest, 1846–1912: A Territorial History (New York: W. W. Norton, 1970), chap. 1–3. An insightful interpretive account of the New Mexican character by a prominent native thinker is Fray Angelico Chavez, *My Penitente Land: Reflections on Spanish New Mexico* (Albuquerque: University of New Mexico Press, 1974). The Presbyterians, like many others at their own time and since, were unsure of what to call these peoples and at various times referred to them as Mexicans, Spanish, and Spanish-speaking. To minimize confusion, this study will simply refer to them as New Mexicans. This, of course, is meant as a cultural label and is not meant to apply to all residents of the territory and subsequent state of New Mexico.

4. Few topics in western history have been as thoroughly studied as Mormonism. Two excellent general accounts are Leonard Arrington and Davis Bitton, *The Mormon Experience: A History of the Latter-day Saints* (New York: Alfred A. Knopf, 1979), and Thomas O'Dea, *The Mormons* (Chicago: University of Chicago Press, 1957). A very good recent study is Jan Shipps, *Mormonism: The Story of a New Religious Tradition* (Urbana: University of Illinois Press, 1985).

5. The standard account of Mormon settlement in Utah is Leonard Arrington, *Great Basin Kingdom: History of the Latter-day Saints, 1830–1900* (Cambridge, Mass.: Harvard University Press, 1958). Also see Arrington's *Brigham Young: American Moses* (New York: Alfred A. Knopf, 1985) and Jan Shipps, "Brigham Young and His Times: A Continuing Force in Mormonism," *Journal of the West* 23 (January 1984): 48–54.

6. John H. Parry, "Plural Society of the Southwest: A Historical Comment," in *Plural Society in the Southwest*, ed. Edward Spicer and R. H. Thompson (Tucson: University of Arizona Press, 1972), 306–7.

7. Kephart recounted his work in a letter to Sheldon Jackson, February 17, 1872, Sheldon Jackson Correspondence Collection of the Presbyterian Historical Society of Philadelphia (hereafter cited as SJCC). Also see Ruth K. Barber and Edith Agnew, *Sowers Went Forth: The Story of Presbyterian Missions in New Mexico and Colorado* (Albuquerque: Menaul Historical Library, 1981), 10.

8. Loefferts Loetscher, *A Brief History of the Presbyterians*, 3d ed. (Philadelphia: Westminster Press, 1974), 92–102; Clifford M. Drury, *Presbyterian Panorama: 150 Years of National Missions History* (Philadelphia: Board of Christian Education, Presbyterian Church, U.S.A., 1952), 106–68. In 1837 theological differences, among other things, divided Presbyterians into New- and Old-School factions, and then, on the eve of the Civil War, each of these groups divided again along sectional lines over the slavery issue.

1

Presbyterian Newcomers

Not long after Presbyterians formally initiated missions in the Southwest, an anonymous mission official composed a long handwritten letter about that work to prospective missionaries. Regarding the native southwesterners who were the targets of this new missionary enterprise, the letter advised that they are people "who are with us—but not of us."[1] This observation, like the label "exceptional populations," reflects more about the Presbyterians than about the peoples they encountered in the Southwest. Like the peoples of the Southwest, nineteenth-century American Presbyterians were heirs to proud, deeply rooted traditions that shaped their views of themselves and all that they encountered.

Although the Old World Calvinist legacy had gradually eroded in the American environment, its emphases on a rigid moral code, social order, and the absolute sovereignty of God remained central to the world-view of most nineteenth-century American Presbyterians. While Presbyterian theology never completely rejected Calvin's emphases on innate human depravity and predestination, most American Presbyterians by the antebellum era assumed the more optimistic stance that salvation belonged to all who truly believed in Jesus Christ. This outlook, of course, made missions an essential responsibility of the church, and Presbyterians since colonial times had generously supported mission activities of their own denominational boards and voluntary interdenominational mission societies.[2]

The American environment similarly altered the Presbyterian understanding of the sovereignty of God. Whereas this basic Calvinist tenet had originally been concerned with the foreordination of individual souls, in the heady atmosphere of antebellum America it became increasingly identified with a linear view of history in which God's will would inevitably triumph. Most Presbyterians refrained from embracing perfectionism, which assumed God's kingdom could be attained in this lifetime. But their attitude toward man's capacity to improve his own condition had drifted far from that of John Calvin. The new understanding of God's sovereignty shaped and confirmed Presbyterian attitudes about their nation's, and indeed their own, role in human history. Colonial Presbyterians supported the American Revolution with near unanimity, and from that time Presbyterians identified closely with the American republican experiment.[3]

Presbyterians shared with most antebellum Protestants belief in a causal relationship between Protestant Christianity and the impressive accomplishments of Western civilization and the United States in particular. Because Protestantism was deemed essential to American republicanism, Presbyterians participated in the crusade to make the United States a Christian nation. This effort was important for more than just the welfare of the republic, for in the evangelical scheme of history the hand of God directed the United States to a special role that would ultimately result in the evangelization of the entire world. Convinced that they must eradicate their nation's shortcomings before the United States could achieve its glorious destiny, antebellum Presbyterians engaged in the revivalism of the second Great Awakening, supported a benevolent empire of voluntary reform agencies, and sent out home missionaries. The new understanding of God's absolute sovereignty envisioned a world in which progress and goodness would inevitably triumph.[4]

Not surprisingly, Presbyterians, like most evangelicals, came to assume that their nation's cultural and moral standards and ideals were preferred by God and superior to those of other peoples. From these assumptions developed the synonymous ideals of the Anglo-Protestant way and Christian civilization. The most notable traits of these concepts were the institutions and ideals of mainstream American society: Protestant churches, public schools, a codified system of laws, private property, hard work, monogamous marriage, patriarchal families, and the Christian Sabbath. Also included were more incidental aspects of Anglo-American physical culture, such as Western clothing and standards of hygiene; permanent, single-family dwellings; modern farming implements and techniques; and the latest conveniences and technological advancements. When these cultural assumptions became intertwined with Protestant religious convictions, the result was a "near absolute ethnocentrism."[5]

The prevailing understanding of culture in mid-nineteenth-century America confirmed this attitude. Like most educated Americans of the time, Presbyterians equated culture with civilization, a high plane of human achievement toward which all societies evolved. This perspective led them to see similarities in the beliefs and behaviors of earlier peoples and modern primitive groups. Similarly, they saw great differences between the achievements of these less advanced peoples and their own cultural attainments.

Unlike later generations whose understanding of cultural variety became colored by racist explanations of innate inferiority, most educated Americans in the mid-nineteenth century maintained that all people were capable of ultimately attaining civilization. The standards for measuring progress along this path were, of course, the traditions, values, and institutions of their own society.[6]

The Presbyterians' religious convictions and understanding of culture intertwined and reinforced each other to weave a distinctive perception of cultural differences. This outlook led Presbyterians to consider culturally distinct peoples inferior, but not permanently so. Confident that Christ's second coming was imminent, Presbyterians felt called by God to aid less fortunate peoples in their journey to Christian civilization. Sectional conflict and the Civil War temporarily deterred this crusade, but it resumed with renewed enthusiasm after Appomattox. Like other northern churchmen, many Presbyterians interpreted Union victory as evidence of divine approval for their ideals. Even unprecedented and troubling socioeconomic and intellectual developments did not dampen evangelical enthusiasm. While industrialization, urbanization, new immigration, Darwinian evolution, and higher criticism of scriptures would eventually undermine Protestant confidence and hegemony, these challenges, just barely apparent after Appomattox, only heightened Protestant resolve to advance their crusade.[7]

To mission leaders urgently planning their new advance, no field seemed more critical than the trans-Mississippi West. Americans had long believed their nation's future lay in the West, and since the colonial period churchmen had considered the frontier a priority area. Moreover, as eastern churchmen in the latter nineteenth century became more aware of the perplexing new developments in their own backyards, they found comfort and reassurance in responding to the needs of a more traditional mission field.[8] The Presbyterian encounter with the unique conditions and peoples of the Southwest resulted directly from this general evangelical concern. In 1864 the Reverend Henry Kendall, secretary of the New School's Home Missions Committee, traveled to California to become familiar with the region's conditions and needs; one of his many stops was in Mormon-dominated Salt Lake City. Two years later, the Reverend David F. McFarland, representing the Old School's Board of Domestic Missions, arrived in Santa Fe.

Troublesome technicalities, however, temporarily delayed initiation of Presbyterian missions among the native southwesterners. Presbyterian home missionaries had long labored among white, English-speaking, and nominally Protestant peoples in frontier areas. But never before had Presbyterian missionaries encountered on American territory a deeply entrenched, non-Protestant European people like the New Mexicans. Even more perplexing to Presbyterians were the Mormons, who had seemingly rejected the advantages of the Anglo-Protestant way for exile in distant Utah. While precedent did exist for Presbyterian missions among Indians, cautious mission officials were uncertain how to deal with the greatly increased number of tribes west of the Mississippi. In the established Presbyterian mission scheme, Indian missions had been assigned to the foreign missions boards. Consequently, domestic (home) mission leaders were less than eager about embracing the southwestern tribes, even though the Board of Foreign Missions was equally unenthusiastic about that prospect.

Three significant developments in 1869 led to adjustments in Presbyterian attitudes and mission machinery that ultimately led Presbyterians to assume responsibility for work among the Southwest's exceptional populations. Many Presbyterians recognized that continued division in their ranks severely handicapped denominational growth and vitality. Consequently, in 1869 representatives of the northern New and Old schools met and reached agreement for the reorganization of the Presbyterian Church in the United States of America or, as it was misleadingly known, the Northern Presbyterian Church. To one churchman, reunion linked "two mighty forces for doing battle against a world of evil." When an overture calling for a one-million-dollar special fund for mission purposes came before the General Assembly, it was rejected and an alternative proposal for a five-million-dollar fund approved instead. Ultimately, more than seven million dollars was raised for the cause.[9]

One of the results of reunion was a new Board of Home Missions that proved more efficient and energetic than its predecessor agencies of the New- and Old-School factions. Two corresponding secretaries led the new board. Henry Kendall, former secretary of the New School's Committee on Home Missions, was a "master of detail and planning." His counterpart, former Old School minister Cyrus Dickson, was widely recognized as one of the church's most powerful orators. Though they did not always agree, Kendall and Dickson proved to be an "extraordinarily effective team," and under their leadership missions in the West became the priority of Presbyterian Home Missions.[10]

While reunion and reorganization set the stage for Presbyterian advance into the West, rapid expansion of railroads actually carried them there. Completion of the first transcontinental railroad in the same year as their own reunion surely must have seemed providential to Presbyterians. The new Union Pacific Railway assured further Anglo-Protestant intrusion and influence in Mormondom's stronghold and soon other rail lines penetrated the rest of the Southwest. By the early 1880s a southern route, linking California to the East, passed through southern Arizona's Pima-Papago country. At the same time the Atchenson, Topeka, and Santa Fe completed lines that skirted the homeland of the New Mexicans and Pueblos en route to

Albuquerque. Three years later tracks of this same company penetrated western Pueblo and Navajo country.[11]

Not the expanding railroads, however, but the efforts of a bearded, bespectacled little man actually awakened Presbyterian interest in the Southwest. Sheldon Jackson was a lifelong Presbyterian and graduate of Princeton Seminary. After being rejected for foreign missionary duty because of fragile health, Jackson in 1858 taught in a Oklahoma mission school for Choctaw Indians. Finding the classroom not to his liking, he spent the next decade as a minister in frontier Wisconsin and Minnesota, except for a brief interlude when he served as a Civil War chaplain. Never content with being merely a local parson, Jackson established an academy, organized and recruited ministers for nineteen new churches, and raised funds for the effort. His aggressive resourcefulness and disregard for established procedures irritated many mission officials, but few questioned the results of his labor.[12]

By the late 1860s, with the Minnesota frontier becoming tame and post–Civil War evangelical fervor and a transcontinental railroad pointing to the West, Jackson sought new and enlarged duties. In 1869 he wrote mission headquarters indicating a willingness to do "pioneer work . . . in Iowa, Nebraska, or Dakota, or anywhere north of the ague line." If the board could not financially support such an effort, Jackson was willing to work on a volunteer basis and raise his own funds. In short, Jackson foresaw the extension of Presbyterianism along the route of the new transcontinental railroad, and he soon became the self-styled superintendent of Presbyterian missions in the Rocky Mountain West. Over the next twelve years Jackson traveled more than 30,000 miles annually, by foot, horseback, buckboard, stagecoach, ox cart, and railroad, promoting and expanding the Presbyterian cause.[13]

Jackson was truly a man of his age. At a time when tycoons like Andrew Carnegie and John D. Rockefeller were revolutionizing American business, Jackson applied many of their techniques to the cause of Presbyterian home missions. He ingeniuously used the new railroad network to accelerate the mission advance. He was also a master salesman who recognized and utilized the power of the press. Like many of his contemporaries in the business world, Jackson utilized new, and sometimes questionable, means to advance his cause.[14]

Jackson's official responsibility as an employee of the Board of Home Missions was to traditional, unchurched Anglo Americans of his vast Rocky Mountain field. Nevertheless, he soon became aware of the array of peoples who had preceded the Anglos in his parish. Severely disappointed when, as a young man, he was rejected for service in the foreign mission field, Jackson never hesitated in advocating Presbyterian home missions among the virtually foreign peoples of the Southwest. Neither lack of precedent nor bureaucratic technicalities deterred Jackson, who recognized that the Board of Foreign Missions had little interest in initiating work among the three southwestern peoples. Rather than let these people continue living in darkness, Jackson spontaneously added them to his ever-growing flock. When members of the Board of Home Missions objected, Jackson barged ahead. His strategy was simple: first occupy the field with missionaries, then secure financial support and official board approval. Only the excuse of long-distance communication and the friendship of Henry Kendall saved Jackson from official board censure for his many unauthorized activities.

Jackson embraced the work in the Southwest with characteristic enthusiasm and spontaneity. He first attempted to establish Presbyterianism in Utah in 1869, when he sent several young ministers to Corrine, a Gentile (non-Mormon) town on the newly completed transcontinental railroad. The next year the board directed Jackson to visit Salt Lake City. Although Mormondom's capital, Salt Lake had become home for a sizable Gentile population, thanks to discoveries of rich mineral deposits nearby. On Jackson's recommendation the board decided to establish a church in Salt Lake, and in October 1871 the Reverend Josiah Welch was appointed to carry out that task. Two years later, again on Jackson's advice, a church was established in Alta, a small, non-Mormon mining community.[15]

To this point, all Presbyterian efforts in Utah had been directed toward the territory's non-Mormon population. Jackson, however, never shared official board reluctance to initiate missions among Mormons.[16] When the young Reverend Duncan J. McMillan visited him in Colorado in 1874, inquiring about a location with a climate that would restore his health, Jackson became a booster for Utah's salubrious air. Shortly thereafter, McMillan initiated missionary labors in Mt. Pleasant, a community 150 miles south of Salt Lake City. A number of disgruntled Mormons had settled in Mt. Pleasant and the surrounding Sanpete valley, and McMillan hoped to win them to Christianity. McMillan's efforts initiated a major expansion of Presbyterian work in central and southern Utah. Moreover, his missionary methods and new developments at the mission in Salt Lake City established a pattern for Presbyterian Mormon missions repeated throughout the territory for nearly two decades.

Developments in New Mexico paralleled those in Utah. At the time Jackson became superintendent of Rocky Mountain missions, the Reverend David F. McFarland had been in Santa Fe more than two years. His efforts there, however, had not established a precedent for Presbyterian missions among New Mexicans or Indians. Indeed, the majority of the members of his small church were Anglos who had come to Santa Fe to serve in the territorial government or as soldiers at Fort Marcy.[17] Shortly after assuming his duties in 1869, Jackson induced the Reverend John A. Annin, a friend from his years in Minnesota, to begin missionary work in Las Vegas. This town was considered important for the Presbyterian cause because it was along the proposed route for the Atchenson, Topeka, and Santa Fe Railroad and was expected to become a major Anglo population center. When the railroad's arrival was delayed and Annin found the community's few Anglos uninterested in his cause, he initiated work among New Mexicans. This unauthorized action aroused the ire of Home Missions officials. In the summer of 1870 Henry Kendall directed Jackson to make an investigatory tour of New Mexico. Fully aware of his friend's ambitions, Kendall warned Jackson to "make no promises." Home Missions, Kendall emphasized, was for white, English-speaking Americans, and the New Mexicans were "not a first priority." Characteristically, Jackson's report from his brief journey to New Mexico called for an expanded Presbyterian effort and at least three more missionaries for that field. Kendall responded that New Mexico would be temporarily abandoned because the board believed their money could gain greater results elsewhere.[18]

The proposed abandonment never occurred, largely due to Jackson's persistence and the home board's fear that other churches might "get ahead."[19] Jackson returned to New Mexico in 1872 and, in spite of official board opposition, helped establish the Reverend James M. Roberts at the important town of Taos. With lieutenants in three of the territory's major Hispanic population centers — Santa Fe, Las Vegas, and Taos — field general Jackson directed a major Presbyterian advance among New Mexicans. By the time of Jackson's third tour of New Mexico in 1874 and 1875, some board members began to share his attitudes toward the Southwest, and he was cautiously advised to expand missions among both New Mexicans and Indians of New Mexico and Arizona.

Despite precedent and a more officially recognized rationale for existence, Presbyterian Indian missions in the Southwest were even slower in developing than the Mormon and New Mexican missions. The greatest obstacle was uncertainty over which missions agency should assume responsibility for the work. In accord with established policy, the Presbyterian Board of Foreign Missions initiated work among the Navajos and the Pueblos shortly after the Civil War. When repeated problems and controversies plagued that work, Sheldon Jackson sought to bring it under his own home missions board. The foreign board resented this encroachment but continued difficulties led it to gradually relinquish control of the Navajo and Pueblo work.[20]

In 1881 the home board's Indian responsibilities increased further when the Dutch Reformed Church transferred to it responsibility for the Pima-Papago field. Jackson wisely persuaded the Reverend Charles H. Cook, a

Methodist who had been a government teacher and trader among the Pimas since 1870, to become Presbyterian and take charge of the home board's work in that field.[21]

These unprecedented advances unofficially broadened the scope of Presbyterian home missions. With missionaries at work among the southwestern peoples, Jackson next turned to winning support for them. Some members of the Board of Home Missions continued to object to Jackson's unauthorized actions. They believed the work rightfully belonged to the foreign board, and they worried that Jackson's ever-increasing commitments were depleting their board's already-strained coffers. At the same time the vast majority of Presbyterians in the East were not even aware of the new southwestern missions.

No one recognized more than Sheldon Jackson the need for full support from the board and Presbyterians at large. Ever the enthusiastic home missions entrepreneur, he devoted considerable energy to promoting his unprecedented mission enterprise. Jackson and his missionaries frequently visited home board headquarters in New York. As they traveled from and returned to their fields, they spoke before local congregations and public audiences in the East and Midwest. Aware that nothing was more convincing than personal contact, Jackson urged mission officials to come west and organized excursions for groups of Presbyterians into his vast field. Jackson's most pervasive and influential promotional device, however, was the *Rocky Mountain Presbyterian*.

The first issue of Jackson's monthly newspaper, published in March 1872, established two principal objectives: to bring western Presbyterians into closer sympathy with one another and to promote the cause of western home missions among eastern readers. Jackson's paper soon surpassed these modest goals. By the time Jackson turned it over to the Board of Home Missions in 1881, the paper's circulation exceeded 20,000, including readers in the British Isles, Asia, and Canada.[22]

Editorials in the *Rocky Mountain Presbyterian* emphasized that the West was an important battleground in the war for the evangelization of the entire world. Reports from local churches and missionaries in the field appeared in every issue and described in detail the challenges and opportunities that faced the missionary advance. Of course, Jackson's paper covered more than just the Southwest. Reports from railroad boom towns in Nebraska and Wyoming, Rocky Mountain mining camps, and Indian missions on the northern Plains and Northwest appeared regularly. But once Jackson became interested in the Southwest and recruited missionaries for that field, reports from them and accounts of Jackson's frequent journeys there became standard fare in the *Rocky Mountain Presbyterian*.

Along with the missionaries' private correspondence and reports to headquarters, Jackson's newspaper shaped the attitudes of mission officials and scores of Presbyterian laypersons toward the Southwest and the exceptional ways of its peoples. Examination of these early accounts of the missionaries' labors will not only reveal how missionaries viewed the southwestern peoples but also help explain the energetic Presbyterian response to them.

Notes

1. Quoted from an undated, handwritten statement entitled "Suggestions for Workers — From the Woman's Executive Committee for Home Missions," Presbyterian Historical Society (hereafter cited PHS), RG 105, Box 2, folder 6. While Presbyterians first used the term "exceptional populations" in the Southwest, they gradually added to the "exceptional" category other non-mainstream peoples, including native Alaskans, the "Mountain Whites" of the southern Appalachians, various urban immigrant peoples, and Cubans and Puerto Ricans.

2. Elwyn A. Smith, *Presbyterian Ministry in American Culture: A Study in Changing Concepts, 1700–1900* (Philadelphia: Westminster Press, 1962), 143; Sidney Ahlstrom, *A Religious History of the American People*, 2 vols. (Garden City, N.Y.: Image Books, 1975), 1:559–64, 2:79–81.

3. Smith, *Presbyterian Ministry in American Culture*, 143, 219. Gary Scott Smith argues that Presbyterian orthodoxy did not erode as much during this period as is suggested herein (*The Seeds of Secularization: Calvinism, Culture, and Pluralism, 1870–1915* [Grand Rapids, Mich.: Christian University Press, 1985], 16–19).

4. For an excellent analysis of the antebellum Protestant effort to make the United States a Christian nation, see Robert Handy, *A Christian America: Protestant Hopes and Historical Realities* (New York: Oxford University Press, 1984), 24–56. Two excellent studies of antebellum reform movements and Protestant support for them are Alice Felt Tyler, *Freedom's Ferment: Phases of American Social History from the Colonial Period to the Civil War* (New York: Harper, 1944), and Ronald Walters, *American Reformers, 1815–1860* (New York: Hill and Wang, 1978). Colin B. Goodykontz, *Home Missions on the American Frontier* (Caldwell, Idaho: Caxton Printers, 1939), remains the most thorough treatment of Protestant home missions in the nineteenth century.

5. Handy's *A Christian America* insightfully analyzes this close identification of Christianity with mainstream American culture; see in particular chapters 2–5. Louis J. Luzbetak labels this attitude "triumphalism" ("Two Centuries of Cultural Adaptation in American Church Action," in *American Missions: A Bicentennial Perspective*, ed. R. Pierce Beaver [South Pasadena, Calif.: William Carey Library, 1977], 337.) Gordon Allport examines the tendency of religious groups to identify with secular aspects of their culture and the relationship of ethnocentrism to religion (*The Nature of Prejudice* [Reading, Mass.: Addison-Wesley

Publishing Co., 1979], 444–55). Michael Coleman coins the term "near absolute ethnocentrism" to describe the attitude of nineteenth-century American Presbyterians toward culturally distinct peoples (*Presbyterian Attitudes toward American Indians, 1837–1892* [Jackson: University of Mississippi Press, 1985]).

6. The nineteenth-century understanding of culture is examined in A. L. Kroeber and Clyde Kluckhohn, *Culture: A Critical Review of Concepts and Definitions* (New York: Vintage Books, 1963), 32–42; Curtis Hinsley, *Savages and Scientists: The Smithsonian Institution and the Development of American Anthropology, 1846–1910* (Washington, D.C.: Smithsonian Institution Press, 1981), 133–35; and Robert Berkhofer, Jr., *The White Man's Indian: Images of the American Indian from Columbus to the Present* (New York: Vintage Books, 1979), 44–59. A thorough analysis of the implications of this outlook for nineteenth-century Presbyterian missions is presented in Coleman, *Presbyterian Attitudes toward Indians*, 86–88, 171–76.

7. Henry W. Bowden, "An Overview of Cultural Factors in the American Protestant Missionary Enterprize," in Beaver, *American Missions in Bicentennial Perspective*, 49–50; James Moorehead, *American Apocalypse: Yankee Protestants and the Civil War* (New Haven: Yale University Press, 1978); George Marsden, *The Evangelical Mind and the New School Presbyterian Experience: A Case Study of Thought and Theology in Nineteenth-Century America* (New Haven: Yale University Press, 1970), 199–211.

8. Ahlstrom, *A Religious History of the American People*, 2:334–39; Robert Handy, *We Witness Together: A History of Cooperative Home Missions* (New York: Friendship Press, 1956), 16–17. Evidence of Presbyterian belief in the importance of western missions is found in the 4th Annual Report of the Board of Home Missions (1874), 22, and Henry Kendall, "Our Country for the World," Sheldon Jackson Scrapbook, 65 vols. (hereafter cited SJS), 48:39.

9. The 1869 reunion is described in many places. A euphoric contemporary account is *Presbyterian Reunion: A Memorial Volume, 1837–1870* (New York, 1870). Richard W. Reifsnyder, "Presbyterian Reunion: Reorganization and Expansion in the Late Nineteenth Century," *American Presbyterians* 64 (Spring 1986): 27–28, is an excellent recent analysis.

10. Reifsnyder, "Presbyterian Reunion," 29–30. See also Clifford M. Drury, *Presbyterian Panorama: 150 Years of National Missions History* (Philadelphia: Board of Christian Education, Presbyterian Church, U.S.A., 1952), 175–96; Thomas S. Goslin, II, "Henry Kendall and the Evangelization of a Continent" (Ph.D. diss., University of Pennsylvania, 1948).

11. Lynn I. Perrigo, *The American Southwest: Its Peoples and Cultures* (Albuquerque: University of New Mexico Press, 1979), 286–94; Robert Reigel, *The Story of the Western Railroads* (New York, 1926); Ira G. Clark, *Then Came the Railroads: The Century from Steam to Diesel in the Southwest* (Norman: University of Oklahoma Press, 1958).

12. Much has been written about Jackson's long missionary career. An uncritical biography written by a contemporary friend and coworker is Robert Laird Stewart, *Sheldon Jackson* (New York: Flemming H. Revell, 1908). Two excellent

recent analyses of Jackson's work are Ted C. Hinckley, "Sheldon Jackson: Gilded Age Apostle," *Journal of the West* 23 (January 1984): 16–25, and Norman J. Bender, "Sheldon Jackson's Crusade," *Midwest Review* 4 (Spring 1982): 1–12. Two Ph.D. disserations — idem, "Crusade of the Blue Banner: Rocky Mountain Presbyterianism, 1870–1900" (University of Colorado, 1971), and Alvin K. Bailey, "The Strategy of Sheldon Jackson in Opening the West for National Missions, 1860–1880" (Yale, 1948) — are very informative. Hinckley has devoted considerable attention to Jackson's later, and better-known, missionary efforts in Alaska.

13. Hinckley, "Sheldon Jackson," 17–23; Bailey, "The Strategy of Sheldon Jackson," 92–124; Drury, *Presbyterian Panorama*, 184–88. In November 1876 Jackson wrote a review of his work at the request of the Presbytery of Colorado. This rather self-serving account is found in "Sheldon Jackson Invades the Rocky Mountains, 1869–76," *Journal of Presbyterian History* 37 (June 1959): 122–28.

14. Hinckley, "Sheldon Jackson," 17–23. For a detailed assessment of Jackson's home missions innovations, see Bailey, "The Strategy of Sheldon Jackson," chap. 4–6 in particular.

15. Although relatively unknown to wider audiences, a great deal has been written about Presbyterian work in Utah. Two uncritical and slanted accounts of the early work by Presbyterian contemporaries are Stewart, *Sheldon Jackson*, 193–218; and Samuel Wishard, *The Mormons* (New York: Literary Department, Presbyterian Home Missions, 1904), 11–20, 27–31. Two later accounts written by Presbyterians are George Davies, "A History of the Presbyterian Church in Utah," *Journal of the Presbyterian Historical Society* 23 (December 1945): 228–48; 24 (January 1946): 44–68; 25 (March 1946): 147–81; 26 (January 1947): 46–67; and Herbert W. Reherd, "An Outline History of the Protestant Churches of Utah," originally published as chap. 4 of *Utah Centennial History* (Chicago: Lewis Historical Publications Co., 1949), 680–82. A more recent account written from a Mormon perspective is Thomas E. Lyon, "Evangelical Protestant Missionary Activities in Mormon-dominated Areas, 1865–1900" (Ph.D. diss., University of Utah, 1962), 78–86. Lyon's dissertation is summarized well in idem, "Religious Activities and Development in Utah, 1847–1910," *Utah Historical Quarterly* 35 (Fall 1967), 292–306.

16. Comments on official board hesitance to embrace work among the Mormons are found in J. M. Coyner, "The Utah Column," *Rocky Mountain Presbyterian* 9 (April 1880), and D. J. McMillan, "The Work in Utah," *Presbyterian Home Missions* 10 (October 1881): 371. Many back-East Presbyterians opposed establishment of missions among Mormons. See Duncan McMillan to S. Jackson, December 19, 1876, SJCC, and L. A. Dorland to Jackson, April 27, 1881, SJCC. The latter letter praised Jackson's efforts among "long wronged Indians" but called for the extinction of Mormonism.

17. Much has also been written about Presbyterian work among New Mexicans. Two contemporary accounts of the early years of Presbyterian advance may be found in Stewart, *Sheldon Jackson*, 219–27, and Robert M. Craig, *Our Mexicans* (New York: Board of Home Missions, Presbyterian Church, U.S.A., 1904), 48–68. Two more recent accounts (both written by Presbyterians who worked in the

New Mexican field) are Lela Weatherby, "A Study of the Early Years of Presbyterian Work with the Spanish-speaking People of New Mexico and Colorado, 1850–1920" (M.A. thesis, Presbyterian College of Christian Education, 1942), 17–25; and Barber and Agnew, *Sowers Went Forth,* 9–27. Also see Douglas Brackenridge and Francisco Garcia-Treto, *Iglesia Presbyteriana: A History of Presbyterians and Mexican-Americans in the Southwest,* Presbyterian Historical Society Publications Series, 16 (San Antonio: Trinity University Press, 1974).

18. Kendall to Jackson, July 8 and September 22, 1870, SJCC.

19. For a while the New Mexico field was a hot potato that neither home nor foreign board wanted ("New Mexico Missions: Stations and Missionaries," undated clipping [ca. 1872], SJS 53:32). In 1874 Santa Fe Presbytery officially complained about this neglect ("Presbytery of Santa Fe," statement issued in November 1874, SJS 54:9–10). Also see Jackson to Rev. and Mrs. James M. Roberts, July 9 and July 16, 1873, SJCC.

20. Presbyterian missions among the Navajos are exhaustively examined in Bruce L. Taylor, "Presbyterians and 'the People': A History of Presbyterian Missions and Ministries to the Navajos" (Ph.D. diss., Union Theological Seminary, 1988). Presbyterian activities among the Pueblos are examined in Mark T. Banker, "Presbyterians and Pueblos: A Protestant Response to the Indian Question, 1872–1892," *Journal of Presbyterian History* 60 (Spring 1982): 23–41.

21. A contemporary account of Presbyterian Pima missions is *Among the Pimas* (Albany, N.Y., 1893). For an account of Cook's efforts and early Presbyterian Indian missions in southern Arizona, see John M. Hamilton, "A History of Presbyterian Work among the Pima and Papago Indians of Arizona" (M.A. thesis, University of Arizona, 1948), 1–32. Also see Minnie Cook, *Apostle to the Pimas* (Tiburon, Calif.: Omega Books, 1976), a biography of Rev. Cook written by his granddaughter.

22. Sheldon Jackson to Readers of *Rocky Mountain Presbyterian* 9 (December 1881) (hereafter cited as *RMP*); Bailey, "Strategy of Sheldon Jackson," 352–73; Bender, *Crusade,* 118–22. The *Rocky Mountain Presbyterian* was published on a weekly basis for a few months in 1873. When Jackson turned his paper over to the Board of Home Missions, its name was changed to *Presbyterian Home Missions* (hereafter cited as *PHM*). In 1883 it became the *Presbyterian Home Missionary* (hereafter cited as *PHMy*).

2

"All This in a Christian Land!"

"Superstition, licentiousness, intemperance, profanity, sabbath-breaking, and intense worldliness prevail to a fearful extent." Thus began the first "Narrative on the State of Religion within the Bounds of the Presbytery of Santa Fe." The three ministers and one elder who gathered for the Presbytery's inaugural meeting in Santa Fe in 1868 attributed this deplorable state to the predominance of Indians and Hispanics in New Mexico Territory. However, the founding fathers of the new Presbytery did not despair. Within a paragraph, optimism chased away gloom, and the narrative concluded on a hopeful note: "the spring of Christian civilization is teeming with bud and blossom."[1]

This account typifies the early Presbyterian response to the Southwest and its peoples. In private correspondence, articles in the *Rocky Mountain Presbyterian*, and reports to home mission officials, Presbyterian missionaries almost always depicted the Southwest in dualistic terms. The missionaries freely and frequently described Indians, New Mexicans, and Mormons with an array of unbecoming adjectives: "degraded," "benighted," "superstitious," "ignorant," and so forth. Yet optimism always tempered these negative assessments. The missionaries' message was clear. These peoples were, indeed, exceptions to the norms of Anglo-Protestant civilization, but through Christian charity and the grace of God they and their cultures could be transformed.

Like all stereotypes, the Presbyterians' dualistic image of the exceptional populations served several functions. For individual missionaries, most of whom were products of highly homogeneous communities, such imagery simplified the confusion of pluralism and affirmed their own cultural identity. More importantly, the perceived negative traits of the peoples among whom they labored confirmed the missionaries' calling, while the ever-present optimism guarded against suspicions that their work might be futile.

When published in Jackson's *Rocky Mountain Presbyterian* or other church publications, such dualistic imagery carried a similar message to a broader audience.

It would be misleading, however, to conclude that the Presbyterians viewed southwestern peoples in dualistic terms simply as a matter of convenience. Wise persons have long recognized that what lies behind one's eyes often influences what is seen even more than what is before them.[2] The Presbyterian missionaries' distinctive cultural baggage, particularly their deep religious convictions and their understanding of culture, profoundly colored their dualistic response to the Indians, New Mexicans, and Mormons of the Southwest. It should be emphasized, moreover, that the ethnocentrism so apparent in Presbyterian perceptions of the exceptional populations was not unique. Most Anglo Americans of the latter nineteenth century shared the missionaries' dismay with cultural and religious pluralism. What distinguished the Presbyterian perspective on the exceptional populations was the other side of their dualistic image of the southwestern natives. While many Anglo newcomers to the Southwest were indifferent and occasionally even hostile to the natives in their way, the Presbyterian missionaries (and many other Anglo Protestant churchmen) felt an obligation to uplift these less fortunate brethren and help them find their way in the new society emerging in the Southwest. From the perspective of a century later, this altruism may appear misguided and even self-serving. But in the context of their own times the Presbyterians were sincere and genuinely humanitarian.

By the time Presbyterians initiated missions among Native Americans in the Southwest in the decade after the Civil War, Anglo Americans had been in contact with Indians for more than a century and a half. Over the years the newcomers to North America had developed two contrasting images of Native Americans. On the one hand, many Americans believed that the only good Indian was a dead Indian. From earliest colonial times, however, some newcomers held a more positive and benevolent attitude toward Indians; this outlook became increasingly widespread in the latter nineteenth century, as the Indian threat steadily diminished. This attitude blamed aggressive whites for the Indian problem. These friends of the Indian saw many negative traits in Indian culture and called for their eradication and replacement with the superior ways of the Anglo Protestants. However, consistent with their understanding of culture, these reformers believed Indians could achieve civilization if given the opportunity and proper guidance.[3] The Presbyterian missionaries who labored among southwestern Indians, by and large, shared this attitude.

Despite the Anglo-American tendency to lump all Native Americans together as Indians, Presbyterian missionaries were very much aware of the cultural distinctiveness of the three southwestern Indian peoples among whom they labored. For example, missionaries among the Pueblos described in detail that peoples' distinctive form of communal architecture, recounted their long history, and described their deeply rooted traditions. Missionary reports from the Navajo and Pima-Papago reveal a similar awareness of the distinctiveness of those peoples.[4]

However, awareness of the distinctiveness of the three southwestern Indian peoples did not remove from Presbyterian minds many of the negative stereotypes that nineteenth-century Americans associated with Indians. Even when missionaries commented on the generally friendly and peaceful nature of these peoples, fears of Indian savagery and hostilities were never far below the surface. At its inaugural meeting in 1868 the Presbytery of Santa Fe lamented that Navajo and Apache warriors committed "cunning theft" and "savage murders." Nine years later missionaries newly arrived to Jemez and Zuni Pueblos exhibited uneasiness about the peoples among whom they labored. From Jemez Dr. J. M. Shields described Indians eating vermin but quickly added, with strained humor, that "so long as they do not eat missionaries, we will not complain." Several months later, Dr. Taylor F. Ealy reported with alarm that incensed Zuni warriors had clubbed a dog to death and disemboweled him with their teeth to exhibit hatred for their traditional Navajo foes. Fearful for the welfare of his family, Ealy wrote, "We lie down and sleep at night because we trust in the Almighty." Missionaries in the field were not the only ones concerned about Indian savagery. After a number of Indian uprisings occurred on the northern Plains in 1878, Henry Kendall warned Jackson to avoid areas of "Indian rampage." Missionary fears of Indian violence, of course, were not completely unfounded.[5]

Missionaries often commented on Indian standards of hygiene. Upon arriving among the Hopis, a young missionary reported that they were "much as I expected ... but much dirtier." Several years earlier, Mrs. H. K. Palmer reported that the Zuni Pueblos were "full of vermin." "The first thing to be done," she wrote, was "to induce them to keep themselves clean enough for us to get nearer than we can now." Apparently this effort failed, because four months later she added, "it requires great care on our part to keep our garments from touching theirs when they come into our house." At about the same time a government teacher among the Pimas, whose salary was partially paid by Presbyterians, reported that her charges were a "half-naked, filthy set of creatures."[6]

Other Indian habits elicited missionary criticisms. When tools and materials for a school building and mission residence were delivered to Zuni Pueblo in 1878, a writer warned Sheldon Jackson to guard them constantly, because "Indians are not to be trusted." From the same pueblo a missionary reported that a Zuni visitor had stolen his family's coffee pot while they were saying grace at a nearby table. In 1881 a missionary reported to Jackson that the Navajos were so "thievish" [sic] that she had "to keep an eye on everything."[7]

Missionary accounts reveal many other Indian stereotypes. The drunken Indian was a stock character in reports from the mission field. Like most Americans, missionaries believed that the Indians had a low alcohol tolerance, and they frequently attributed Indian difficulties and failures to this problem. Missionaries likewise often blamed neighboring Mexicans and Anglo traders for supplying alcohol to the Indians.[8]

Missionaries were equally unappreciative of other aspects of the traditional Indian lifestyle. For example, after a four-hour conference with Zuni leaders to arrange for new missionaries there, Sheldon Jackson commented condescendingly that "the more time the Pueblos can talk and smoke the greater impressiveness and dignity of the occasion." "Americans," he concluded, "would have done the business in fifteen minutes." The division of labor among the Indians particularly distressed missionaries. After explaining that Zuni men hunted, sewed, and knitted while women worked in the fields, ground flour, and carried water, one missionary expressed her desire "to reverse their labors."[9]

The great interest of eastern Presbyterian women in the southwestern field led missionaries (many of whom were women) to comment often on the plight of Indian women and to show how far removed they were from the Anglo-American ideal of "true womanhood." Missionaries described native women as inferior looking and unattractive. More seriously, they charged that many Indian squaws were sexually promiscuous with both Indian and American men. The spread of venereal disease among southwestern Indians was often cited as evidence of such blatant immorality. Finally, the missionaries charged that Indian women often failed to rear their children properly. Zuni children, wrote one missionary, were "as wild as jackrabbits" and "know very little [about] what it is to be happy and comfortable."[10]

Missionaries believed that the root cause of all of these maladies was Indian paganism. While they commented frequently on Indian religious practices, few missionaries attempted to understand the native religion on its own terms. Instead, descriptions of native beliefs and practices revealed more about the missionaries' religious predilections than those of the Indians. Sheldon Jackson, for example, often used biblical examples to illustrate his descriptions of native religion. He charged on many occasions that the Pueblos worshiped Baal. After visiting one of "their heathen temples" (i.e. a sacred, underground kiva) at Taos Pueblo, he described an altar "where they formally sacrificed little children." Jackson asserted that all southwestern Indians were "sun worshipers . . . in one way or another" and were usually at the mercy of their "sorcerers and medicine men."[11]

Most missionaries in the field shared Jackson's views of Indian religion. The Zunis, wrote Mrs. T. F. Ealy in a letter to Presbyterian Sunday School children, "worship the sun . . . and believe when it is down at night that they can do whatever they please." Indian rituals and dancing particularly shocked the missionaries. Mrs. Ealy complained to Jackson in 1878 that she was tired of the Zunis dancing every day. Several months later, her husband wrote that his Indians had carried a sacred image sixty miles to a sacred lake, on the misguided hope that their efforts would bring rain.[12]

Occasionally missionaries in the field took a more balanced view of Indian religion. John Menaul, a native of Ireland who labored fifteen years at Laguna Pueblo, publicly challenged the assertion that the Pueblos were sun worshipers. Instead he (more correctly) labeled them pantheists. While he, too, was highly critical of Laguna rituals, Menaul understood better than most missionaries their integral role in Pueblo life and identity. Menaul recognized that Pueblo devotion to tradition was a major obstacle to conversion but optimistically asserted that once the native traditions were broken the Lagunas' "stability of character" would be of "inestimable value to their regenerated lives."[13] Charles H. Cook, a German immigrant who worked among the Southern Arizona Indians for more than forty years, often expressed similar sentiments about the Pimas and Papagos.

Missionaries quickly recognized that some southwestern Indians were more than mere pagans. The Spanish Catholic friars who had labored in the Southwest since the seventeenth century had enjoyed limited success among the Pueblos and Papagos, who combined their native traditions and rituals with aspects of Catholicism. To fiercely anti-Catholic American Protestants, this syncretic mixture of paganism and papism was worse than paganism itself. Although critical of Catholicism's presence among the Indians, missionaries invariably minimized its influence. After visiting Jemez, Laguna, and Zuni Pueblos in the spring of 1879, Sheldon Jackson quoted from an 1812 report of a Mexican bishop describing the deplorable state of Catholicism among the Pueblos, adding that little had changed since that time.[14]

Missionaries in the field usually shared Jackson's views about Indian Catholicism. John Menaul, whose Irish heritage intensified his anti-Catholicism, labeled Pueblo Catholicism "baptized heathenism." The Spaniards, he emphasized, had not Christianized the Pueblos but "simply baptized, married, administered the sacraments, and buried them." The Pueblos, he concluded in 1880, know no more about "revealed religion" than they did two centuries before. Similar comments came from Dr. H. K. Palmer at Zuni; in 1878, he wrote that the Zunis knew nothing about God or Jesus

Christ and just a little about Mary. Early reports about the state of Catholicism among the Papagos carry similar sentiments.[15]

For all of their disdain for Indian culture, however, Presbyterian missionaries believed Native Americans could achieve the ideals of Christian civilization. In an 1875 article in Jackson's paper, one writer suggested that "no people on earth were more eager for the gospel" than American Indians. This eagerness he attributed to their recognition that knowledge of the Bible and God was responsible for the whites' "irresistible supremacy" over the Indians.[16]

Presbyterians believed the southwestern Indians were particularly inclined to embrace the Christian gospel. They time and again commented on the distinctiveness of the Pueblos and their capacity for civilization. For example, Sheldon Jackson and other observers pointed to the Pueblos sedentary lifestyle, their relatively advanced arts, and their peaceful ways. One writer, after contrasting Pueblos with other American Indians, concluded that this was "the most promising field for missionary effort" ever encountered by Presbyterians "among Indians or other heathen peoples."[17]

Missionaries in the field expressed similar sentiments. In 1878 J. M. Shields wrote that the Jemez Pueblos were "quite as good in nature as other people." Their problem, he concluded, was ignorance. But after comparing them to people who had the advantages of education and Christianity, Shields concluded that "we wonder that these neglected Indians are as good as they are." From the Navajo field, Mrs. J. D. Perkins wrote in 1881 that her people were "bright, active, willing to learn, and quite industrious." A year later, she reported that the children in her school were "far more capable than is generally assumed." A decade earlier, Charles Cook described the Pimas as "intelligent, peaceable, and industrious."[18]

Like most humanitarians of the period, missionaries in the field and their supporters in the East often suggested that land-hungry Americans, dishonest Indian agents, and shortsighted federal Indian policy exacerbated the Indian problem. Upon arriving in Arizona in 1871, Charles Cook described white prejudice against Indians and its unfortunate consequences. Eleven years later, the superintendent of a Presbyterian boarding school for Pueblos in Albuquerque suggested that Indian suspicions and hesitance to embrace Christianity and white civilization were understandable in light of the long and sordid history of their relations with whites. Some missionaries, including A. H. Donaldson, who labored among the Navajos, felt a special calling to the Indian field because of their countrymen's treatment of Native Americans.[19]

For all of their concern about past injustices, Presbyterian missionaries and their supporters were more interested in the Indians' present and future. To them the Presbyterian arrival among the southwestern Indians had come none too soon. Presbyterians shared the concern of most nineteenth-century Americans that Indians were a "vanishing race" that would soon disappear.[20] The great task for concerned Christians in the decade after the Civil War was to find a ready means to spread the Good News of Christian salvation among these unfortunate, but "salvageable," peoples. Only the leavening influence of the Gospel could save the southwestern Indians from a fate too awful to contemplate and lay the foundation for new, regenerated lives for them.

While Presbyterians considered Indians an unfortunate people who were simply stalled in a primitive stage of development, their understanding of New Mexicans and Mormons was more complex and less benevolent. These peoples, the Presbyterians asserted, were products of their own vaunted Western civilization. But geographical isolation and peculiar circumstances and choices had caused them to stray far from the path of progress.

Many outside influences colored Presbyterian perceptions of New Mexican culture. As heirs to the English tradition of the "black legend," Presbyterians considered Spaniards unusually cruel and their culture innately flawed. One early Presbyterian visitor observed that New Mexico, since the Spanish arrival, had been the "scene of debauchery, iniquity, violence and bloodshed." Even more damning to Americans with serious qualms about race mixture was Spanish-Indian miscegenation and cultural intermingling that fostered the New Mexican "conglomerate of Moor, Spanish, and Indians." Ardent anti-Catholicism, which flourished in nineteenth-century America, added more negative tones to the Presbyterian outlook. Finally, as members of Victorian society Presbyterians held a more rigid moral code than the less inhibited New Mexicans.[21] Because of these influences, Presbyterians came to New Mexico expecting to find a benighted and degraded people. Their accounts reveal that they were not disappointed.

Like many other Anglo observers, the missionaries frequently described New Mexicans as indolent and lethargic. Illustrations in the *Rocky Mountain Presbyterian* usually depicted New Mexicans at siesta time, and accompanying stories elaborated on this theme. One observer suggested that New Mexicans "have been on strike for generations," while another lamented that they "have not caught the spirit of the age." A missionary in Tierra Amarilla observed that the forty men of that town together "worked less during the four winter months than one industrious American farmer."[22]

Closely related to the lazy New Mexican in the missionary mind was the frivolous New Mexican. Missionaries frequently commented on New Mexican proclivities for tobacco, alcohol, card playing, dancing, cock fighting, horse racing, and other forms of merry making. "Mexican paradise," suggested one observer, was playing monte, while leaning against the shady side of the house in summer.[23] The behavior of New Mexican women particularly disturbed missionaries. While lamenting that women did most of the menial labor, one missionary expressed her concern that "with few exceptions" they smoked, drank, and gambled with the men. Even more serious to Victorian Presbyterians was evidence of moral and sexual laxity. Sheldon Jackson frequently charged that chastity was rare among New Mexican *senoritas*. After noting that many of the native girls were bright-eyed and sweet voiced, another observer reported "if they cannot sing, they can enchant." Similar thoughts led an anonymous contributor to the *Rocky Mountain Presbyterian* to urge that only married males be sent to work in the New Mexico field. The "scant dress" of the native women, he warned, "is itself a trial of virtue."[24]

Like many other Anglo visitors to New Mexico, missionaries criticized the natives' relatively simple material culture. An article from *Harper's Magazine* reprinted in the *Rocky Mountain Presbyterian* suggested the typical New Mexico home was "a cheerless, one-story rectangle" that would "make a traveler more homesick than a dinner in a railroad restaurant." This writer attributed adobe architecture to the laziness of the New Mexicans. "Had the sun always shone and the winds blown steadily from the South," he concluded, the New Mexican "would not have built at all." Other observers commented on the lack of furnishings and presence of livestock, vermin, and filth in New Mexican homes.[25]

New Mexican farming methods and simple technology also dismayed missionaries. Sheldon Jackson and others described natives plowing with crooked sticks, cutting grain and hay with sickle and hoe, and driving a herd of sheep or goats over a threshing floor of hardened earth. Jackson suggested that these methods "would drive an eastern farmer to despair." Not surprisingly, missionaries often likened the primitive methods of the New Mexican farmer to those of Biblical times, particularly "the days of Ruth and Boaz."[26]

Few aspects of New Mexican culture were too incidental to escape Presbyterian criticism. Missionaries often commented on the ever-present burro—that "degenerate son of the ass family"—with its incessant braying and stubborn disposition. Even more disagreeable was the traditional New Mexican ox-cart, with its squeaking axles and snaillike pace. One writer suggested it had no equal "on earth, in the heavens above, or below the earth" and concluded that "there is nothing about it that is either square, straight, round or plumb." Not surprisingly, Anglo Presbyterians also disliked traditional New Mexican food. After eating a "villainous supper" between Santa Fe and Albuquerque, Sheldon Jackson likened it to "red hot iron." A "new beginner" on this diet, he concluded, should have a "copper lined stomach."[27]

For all of their criticisms of New Mexican culture, early Presbyterian visitors rarely suggested that the natives' condition was hopeless or permanent. Praise of New Mexican hospitality and civility almost always tempered descriptions of native indolence, frivolity, and backwardness. More importantly, missionaries from the field emphasized that only a lack of opportunity prevented New Mexicans from being as "intelligent, moral, and useful as other citizens of the land."[28] To missionary eyes the culprit was not the New Mexican himself but the institutions that had led him astray from the path of progress and perpetuated his deplorable condition.

Presbyterian assessments of the causes of New Mexico's maladies invariably pointed first to the "dense and universal ignorance" that prevailed in the territory. Missionaries reported that levels of illiteracy were high and most New Mexican towns and villages were without schools. They customarily attributed this situation to the stifling influence of the Roman Catholic church. Presbyterians charged that Catholics had undermined efforts to establish public, non-sectarian education in the territory. They further alleged that the few public schools in New Mexico were under Catholic control and that these and the few private Catholic schools in the territory were inadequate. Charges that schools served as political rewards, that native teachers were unprepared, and that the "Romish Catechism" was the "only textbook" in most schools of the territory appeared frequently in the *Rocky Mountain Presbyterian* and missionary correspondence.[29]

Of course, this state of affairs did not surprise Presbyterians. The Catholic hierarchy, they asserted, "abhorred the idea of education for the common people" and had long hindered the public school movement in the United States. One writer commented that "smallpox is not more dangerous or offensive" to the priests than an educated populace. Presbyterians offered evidence from abroad to substantiate these contentions. An article in the *Rocky Mountain Presbyterian* in 1878 contrasted two Irish counties: predominantly Protestant Donnegore county, with a 95 percent literacy rate, and largely Catholic Tullahobegley County, where 91 percent of the people were illiterate. The same article reported that 63 percent of Italians could not even write their own names.[30]

Presbyterians charged New Mexico's Catholic church with even more serious shortcomings. Indeed, most early Presbyterian observers suggested that Romanism was the principal cause for *all* of the territory's ills. David McFarland, first Presbyterian missionary in the territory after the Civil War, suggested that for 200 years Catholicism's "degrading and demoralizing influences" had produced the "licentious vices fearfully present" in New Mexican culture. Several years later John Annin attributed New Mexico's shortcomings to the "very reason that explains the greater prevalence of beggary [sic] and poverty in Naples than in Boston and the superiority of Edinburg over Madrid or Rome."[31]

Most Presbyterians blamed a corrupt corps of priests for the maladies of the New Mexican church. Reports from the field frequently charged that greedy priests performed their duties only when paid. Consequently, mass was rarely celebrated in many impoverished New Mexican villages. One indignant missionary wrote that excessive fees for baptisms, weddings, and funerals "robbed [New Mexicans] as soon as they are born." Even more exorbitant fees were assessed, he alleged, for cases of "more questionable nature." As an example, he reported that one priest demanded, and received, $500 to perform the marriage of a man to his own daughter.[32]

Although priests were considered the major culprits, few aspects of New Mexican Catholicism escaped Presbyterian criticism. Particularly disagreeable were the "large, curiously formed" adobe churches with their array of crucifixes, *retablos,* and *santos.* One observer likened the latter to "gods in heathen temples" and suggested they violated the commandment prohibiting the worship of graven images. Sheldon Jackson showed even less respect for traditional New Mexican church art. After describing a large crucifix at the Cathedral of Taos with one of Christ's arms broken and dangling, Jackson supposed that the priest was "without sufficient interest to glue it on again." He described a representation of the Virgin in the same church as a "rude wooden figurine [with] frousy hair fastened on with common carpet tacks."[33]

Presbyterians also criticized the worship that occurred in New Mexico's adobe churches. One account reported "superstitious" worshipers "kneeling, mumbling, and trembling." Another writer concluded, after observing "pomp and ceremony" in Albuquerque's Old Town cathedral, that Catholicism's hold "on minds so simple" was understandable. Presbyterians particularly objected to New Mexican sabbaths and feast days. Following a visit to Albuquerque in 1872, John Menaul wrote: "Sabbath there consists of cock-fighting first, then mass," followed in the afternoon by "more cockfighting and horseracing," and concludes with "dancing and drinking till near morning." Even more disgusting were New Mexican feast days that Presbyterians alleged were occasions for drinking, gambling, dancing, and quarreling.[34]

Presbyterian observers reserved their most sensational rhetoric for *Los Hermanos de Jesus Nazareno,* the lay brotherhoods, better known as *los penitentes,* that played such a vital role in nineteenth-century New Mexican Catholicism. To Sheldon Jackson, they were a "secret society of the most ignorant of the Catholics," while a missionary in Las Vegas simply called them a "race of fanatics." With few exceptions, missionary accounts focused on penitential Holy Week activities and overlooked the penitentes' important contributions to community order and stability during the remainder of the year. Missionaries described in graphic and gory detail the blood-soaked backs of flagellants, processions of near-naked men bent low under heavy wooden crosses, and eerie *teniebla* ceremonies in dark, secret *moradas*. A missionary at Taos called the penitente procession "one of the most awful sights a human being could witness." According to another, the "most weird, dirge-like music ever made by a mortal flute player" accompanied penitente rituals. Sheldon Jackson added that "groaning, shrieking, and striking of sticks and stones" characterized the secret ceremonies in the *moradas.*[35]

Not surprisingly, shocked and ethnocentric Presbyterians (like most American newcomers to New Mexico) often misunderstood and exaggerated about particularly shocking aspects of penitente activities. Their most sensational and oft-repeated charge was that the brothers actually crucified one of their own members in commemoration of the death of Christ. Most observers reported that the *Cristo* was bound tightly from head to foot with leather thongs and that he usually died from the experience. Alexander Darley, who many considered an authority, informed Sheldon Jackson in a personal letter in 1875 that "once in five years there must be a crucifixion unto death of at least one person." Three years later, he admitted that he really did not know if victims survived or not but that he "had heard stories that many die." Other accounts were less cautious. An article in the October 1876 *Rocky Mountain Presbyterian* quoted a surgeon from Ft. Lyon, Colorado, who estimated "at least 100 die each year" from penitente rituals. The month before, the same paper reprinted a report from the *Denver Tribune* that two died from the previous Easter's activities and that at least three more were likely not to recover.[36]

Presbyterians further charged that penitentes callously engaged in these activities to expiate past and future sins. One missionary reported that members of the brotherhood met secretly and confessed their crimes before one another with the understanding that these would never be revealed to outsiders or civil authorities. Thereafter fellow brothers determined the type and degree of penance sufficient "to fit the crime." Once a penitente completed his annual penance, Darley added, he "could commit any crime and be forgiven." Another observer attempted to explain this preference for "literal rather than metaphorical" bearing of the cross by suggesting that it was "far easier for natural man to endure agonies than to cease sinning."[37]

While Presbyterians customarily portrayed New Mexican Catholicism in monolithic terms, a few observers correctly recognized the ominous divisions that threatened that church. Of the countless descriptions of penitentes, for example, two reported efforts by the institutional church and Archbishop Jean Baptise Lamy to suppress that movement. The French-born Lamy had been appointed archbishop after the American takeover, and his reaction to traditional New Mexican culture and Catholicism was as ethnocentric and harsh as that of the Protestants. Lamy's attempts to reform the church that he inherited seriously divided New Mexico Catholics.[38]

Presbyterian reporters gave mixed reviews to Lamy's effort. Some reports from the field praised the archbishop as a "man of unquestionable ability" and concluded that his "sincere and jealous" effort to remedy the ills of the New Mexican church had enjoyed some success. Other observers, including W. G. Kephart (the first Presbyterian missionary in the territory), were more critical. They charged that Lamy and the foreign priests that he brought to New Mexico (particularly the Jesuits) burned Bibles and tracts missionaries had distributed and intimidated natives who associated with them.[39]

Presbyterian observations about Lamy's archrival, Padre Antonio Jose Martinez of Taos, are particularly intriguing. A leader of the anti-American faction at the time of the American takeover, Martinez challenged Lamy's condemnation of penitentes, New Mexican religious arts, and other aspects of New Mexico's traditional culture. Lamy finally excommunicated the Taos priest. After Martinez's excommunication and death, his followers in the Taos area, a deeply religious people then without church and leader, became some of the first native New Mexicans to show interest in Presbyterianism. Consequently, even as they condemned much that Martinez defended, some Presbyterian observers praised the Taos patriarch as the forerunner of New Mexican Presbyterianism. They lauded his liberal views and asserted that he was "Protestant in all except name" and had "taught many of his people the better way."[40]

To win Presbyterian support, Sheldon Jackson and the early New Mexico missionaries regularly emphasized the practical and patriotic, as well as the religious, importance of their work. Like other western boosters New Mexico missionaries praised the territory's mild climate, mineral wealth, and potential for agriculture and farming. The imminent arrival of the railroad, they were sure, would initiate a new era of prosperity that would benefit American business as well as New Mexico. Other reports from the field stressed the urgent necessity of teaching American institutions and values to the culturally disparate New Mexicans. Soon, suggested one missionary, New Mexico would achieve statehood and have representatives in Congress; unless conditions changed, he warned, the latter would almost assuredly vote in the interest of Catholicism and its effort "to subvert our system of education and destroy our government." Finally and most importantly, missionaries stressed the religious reasons for their work. John Annin succinctly summed up these goals in 1870 when he reported that the Territory had a population of 100,000 — "each one with a soul to save."[41]

Whether talking about development of New Mexican resources, incorporation of the New Mexicans into the American mainstream, or conversion of the natives to Protestant Christianity, Presbyterian missionaries were confident of the ultimate success of their cause. In spite of their disregard for New Mexican culture, the missionaries always believed that New Mexico's people could be regenerated. Time and again they emphasized that New Mexicans had "great innate intelligence," that many of them "look[ed] for something better," and that it was "only the Gospel that [made] us different from them."[42] For the good of the New Mexicans, the American republic, and the Presbyterian church, Presbyterian missions among New Mexicans had to be supported and expanded.

Presbyterian cultural biases and linear understanding of history offered ready explanations for the relatively laggard cultural development of Indians and New Mexicans and led Presbyterians to establish missions that would bring those peoples to true religion and the Anglo-Protestant way. The Mormons of Utah, however, posed a far different problem. Mostly of Anglo-American and western European stocks, and often converts from Protestant Christianity, they had rejected Christian civilization for the "dark," "corrupt," and "foreign" religion and society of their desert Zion. Moreover, the success of their Great Basin Kingdom, the flocking of new converts there from the East and overseas, and relative Mormon imperviousness to Protestant missionary overtures perplexed Presbyterian observers. These very reasons made Mormons the most challenging and threatening of the exceptional populations.[43]

Presbyterian observers went to great lengths to explain how this corrupt and misleading religion emerged in the pure air of Christian America. Like most non-Mormons of the time, they depicted the Mormon patriarch, Joseph Smith, in darkest terms. One leading Presbyterian called him an "impostor of the lowest order," and an article in the *Rocky Mountain Presbyterian* charged that Smith's "ignorant, lazy, and superstitious" family "dabbled in witchcraft" and often bilked gullible contributors with fraudulent searches for buried treasure. Regarding the mysterious origins of the *Book of Mormon,* Presbyterians alleged that it was plagiarized from an unpublished "historical romance of the first settlers of America" written by one Solomon Spalding.[44]

A religion born from such questionable beginnings could have few redeeming characteristics, and Presbyterian missionaries in Utah regularly and roundly criticized Mormon doctrine and ritual. One longtime Salt Lake City missionary reported that the Mormon religion was "made up of 20 parts: 8 parts diabolism, 3 parts animalism from the Mohammedan system, 1 part bigotry from old Judaism, 4 parts cunning and treachery from Jesuitism, 2 parts Thugism from India, and 2 parts Arnoldism." Steeped in Calvinist theology, Presbyterians particularly objected to Mormonism's anthropomorphic, materialistic concept of God and Arminian understanding of the nature of man.[45]

Even more alarming than Mormon theology, however, were Mormon religious practices and rituals. The *Rocky Mountain Presbyterian* devoted considerable space to sensational exposés of secret rituals performed in endowment houses and Mormon temples. Reports from anonymous insiders described in detail the anointing of private parts of the body with special oils, the teaching of secret oaths and handshakes to neophytes, and threats of dire consequences if these secrets were ever revealed to non-Mormons. Presbyterian observers often commented incredulously on Mormon baptism practices, particularly "baptism for the dead," and "celestial" marriage ceremonies in which husband and wife were "sealed for eternity."[46]

Mormon contentions that their holy books and revelations to their leaders were additions to the revealed truths of the Bible galled Presbyterians and other Protestants, as did their assertion that the Judeo-Christian scriptures were the basis for many of their peculiar ways. For example, one missionary reported that Mormons distorted the biblically based practice of "laying on hands" when a person is ill and that this led to total neglect of doctors and medicine, causing a very high death rate among infants and children.[47]

Presbyterians reserved their most scathing criticism, however, for Mormon contentions that the practice of polygamy restored Old Testament marital patterns. Presbyterians considered Mormon assertions that polygamy on earth heightened one's place in heaven, that God was "the celestial patron of polygamy," and that even Christ had engaged in polygamous relationships especially heretical.[48]

Polygamy's degrading social impact stirred even more frequent and fervent Presbyterian comment. Not only were monogamous Presbyterians morally offended by polygamy, but they (along with many other Americans) also correctly realized that it was *the* issue certain to win eastern sympathy and support for their cause. Consequently, Presbyterian antipolygamy literature was often long on rhetoric and occasionally short on accuracy. Sheldon Jackson, as he did in the other two fields, led the way with many sensational charges. The "Rocky Mountain Superintendent" likened polygamous wives to slaves who worked without wages and increased the wealth of their husbands. Because of this and polygamy's many other degradations, Jackson suggested, many Mormon women became insane and attempted suicide. Escape from this unfortunate situation was out of the question, however, because "before (a woman) would get many miles, she would be shot and her body left for the ravens and wolves."[49]

Missionaries in the field and church officials who toured Utah elaborated on Jackson's concerns. The *Rocky Mountain Presbyterian* reminded Christian women in 1877 not to forget that "thousands of their own sex are shut up in the harems of Utah." The following year, home board secretary Henry Kendall charged that "before the civilized world" every plural wife "is a harlot and her children bastards." While most observers portrayed Mormon women as victims of polygamy, one leading Presbyterian scholar reported that polygamous wives were unusually unchaste and often "leave their husbands at breakfast and marry another by tea time."[50]

Missionaries often asserted that the most innocent and unfortunate victims of polygamy were Mormon children. The combination of multiple wives and divine emphasis on male virility produced abnormally large Mormon families. Presbyterians alleged that children in overcrowded Mormon homes suffered from a lack of love, education, and physical care. One report suggested that "food and shelter are of such meager, insufficient quality that a decent, respectable, childhood is out of the question." Another account suggested "there is no such thing as a Mormon home" and likened Brigham Young's "Beehive House" to a hotel. A major cause of this deplorable situation, Presbyterians believed, was the failure of Mormon fathers to fulfill their paternal responsibilities. One account suggested that since most Mormon husbands were older than their wives, Mormon society had become a "community of widows and orphans." Others charged that Mormon fathers simply neglected their children.[51]

Presbyterians believed that such abnormal home lives produced ignorant, immoral, and wicked youths. One account alleged that crowded Mormon homes had little room for privacy and modesty and that without these "safeguards of virtue" many Mormon youths engaged in incest and other undesirable activities. Secondly, Presbyterians charged that the excess of children and the jealous authority of church leaders undermined any effort to establish schools that might uplift and enlighten Utah's unfortunate youth. Finally, missionaries reported that "the bitter realization of neglected childhood" led many Mormon youths to reject all religion and embrace atheism and infidelity.[52]

Like their colleagues in New Mexico, Utah missionaries usually absolved the general population of blame for the many ills that they described. Missionaries, of course, criticized everyday Mormons for slavishly adhering to a corrupt religion. But the true villains were the Mormon hierarchy who exacted this loyalty from their "ignorant and misguided" peoples. One missionary asserted that "no pope ever exercized a sway so autocratic . . . and no priesthood were ever so unquestioningly obeyed" as the Mormon patriarchs. One of his colleagues likened the L.D.S. leadership, with its divine revelations, union of church and state, and tabernacles and temples, to the "Jewish theocracy in the days of Moses." After visiting the Utah field in 1881, the recording secretary of the home missions board denounced the Mormon priesthood as "ignorant," "arrogant," "avaricious," "abominable," and "bloodthirsty." While most attacks were directed against the Mormon hierarchy in general, Presbyterian disdain was particularly directed toward Brigham Young. He was, one anonymous Presbyterian suggested, a "cunning, designing, selfish man, influenced by lust for women, gold, and power."[53]

Practically every action by L.D.S. officials was fair game for Presbyterian attack. Missionaries charged that Mormon tithing (customarily 10 percent) allowed bishops and priests to live in luxury, while it impoverished "hard-working but ignorant" Mormon people.[54] Divine revelations by Mormon leaders stirred similar criticisms. One missionary quipped that whenever disputes arose or previous church policy conflicted with new plans a "revelation is readily at hand." The same person described "Sabbath discourses" by Mormon priests as "a compound of agriculture, politics, tirades against Gentiles, ecclesiastical rules, threats to the disobedient, and exhortations to pay up tithing." After commenting on similar qualities in Mormon sermons, another writer concluded that for all their religiosity Mormons had "no true communion with God . . . no true worship . . . no blessed comforting Gospel."[55]

The most sensational charge against L.D.S. officials was that they followed the policy of blood atonement in dealing with apostates. Sheldon Jackson reported that it was a "prominent article of their faith" that good Mormons must kill those who reveal church secrets in order to "save them from a fate worse than going to Hell." Consequently, he charged that every town in Utah had "been stained with the blood" of those who became obnoxious to church leaders. Other missionary accounts occasionally made similar charges, but one particularly outspoken missionary (who rarely saw any virtue in the Mormon leadership) conceded in 1878 that, while blood atonement had been common in the 1850s, it had virtually disappeared in more recent years due to pressure from U.S. courts.[56]

After painting such a dark and degrading picture of Mormonism, missionaries strained to explain how it maintained loyalty from its adherents and, indeed, how it continued to win converts in unprecedented numbers. First, they charged that L.D.S. leaders had masterfully convinced Mormons of the superiority of their ways over the vice and extravagance of the Gentile world. Second, Presbyterians conceded that Mormons outdistanced them (and all of other American churches) in winning immigrants from England and western Europe to their faith. Of course, Presbyterians charged that Mormons often deceived immigrants with promises of free farms and passage and of an easy life. Only after reaching Utah did the newcomers learn about the more peculiar aspects of Mormon doctrine (i.e., polygamy) and that they were at the mercy of their new church. Finally, Presbyterians charged that the absence of public education and Mormon control of the few "common schools" existing in Utah prevented ignorant Mormons from ever becoming aware of the shortcomings of their church and their own degradation.[57]

The acceptance of plural marriage by many Mormon women particularly challenged Presbyterian powers of persuasion. The standard explanation suggested that Mormon women tolerated polygamy because they believed it necessary to attain God's approval and eternal salvation or that they simply feared the consequences of resisting established ways. To substantiate these contentions, the *Rocky Mountain Presbyterian* frequently printed articles from former polygamous wives, including Anna Eliza Young, who married Brigham Young when she was nineteen, only to flee from him and Utah five years later. Evidence that many plural wives truly supported polygamy occasionally trapped Presbyterians in curious contradictions. For example, though many previous issues of the *Rocky Mountain Presbyterian* defended Mormon women as victims of polygamy, missionary George Bird reported in the November 1878 issue that Mormon women voted "in solid phalanxes for Mormonism and polygamy." Consequently, he called for repeal of the law which made Utah one of the few places in the United States where women were allowed to vote.[58]

Presbyterians regularly warned their readers of the greater threat of Mormonism. Mormons, they charged, violated the principle of church-state separation and dominated politics in Utah and were spreading their influence to adjoining territories. Furthermore, Mormon missionaries in the East and overseas annually won new converts, including many from Anglo-Protestant strongholds. The *Presbyterian Home Missionary* reported in 1883 that a special train recently departed Chattanooga, Tennessee, with 150 converts bound for Utah, and that 90 Mormon missionaries in Georgia, Virginia, and Tennessee expected to win more than 600 converts. Even more sensational were charges of Mormon treason. In 1877 the *Rocky Mountain Presbyterian* reprinted words from a Mormon prayer calling for "God to destroy the U.S.A." Six years later Sheldon Jackson reported that, following the shooting of President James A. Garfield, Mormons prayed for his death. "Charles Guitteau," concluded Jackson, "is their hero."[59]

The formidable Mormon challenge dampened, but did not destroy, Presbyterian optimism. Utah missionaries occasionally (though not as frequently as their colleagues in the Indian and New Mexican fields) commented favorably on certain Mormon traits. George Gallagher, author of many of the most vitriolic comments on the preceding pages, conceded in 1878 that many Mormons were "devout, honest, sincere, and conscientious." Similar sentiments were expressed in the preface to the *Handbook on Mormonism*, a book Presbyterians recommended widely in the early 1880s. More begrudging, but still complimentary, was Presbyterian praise for the transformation of "unsightly wastes into a garden of plenty." Several writers compared Mormons favorably to Anglo frontiersmen and miners. Finally, like their colleagues in New Mexico, Utah missionaries waxed eloquent about that territory's natural beauty and great mineral and agricultural potential. Even though occupied by Mormons, such a land could not be overlooked.[60]

These rare positive comments notwithstanding, some Presbyterians joined the chorus advocating extreme, secular remedies for the Mormon problem. Many called for congressional censure against polygamy and the political power of L.D.S. officials. Others warned that statehood for Utah would result in inevitable conflict, not unlike the Civil War. While several missionaries realized that anti-Mormon legislation might appear to violate the sacred American principle of religious freedom, all agreed with the longtime missionary-educator J. M. Coyner, who observed in 1875 that "any sect, Mormon or otherwise, [that] violates not only the laws of the land, but the established laws of common civilization" forfeited this basic American freedom.[61]

Nevertheless, most missionaries also shared Coyner's conviction that political action was simply a means to an end and that persecution could never suppress Mormonism. "True reformation," he suggested, required substitution of "truth for error, right living for wrong living, and showing a better way, in which men will be inclined to walk of their own free will." On another occasion, Coyner reminded readers of the ultimate arsenal for the Presbyterian cause: "God's divine plan." Thus, he could speculate that perhaps God allowed polygamy to exist in Utah as a "beacon to warn the nation of the dangers that besets the home of their fathers."[62] Faith like this carried Presbyterian missionaries in Utah into battle against frightful odds.

These then were the exceptional populations. To be sure, the southwestern Indians, New Mexicans, and Mormons were not without their shortcomings, and, indeed, it was the seed of truth in the Presbyterian images that made them so believable and powerful. However, the Presbyterian decision to lump three such distinctive peoples together into the single category "exceptional populations" and the criteria for their judgments suggest that what lay behind Presbyterian eyes, more than what lay before them, shaped Presbyterian perceptions of the Southwest. Present-day observers would nevertheless be wise to heed H. Richard Niebuhr's warning about the evil habit of criticizing past generations. One need not share the missionaries' views to recognize that they were sincere and serious. To assume that they intentionally distorted what they saw does injustice to them and history. No less than the present-day reader who is uncomfortable with the blatant ethnocentrism so apparent in this chapter, the missionaries were products of their own age. Nineteenth-century Anglo Americans were intensely ethnocentric; and as the century progressed, deep and unconscious social and psychological influences and uncertainties heightened this ethnocentrism and fostered the sense of urgency so apparent in missionary accounts.

Furthermore, observation of late nineteenth-century popular literature quickly reveals that heated rhetoric was standard fare for the time. Ethnocentrism and exaggeration were not unique to Presbyterians nor Anglo Protestants in general. Indeed, the table often turned the other way and they became the target of emotional and misleading rhetoric. For example, *La Revista Catolica,* a weekly Jesuit paper published in Las Vegas, New Mexico, charged in 1875 that the "babel" of American Protestantism had fostered "absurd," "ridiculous," and "blasphemous" doctrine, immoral practices (including divorce and polygamy), and "many other heresies." Nearly a decade before, a Mormon official defended polygamy as far more desirable than "the institutions of pseudo-Christianity" with their "hypocrasy [sic] and depravity and [their] debauching, demoralizing, and corrupting influence."[63]

Although they have received scant attention from historians, the first line of Presbyterian recruits to the Southwest were more than mere voices crying in the wilderness. In the subsequent half century, Sheldon Jackson's oft-repeated lament "all this in a Christian land!" stirred scores of young men and women to join the missionary advance into the Southwest and thousands of "back east" Presbyterians to contribute nickels, dimes, and family fortunes to that cause. This and similar responses by other Protestant churches are best understood in the context of the humane, but painfully human, struggle of Anglo Americans to reconcile their religious and secular ideals with the ever-increasing cultural diversity of their nation.

Notes

1. Minutes, Presbytery of Santa Fe, December 19, 1868, 17–19. At that time the bounds of the Presbytery of Santa Fe were not precisely defined, but the comment applied generally to all of New Mexico Territory.

2. This old adage was formally described by Walter Lippman, *Public Opinion* (New York: Macmillan, 1927), 90. Gordon Allport elaborates on Lippman's premise in *The Nature of Prejudice* (Reading, Mass.: Addison-Wesley Publishing Co., 1979), 444–55, 191.

3. Historians have devoted considerable attention to the later nineteenth-century Indian Reform movement. See in particular Prucha, *American Indian Policy in Crisis;* Prucha, ed., *Americanizing the American Indians: Writings by the "Friends of the Indian," 1880–1900* (Lincoln: University of Nebraska Press, 1973); Keller, *American Protestantism and U.S. Indian Policy;* and Robert W. Mardock, *The Reformers and the American Indian* (Columbia: University of Missouri Press, 1971).

4. For Presbyterian comments on Pueblos see S. Jackson, "An Appeal for the Pueblo Missions," *RMP* 7 (October 1878); Minutes, Presbytery of Santa Fe, December 19, 1868, 18; "Interesting Visit to the Pueblo Village of Taos," *RMP* 7 (October 1878); "The Pueblos of New Mexico," *RMP* 7 (March 1877). While the Presbyterians devoted considerable attention to Pueblo history, they erroneously suggested that the Pueblos were descendants of the Aztecs of Mexico. An accurate description of Navajo culture by missionary A. H. Donaldson is found in "The Navajo Mission, 1879," SJS 55:111–12. For early descriptions of Pima-Papagos, see William Meyer to S. Jackson, May 1880, SJCC; and 1st Annual Report of the New Mexico, Arizona, and Colorado Missionary Association, 1869, SJS, vol. 53.

5. Minutes, Presbytery of Santa Fe, December 19, 1868, 18; J. M. Shields, "Home Mission Letter to Children," *RMP* 7 (July 1878); T. F. Ealy to S. Jackson, October 22, 1879, SJCC; H. Kendall to S. Jackson, June 14, 1878, SJCC.

6. Charles A. Taylor to S. Jackson, July 22, 1880, SJCC; Mrs. H. K. Palmer, "The Journey to Zuni in an Ox Wagon," December 1, 1877, SJS 55:36; Mrs. Flora D. Palmer, "Zuni Pueblo, N.M., April 8, 1878," SJS 55:16; Letter of Mrs. B. M. Armstrong from Pima Agency, September 24, 1879, reprinted in 9th Annual Report of Ladies' Union Mission School Association, SJS 53:420–21.

7. J. V. Lauderdale to S. Jackson, August 21, 1878; H. K. Palmer, "Among the Aztecs," *RMP* 7 May 1878; Mrs. J. D. Perkins to S. Jackson, November 7, 1881; all in SJCC.

8. Mrs. J. D. Perkins to Sheldon Jackson, April 1, 1882, SJCC, commented on the disturbances of drunk men at her school among the Navajos. Similar comments from a missionary to the Pimas are found in "Words from Workers — Arizona," *Home Mission Monthly* 2 (January 1888): 58–59 (hereafter cited as HMM). Also see Bender, *Crusade*, 242–43.

9. S. Jackson, "The Ancient Cities of Cibola," *RMP* 8 (February 1879); Mrs. T. F. Ealy, "To the Boys and Girls," SJS 55:108–9.

10. Mrs. Flora D. Palmer, "Zuni Pueblo, N.M., April 8, 1878" SJS 55:14; Mrs. Palmer, "Zuni Mission" *RMP* 7 (May 1878); Bender, *Crusade*, 243–44.

11. S. Jackson to Children and Friends in the Sabbath Schools, 1873, SJCC; "The Aztec Village of Zuni," *RMP* 7 (April 1878); "Aztecs and Indians: Lecture by S. Jackson, July 31, 1880," SJS 57:1; "Sun Worship in the U.S.," *RMP* 7 (October 1878).

12. Mrs. T. F. Ealy, "To the Boys and Girls," SJS 55:109; Mrs. T. F. Ealy to S. Jackson, November 18, 1878; and T. F. Ealy to S. Jackson, June 25, 1879, SJCC.

13. John Menaul, "Laguna Pueblo, N.M.," *RMP* 9 (October 1880); idem, 3rd Annual Report of Laguna Mission, March 1, 1879, SJS 58:76–77; idem, "Laguna Aztec Mission, 1877," SJS 53:339.

14. S. Jackson, "Interesting Visit to the Pueblo Village of Taos," *RMP* 7 (October 1878); idem, "The Ancient Cities of Cibola," *RMP* 8 (January 1879); idem, "The Ancient Province of Hah-Koo-Kee-Ah," *RMP* 8 (March 1879).

15. John Menaul, "Pueblo of Laguna, N.M.," *RMP* 9 (October 1880); idem, 3rd Annual Report of the Laguna Mission, March 1, 1879, SJS 58:73–74; Dr. H. K. Palmer, "Pueblos Missions," *RMP* 7 (July 1878); idem, "A Zuni Experience," *RMP*

8 (October 1878). William Meyer comments briefly on Catholic influence among the Papagos in a letter to S. Jackson, May 1880, SJCC.

16. "The Indians," *RMP* 4 (September 1875).

17. S. Jackson, "A Missionary Tour through New Mexico," *RMP* 4 (November 1875); "Pueblo Indians of New Mexico," article in 3 parts, signed by "Verdad," SJS 53:55. Similar sentiments are expressed by Julia McNair Wright, "Pueblo Missions — N.M.," *RMP* 9 (January 1880).

18. "Home Missions Letter to Children: Letter from J. M. Shields, June 14, 1878," *RMP* 7 (July 1878); "Among the Navajos," *PHM* 10 (May 1881): 292; Mrs. J. D. Perkins, "Extract from Report of Navajo Mission," *PHM* 11 (February 1882): 17; 3d Annual Report of New Mexico, Arizona, Colorado Union Missionary Association, 1871, SJS 53:116.

19. 3rd Annual Report of New Mexico, Arizona, and Colorado Union Missionary Society, SJS 53:120; J. S. Shearer, "New Mexico," *PHM* 11 (May 1882), 110; "Rev. A. H. Donaldson," SJS 57:48.

20. "The Indians," *RMP* 4 (September 1875); William H. Tonge to Sheldon Jackson, January 19, 1876, SJCC. Lee Clark Miller examines the concept of the Indians as a vanishing race in *Witness to a Vanishing America: The Nineteenth-Century Response* (Princeton: Princeton University Press, 1981), chap. 4.

21. "Pueblos of New Mexico," SJS 53:53–54; Rev. William Porteus, "Westward Ho! A Trip through New Mexico," undated item, ca. late 1870s, SJS 54:49. For an analysis of the "black legend" and its influence on American attitudes, see Phillip W. Powell, *Tree of Hate: Propaganda and Prejudices Affecting U.S. Relations with the Hispanic World* (New York: Basic Books, 1971). Nineteenth-century American anti-Catholicism is examined in Ray Billington, "Anti-Catholic Propaganda and the Home Missionary Movement, 1800–1860," *Mississippi Valley Historical Review* 22 (December 1935): 361–84. Also see David B. Davis, "Some Themes of Counter-Subversion: An Analysis of Anti-Masonic, Anti-Catholic, and Anti-Mormon Literature," ibid. 47 (September 1960): 205–24; John P. Bloom, "New Mexico Viewed by Americans," *New Mexico Historical Review* 34 (July 1959): 165–98 (hereafter cited as *NMHR*).

22. See, for example, the illustration "New Mexico Street Scene," *PHM* 11 (July 1882): 132. Porteus, "Westward Ho," 49; "Monthly Concert — New Mexico," *PHM* 11 (June 1882): 128; S.A.R., "Habits and Customs in New Mexico, 1876," SJS 54:130.

23. Porteus, "Westward Ho"; "Monthly Concert." Randi Walker thoroughly analyzes Protestant missionary perceptions of New Mexicans in "Protestantism in the Sangre de Cristos," 85–89. Also see John Porter Bloom, "New Mexico Viewed by Americans."

24. S.A.R., "Habits and Customs in N.M."; Porteus, "Westward Ho"; "Light Dawning in New Mexico," *RMP* 4 (October 1875). Two contrasting studies of Anglo-American perceptions of New Mexican women are James M. Lacy, "New Mexican Women in Early American Writings," *NMHR* 34 (January 1959): 41–51; and Beverly Trulio, "Anglo-American Attitudes toward New Mexican Women," *Journal of the West* 12 (April 1973): 229–39.

25. William H. Rideing, "New Mexico: Its People and Culture," *Harper's Magazine*, reprinted, *RMP* 7 (March 1877); Sheldon Jackson, "A Trip of 2,000 Miles through New Mexico," SJS 53:347; "Home Missions — Presbyterial Society of Presbytery of Cincinnati — Topics for June — New Mexico and the North American Indians," June 7, 1882, SJS 55:9–10.

26. Sheldon Jackson, "Home Missions: A Trip along the Frontier," September-October 1872, SJS 53:60–61; idem, "A Ride of 2,000 Miles through New Mexico," SJS 53:347–48; "Ought New Mexico Be Admitted to the Union?" *RMP* 5 (April 1876); Thomas Thompson, "Pioneer Work in Southern New Mexico," June 1898, SJS 10:411–14.

27. Robert West, "Notes of New Mexico," SJS 54:14–15; Jackson, "A Trip of 2,000 Miles."

28. Typical Presbyterian descriptions of New Mexican hospitality and civility are D. F. McFarland, "Correspondence of the Presbyterian," 1866, SJS 53:12; and J. M. Roberts, "An Appeal for Ocate, N.M.," 1878, SJS 56:11. Suggestions that the New Mexicans were "redeemable" are found in "Ought New Mexico Be Admitted to the Union?"; "Supplement to Del Norte College Record," PHS, RG 32, Box 24, F-13; "Missionary Convention," clipping from the *Daily Democrat*, December 15, 1883, SJS 48:25; James M. Roberts, "From Fernando de Taos, N.M.," 1878–79, SJS 54:61.

29. C. R. Bliss, "New Mexico," *RMP* 8 (October 1879); "Ought New Mexico Be Admitted to the Union?"; clipping from John Annin's *Revista Evangelica*, Fall 1878. Similar views presented by a Congregationalist are found in E. P. Tenney, "11,520 Whacks and 43,897 Jolts," SJS 54:11.

30. "Ought N.M. Be Admitted to the Union?"; George Darley, "The Roman Catholic Church and Our Public Schools," sermon, Darley Collection, Western History Collection, University of Colorado; "Romanism and Education," *RMP* 7 (December 1878).

31. "Correspondence to the *Presbyterian*," 1866, SJS 53:12; John Annin, "New Mexico, No. 11," *Presbyterian*, 1870, SJS 53:18.

32. "Light Dawning in N.M.," *RMP* 4 (October 1875); Rev. Alexander M. Darley, "New Mexicans," *RMP* 9 (October 1880).

33. "Jottings in New Mexico," SJS 54:30–31; Sheldon Jackson, "Home Missions: A Trip along the Frontier, September-October 1872," SJS 53:61–62. *Retablos* are paintings of saints on flat boards, and *santos* are wood carvings of saints. These traditional New Mexican religious art forms developed during New Mexico's long period of isolation and bore distinctive medieval traits.

34. "Statement Issued by the Presbytery of Santa Fe, November 1874, for Circulation in Church Publications," SJS 54:9; "From N.M.," author unknown, to Bro. Gage, February 13, 1881, SJS 54:25; John Menaul to Mrs. M. L. Sheafe, October 26, 1872, SJCC.

35. Presbyterian accounts of penitentes are voluminous. The information in this paragraph is drawn from the following sources, which are fairly typical of other Presbyterian accounts. Jackson, "Home Missions: A Trip along the Frontier," 62; Mrs. Susan T. Perry, "Scenes in New Mexico," 1881, SJS 54:18; Letter from

Miss Jennie Flott, reprinted in *RMP* 2 (July 1873); S.A.R., "The Penitentes," *RMP* 5 (June 1876); "The Penitentes — Vivid Description of Passion Week in Conejos, Colorado," *RMP* 7 (April 1878). The sensational *Passionists of the Southwest*, written by Presbyterian Alexander Darley in 1893, is one of the first accounts of the organization by an outsider. In recent years historians and other social scientists have devoted considerable attention to the penitente phenomenon. Marta Weigle's *Brothers of Light, Brothers of Blood* (Albuquerque: University of New Mexico Press, 1976) refutes many of the emotional Presbyterian charges. She briefly assesses Protestant responses to penitentes on pp. 68–75. *Moradas* are penitente meeting places, usually located near a Catholic church and often closed to non-penitentes. *Teniebla* ceremonies take place in *moradas* on Good Friday evening and represent the darkness and earthquake that followed the crucifixion of Christ.

36. Alexander M. Darley to Sheldon Jackson, May 5, 1875, SJCC; "The Penitentes: A Vivid Description of Passion Week in Conejos, Colorado"; "The Cruelties of Heathenism in the United States," *RMP* 5 (October 1876); "Crucifixion as a Religious Rite in the U.S.," *RMP* 5 (September 1876). Weigle describes the simulated crucifixion of penitente rituals and suggests that accounts like those of the missionaries were sensational and misleading. She reports that the chosen brother was usually a young, hardy member of the brotherhood and that he was bound to the cross for only a short period. "The human *Cristo,*" she emphasizes, "was not supposed to die," but she does not deny that death occasionally occurred (*Brothers of Light*, 171–73).

37. "The Cruelties of Heathenism in the U.S."; J. A. Merritt to S. Jackson, March 19, 1875, SJS 54:83; Letter from Miss Jennie Flott; S.A.R., "The Penitentes." Weigle suggests that penitential activities were simple and sincere and that they were "not masochistic self-indulgences or self-tortures" (*Brothers of Light*, 162, 178).

38. S.A.R. "The Penitentes"; Perry, "Scenes in New Mexico." Much has been written about Archbishop Lamy. An uncritical, but thorough, biography is Paul Horgan, *Lamy of Santa Fe* (New York: Farrar, Straus and Giroux, 1975). Horgan describes Lamy's reaction to New Mexico Catholicism and culture on pp. 127–31.

39. "New Mexico: Letter of a Missionary Recently Gone to N.M.," probably written by John Annin in 1871, printed in the Presbyterian mission magazine *The Field Is the World*, SJS 53:165; Rideing, "New Mexico: Its People and Culture"; W. G. Kephart to Sheldon Jackson, February 17, 1872, SJCC; "New Mexico: Letter of a Missionary Recently Gone to N.M."

40. The Lamy-Martinez feud has received considerable attention from historians. Horgan in *Lamy of Santa Fe* offers a very pro-Lamy assessment, as did the novelist Willa Cather in her fictional account *Death Comes to the Archbishop*. A strongly pro-Martinez response is Ray John de Aragon, *Padre Martinez and Bishop Lamy* (Las Vegas, N.M.: Pan American Press, 1978). A more balanced account is Fray Angelico Chavez, *But Time and Chance: The Story of Padre Martinez of Taos* (Santa Fe: Sunstone Press, 1981). Contemporary Presbyterian praise of Padre Martinez is found in "A History of Church of Taos, N.M., *RMP*

7 (January 1878); and "The Religious Condition of N.M.: Past and Present," *PHM* 11 (June 1882): 129. The unpublished writings of Dora Ortiz Vasquez, a descendent of Padre Martinez, makes a case for the contention that Martinez laid the foundation for New Mexican Presbyterianism; much of her work is held by the Menaul Historical Library, Albuquerque, N.M.

41. "New Mexico by a Home Missionary," *RMP* 4 (November 1875); John Annin, "New Mexico," series of articles written for the *Presbyterian*, 1870, SJS 53:19–25; "Dr. Kendall's Speech for Home Missions," SJS 48:35–36; Hon. S. B. Elkins, "Resources of New Mexico," *RMP* 7 (March 1877); W.R.T., "On the Wing: Two Weeks in Santa Fe," SJS 53:3; Annin, "New Mexico," 1870, SJS 53:18–19; idem, "New Mexico, No. 2," 1870, SJS 53:19.

42. S.A.R., "Habits and Customs in New Mexico," 1876, SJS 54:130; "Ought New Mexico Be Admitted to the Union?"; James M. Roberts, "From Fernando de Taos," 1878–79, SJS 54:61; "Supplement to Del Norte College Record," PHS, RG 32, Box 24, F-13; "Missionary Convention," clipping from the *Daily Democrat,* December 15, 1883, SJS 48:25.

43. Early Presbyterian responses to Mormons paralleled those of most Anglo Protestants of the period. There have been a number of excellent analyses of this anti-Mormon reaction. See, for example, Leonard J. Arrington and Jan Haupt, "Intolerable Zion: The Image of Mormonism in Nineteenth-Century American Literature," *Western Humanities Review* 22 (Summer 1968): 243–57; Jan Shipps, "From Satyr to Saint: American Attitudes toward the Mormons, 1860–1960" (paper presented at 1973 Annual Meeting of Organization of American Historians; copy in L.D.S. Archives, Salt Lake City); Davis Bitton and Gary L. Bunker, "Double Jeopardy: Visual Images of Mormon Women to 1914," *Utah Historical Quarterly* 46 (Spring 1978); Davis Bitton and Gary L. Bunker, *The Mormon Graphic Image, 1834–1914: Cartoons, Caricatures, and Illustrations* (Salt Lake City: University of Utah Press, 1983).

44. Rev. F. F. Ellinwood, "Utah and the Next Vexed Question," ca. late 1860s, SJS 59:85; "The Origins of Mormonism," *RMP* 6 (July 1877); George W. Gallagher, "Home Missions among the Mormons," *RMP* 5 (November 1878). The Spalding thesis regarding the origin of the *Book of Mormon* was widely held by many non-Mormons of the time. Sociologist Thomas O'Dea suggests this theory "is supported by tenuous arrangements of circumstantial evidence and even more questionable analysis of internal content" and that few present-day scholars take it seriously (*The Mormons,* 24).

45. J. M. Coyner, *The Utah Review* 1 (February 1882), quoted in Dwyer, *The Gentile Comes to Utah* (Salt Lake City: Western Epics, 1971), 184.

46. Gallagher, "Home Missions among the Mormons"; George R. Bird, "Mormon Utah and Presbyterian Missions," *RMP* 7 (June 1879); "Mormonism," lecture presented by the Reverend Joseph Cook in Boston, December 23, 1878, reprinted in *RMP* 8 (April 1879); J. M. Coyner, "The Utah Column: The Endowment Expos," SJS 60:36–39; George W. Gallagher, "Letters on Mormonism," December 1878, SJS 60:44–45. A brief summary of Presbyterian objections to Mormonism is presented in T. Edgar Lyon, "Evangelical Protestant Missionary Activities in Mormon-

dominated Areas, 1865-1900," 81-82. The origins of distinctive Mormon rituals is analyzed by O'Dea, *The Mormons,* 54-63.

47. Gallagher, "Home Missions among the Mormons."

48. "Mormonism," *RMP* 8 (April 1879).

49. Sheldon Jackson to the Ladies of the Presbyterian Church of Brooklyn, N.Y., ca. 1877 or 1878, SJCC. In "Mormon Polygamy: A Review Article," Davis Bitton examines the vast literature on Mormon polygamy, including a number of recent revisionist studies (*Journal of Mormon History* 4 [1977]: 101-18).

50. "Monthly Concert," *RMP* 6 (April 1877); "Home Missions Address of Dr. Kendall," SJS 48:48; Dr. Phillip Schaff, "The Fruits of Polygamy," SJS 60:56. Another article, "Women's Mission to the Women in the Harems of the U.S.," *RMP* 7 (March 1878), reprinted from an article in the *New York Herald,* carried comments condemning polygamy by a former wife of Mormon Apostle Orson Pratt.

51. "The Women of Utah," *RMP* 7 (June 1876); Ellinwood, "Utah and the Next Vexed Question"; Gallagher, "Home Missions among the Mormons."

52. "The Women of Utah"; Julia McNair Wright, "To Our Young Folks," *RMP* 8 (December 1879). Mrs. Wright was a prominent Presbyterian and frequent visitor to her church's mission fields. In this article she called for Presbyterian youths to support missions among the children of Utah. Comments on the status of education in Mormon Utah are found in Mrs. A. G. Paddock, "Free Schools in the Mormon Capital," ca. late 1870s, SJS 54:79-80; and "Mormon Deviltry," probably written by Duncan McMillan, *Cleveland Leader,* January 14, 1882, clipping in SJS 60:90.

53. Bird, "Mormon Utah and Presbyterian Missions"; George W. Gallagher, "Letter on Mormonism," *RMP* 8 (April 1878); O.E.B. [O. E. Boyd], "Utah in 1881: Mormonism as Seen by the Recording Secretary of the Board of Home Missions," *PHM* 10 (November 1881): 394-95. The description of Young is from an untitled and undated clipping in the SJS 60:12. Thomas O'Dea examines the complex hierarchy of the L.D.S. church in *The Mormons,* 174-85.

54. Bird, "Mormon Utah and Presbyterian Missions"; "Our Schools in Utah: Report of Women's Synodical Home Missionary Society of Michigan," October 11, 1883, PHS, RG 105, Box 1, F-4; "Home Missions Address of Dr. Kendall," 48:47-48; untitled clipping dated 1879, SJS 60:20.

55. Bird, "Mormon Utah and Presbyterian Missions"; "The Land of the Saints," *RMP* 5 (May 1876).

56. Sheldon Jackson to Ladies of Presbyterian Churches of Brooklyn, New York, ca. 1877-78, SJCC; "Mormon Deviltry"; Bird, "Mormon Utah and Presbyterian Missions." Thomas O'Dea comments on the Mormon practice of blood atonement and substantiates Bird's contention that the practice had been largely abandoned by the 1870s (*The Mormons,* 101).

57. The ability of L.D.S. leaders to convince their people of the superiority of their ways is described in Ellinwood, "Utah and the Next Vexed Question"; Rev. W. C. Cort, "Home Mission Work in Southern Utah," *PHM* 11 (April 1882): 79. Mormon tactics in winning converts and immigrants are described in "Two Thousand Mormon Recruits," *PHM* 10 (November 1881): 393. The status of Utah

education is covered by Mrs. A. G. Paddock, "Free Schools in the Mormon Capitol," ca. late 1870s, SJS 54:79–80. "Mormonism," a lecture by the Reverend Joseph Cook, December 23, 1878, summarizes these arguments about Mormonism's hold over its people and adds to them Utah's geographical and political isolation (*RMP* 8 [April 1879]).

58. "The Mormon Wives of Utah," *RMP* 5 (April 1876); "Mrs. Anna Eliza Young Writes an Open Letter to Mrs. Rutherford B. Hayes," *RMP* 8 (September 1879); "Mormonism: Mrs. Anna Eliza Young Interviewed by *Denver Tribune,*" *PHM* 10 (January 1881): 218; J. M. Coyner, "Women Pleading for Polygamy," February 1879, SJS 60:72–74; George W. Bird, "Home Missions among the Mormons," *RMP* 7 (November 1878).

59. Charges of Mormon domination of Utah politics are made by J. M. Coyner's "Utah Column" in *RMP* 9 (October 1880) and 10 (April 1881). Concern about the growing strength of Mormon mission efforts is expressed in "Train Load of Mormon Converts," *PHMy* 12 (May 1883), 111; and "Mormons in Palestine," *RMP* 2 (January 1873). See the following for charges of Mormon treason: "The Mormon Prayer: Treason and Irreligion," *RMP* 7 (April 1877); J. M. Coyner, "The Utah Column," *RMP* 6 (September 1879); S. Jackson, "Extent of the Danger," ca. 1883, SJS 60:25. Gustive Larson suggests that Mormon control of Utah political structures was an even greater cause for American anti-Mormon hostility than polygamy (*The "Americanization" of Utah for Statehood* [San Marino, Calif.: Huntington Library, 1971]).

60. Gallagher, "Home Missions among the Mormons." Excerpts from the *Handbook on Mormonism* are carried in the *PHM* 11 (May 1882): 111; Ellinwood, "Utah and the Next Vexed Question"; "Two Thousand Mormon Recruits." The best example of boosterism by a Utah missionary is J. M. Coyner, "The Utah Column: A Pen Picture of Utah," *RMP* 8 (December 1879).

61. Calls for political action against Mormonism are found in John Eaton to S. Jackson, October 12, 1881, SJCC; "Mormon Deviltry." Concerns about Utah statehood are expressed in J.M.S., "What Is to Be Done for Utah?" *RMP* 2 (September 1873); Cook, "Mormonism"; J. M. Coyner, "Women Pleading for Polygamy," February 1879, SJS 60:72.

62. See Coyner's "Utah Column," *PHM* 10 (February 1881) and 10 (July 1881).

63. Randi Walker analyzes the anti-Protestant rhetoric of *La Revista Catolica* ("Protestantism in the Sangre de Cristos," 257–58). The Mormon leader quoted was John Taylor, who later succeeded Brigham Young as president of the L.D.S. church. Taylor's statement is recorded in the L.D.S. *Journal of Discourse,* 24:4–5, and quoted in Larson, *The "Americanization" of Utah for Statehood,* 44. Taylor included prostitution, foeticide, and infanticide in his list of "institutions of pseudo-Christianity."

3

The Presbyterian Panacea

Presbyterian missionaries who arrived in the Southwest in the 1870s were confident that the Christian gospel and Anglo-American cultural traditions and values could quickly regenerate the exceptional populations. They soon found, however, that administering this remedy would be more difficult than assumed. Language barriers, for example, prevented the missionaries from immediately taking their message to Indians and New Mexicans and even many of the Mormons, who had only recently immigrated to the United States. More seriously, cultural differences fostered suspicions and distrust that left a wide chasm between the Presbyterian newcomers and all three of the native groups.

Years later Sheldon Jackson recollected these problems in the early work among the exceptional populations and remembered lamenting to Henry Kendall, "They won't come to hear preachers; send us a teacher."[1] Jackson and the missionaries saw two distinct advantages in establishing mission schools among the exceptional populations. First, they believed schools would help bridge language and cultural gaps and enable them to reach the southwestern natives. Second, the missionaries were confident that their version of Christian education offered the best means to regenerate these anomalous peoples.

Like the perceived ills it was intended to cure, this mission school remedy indicates a great deal about Gilded Age American Presbyterians. Since the days of John Calvin and John Knox, Reformed Protestants had been strongly committed to education. In the American colonies and thereafter in the young United States, Presbyterians numbered among the most vocal proponents of schools. Traditional Calvinist demands for an educated clergy led Presbyterians to call for schools that would serve that purpose; most notable of these was William Tennent's "Log College" in Neshaminy, Pennsylvania, which eventually became Princeton College and Seminary.[2] In the heady era of the American Revolution, many Presbyterians also saw an opportunity to benefit the broader society by supporting schools. Certain that a virtuous citizenry was essential to republican society, Presbyterians established academies and colleges to foster this necessary sense of civic responsibility and disinterested benevolence among the nation's youth.[3]

The general decline of religion in the wake of the American Revolution dampened Presbyterian optimism but not their commitment to education. Although their church officially endorsed action separating church and state, many Presbyterians worried that these acts might precipitate a decline in morality. Consequently, conservative Presbyterians called for their church to support schools as necessary "bastions of Calvinist orthodoxy." Other Presbyterians soon recognized many other ills that only education could cure. Pioneer missionaries established backwoods schools as antidotes for the "barbarism" that flourished in newly settled areas. Urbanization and increasing cultural heterogeneity provided yet another concern. Consequently, antebellum Presbyterians supported Sabbath and charity schools intended to uplift the urban poor and Americanize immigrant peoples.[4]

During this same period Presbyterian foreign missionaries, laboring under both the American Board of Commissioners of Foreign Missions (ABCFM) and their denominational boards, relied heavily on mission schools to reach a wide array of "foreign" people, including American Indians. Since colonial times Presbyterian missionaries had conducted schools among several native tribes, and in 1803 the Presbyterian Committee on Missions formally endorsed a plan for mission schools that would "produce a revolution in the habits of the Cherokee nation." Within a few years Presbyterian missionaries were conducting schools among a number of Indian peoples, most notably the five civilized tribes of the Southeast.[5]

Despite their historic commitment to education Presbyterians initially divided in their response to the advent of widespread public-supported primary schools. While more progressive New Schoolers generally supported this development, orthodox Old Schoolers feared that the new public schools were too secular. Consequently, in 1846 they adopted a plan to establish a network of Presbyterian parochial schools. Under this program they established 246 schools, but many frustrations undermined that effort and by the Civil War most Presbyterians were convinced that the responsibility of education belonged to the whole society. Consequently, at the time of the 1869 reunion Presbyterians threw their considerable influence behind the movement for public-supported grammar and secondary schools. At the same time, they retained their concern for higher education through a number of colleges and other postsecondary institutions.[6]

Presbyterian missionaries who arrived in the Southwest in the decade after the Civil War all commented on the absence of public schools, usually lamenting that the few schools they found were in no way like those they had known. In New Mexico Archbishop Lamy in the 1850s had established a small network of parochial schools to combat the New Mexicans' "ignorance, prejudice, self-interest, and passion." While Presbyterians shared Lamy's attitudes, they strongly objected to his parochial schools. Not only did they promote the wrong faith; they also were inadequate, for they could educate only a handful of the territory's youth. Furthermore, Lamy and the priests he brought to conduct the schools became staunch foes of all legislation for a public educational system for the territory. The Presbyterians hoped that any state-supported system would be conducted along the lines of the Anglo-Protestant–dominated public schools they had known in the East. Consequently, the Hispanic Catholic majority and Anglo-Protestant minority sparred over this issue for more than forty years. During that period much of New Mexico's youth had limited prospects for an education. In 1870, for example, there were only forty-four primary schools in the entire territory (thirty-nine were parochial or "Catholic controlled"), and only 17 percent of the territory's school-age population was actually in school.[7]

A similar situation existed in Mormon Utah. Though Joseph Smith and Brigham Young had often commented on the importance of education, the first Presbyterian missionaries in Utah found few schools. Mormons were more preoccupied with subduing their Great Basin Kingdom than with establishing schools for their children. Moreover, Young himself advised that free, tax-supported schools were "not in keeping with the nature of our work." Consequently, with the exception of a few counties that made provisions for public schools, the schools of Utah were private enterprises in which parents contracted for the education of their children. In 1862 only 32 percent of Utah Territory's school-age children were in school. Even more disturbing to Presbyterians was the realization that a major purpose of the existing schools in Utah was to protect and preserve Mormon social unity. As in New Mexico, Anglo-Protestant endorsement of public education spurred Mormon opposition to it, and the school question became a focal point in the broader Gentile-Mormon conflict.[8]

The status of formal education among the Indians was even more deplorable to Presbyterians. The southwestern Indians had long had a system of socializing and teaching their traditions to their youth, but this, of course, fell short of the Anglo-Protestant definition for education. Spanish Catholic friars during the seventeenth and eighteenth centuries made some effort to educate Indians, but their influence was minimal. By 1800 Spanish mission efforts in the Southwest had virtually collapsed.[9] Following Mexican independence from Spain, Mexican authorities devoted little attention to the educational needs of the Indians of their own "far North."

When the United States acquired the Southwest, Americans were still struggling to come to terms with their own Indian problem. Since the British colonial period, church and state had often cooperated in the business of civilizing Indians, and mission schools were considered essential "nurseries of morality" in this process. Baptists led the way in establishing missions among the southwestern Indians, but their work at Laguna Pueblo and among the Navajos was only marginally successful and was discontinued with the outbreak of the Civil War.[10]

By the time Sheldon Jackson brought the cause of Presbyterian Home Missions to the Southwest in the early 1870s, little progress had been made in educating the southwestern Indians. The Catholics operated several schools among the Pueblos, the Presbyterian foreign board had made a halting start among the Navajos, and Charles H. Cook, a Methodist who received support from a variety of interdenominational Protestant groups, worked as government teacher among the Pimas. Jackson immediately urged his superiors in New York and readers of the *Rocky Mountain Presbyterian* to assume responsibility for sorely needed mission schools among the southwestern Indians.[11]

Appeals for Presbyterian mission schools for the exceptional populations initially fell on deaf ears. Eastern Presbyterians and home missions officials, in particular, were preoccupied with other concerns, most notably the Old-New School reunion and the effects of nationwide economic woes on their church's mission budgets. Furthermore, Presbyterian commitment to the cause of public education led the reunited church to prohibit its new home missions board from establishing primary schools.[12]

Missionaries in the field, however, saw in the absence of public education in the Southwest their one opportunity to reach and regenerate the exceptional populations. The missionaries likened their work to that of their colleagues in foreign missions fields, where mission schools had long been central to missionary efforts. Furthermore, they pointed to similarities between the exceptional populations and southern freedmen, among whom their church had recently initiated a number of mission schools.[13]

Like most of their contemporaries, these missionaries did not sharply distinguish between public and private education. In the East Protestants generally supported existing public elementary schools and ministers often served as teachers. Conversely, where public schools were lacking, churchmen easily moved in to fill the void.[14] Such attitudes led the early missionaries in the Southwest, almost without exception, to turn to education as the major thrust of their work.

Home board unwillingness to endorse mission school work in the Southwest only temporarily discouraged the missionaries. Far distant from cautious missions officials in New York City and convinced that they could reach the exceptional populations only through schools for their children, the missionaries barged ahead. Jackson not only encouraged this unauthorized course but promised to secure financial support to supplement what the schools could earn in tuition revenues. Jackson found his most ready source of support among the women of his church. Initially, small local interdenominational organizations, like the Female Bible Society of Auburn, New York, responded to his pleas. But by the early 1870s larger, regionally organized groups, such as the Presbyterian Ladies Board of Missions of New York and the interdenominational Ladies Union Mission School Association, became the most reliable supporters of the school work in the Southwest. These organizations were not official Presbyterian agencies, and their ability to raise funds and administer the schools was limited. But without their help the Presbyterian mission school effort in the Southwest would never have begun.[15]

The spontaneity with which Presbyterian missionaries embraced school work is illustrated by the experience of David F. McFarland, the first missionary to arrive in the Southwest after the Civil War. Less than two weeks after reaching Santa Fe in November 1866, McFarland opened a school. Under the employ of the Board of Domestic Missions (Old School), McFarland came to New Mexico to labor among newly arriving Anglos. His missionary commitment, however, would not allow him to overlook the territory's natives. The ten students to whom he taught the "rudimental branches of English education" in the winter of 1866 and 1867 included both Anglos and New Mexicans. By spring McFarland's Santa Fe church assumed responsibility for his school, and his wife, Amanda, arrived to assist him in conducting it. McFarland purchased from the Baptists a dilapidated building that had been their house of worship before the Civil War, and it served as both church and school building.[16]

McFarland's mission in Santa Fe first stirred eastern women to support school work among the exceptional populations. Evangeline Alexander, a member of his congregation and wife of a military officer stationed at Ft. Marcy, wrote her mother in Auburn, New York, about New Mexico's destitute native peoples. The mother, a leader in the Auburn Female Bible Society, persuaded that group to send $500 to McFarland for support of a colporteur to distribute Bibles and religious tracts among the New Mexicans. After failing to secure a person for this position, McFarland advised the women of Auburn that a "Christian lady" conducting a "free school in Santa Fe" would do more to "interest the Mexican people, and open the way for Bible distribution and for Bible truth ... than 100 Agents or Bible readers could possibly do." His own school, he advised, could not meet this task because he had to charge tuition in order to defray his own expenses. Consequently, the Auburn women contracted Charity Ann Gaston, formerly a missionary among the Choctaws of Oklahoma territory, to open a free school in Santa Fe. She arrived in New Mexico in November 1867. Difficulties in securing a place to teach temporarily delayed the opening of Miss Gaston's school, and as late as the following fall she continued to assist in McFarland's parochial school. Although the minutes of the December 1868 meeting of the Presbytery of Santa Fe reported that the "free school is doing well," Miss Gaston soon thereafter left Santa Fe to become a teacher among the Navajos for the Presbyterian foreign mission board. The circumstances that led to the closing of the free school are unclear. However, it apparently became expendable when McFarland and the new Presbytery envisioned a more ambitious and enlarged educational effort.[17]

In December 1868 the Presbytery of Santa Fe assumed control of McFarland's school, which then had more than forty pupils (including a number who boarded in the McFarland home.) Despite considerable Catholic opposition, the Presbytery claimed the school a "great success." They renamed it Santa Fe Collegiate Institute and announced their intentions to make it "a college of the highest order." After nearly two years' delay in securing a charter, the school adopted the even more presumptuous title Santa Fe University, Industrial and Agricultural College. The former Collegiate Institute was to become the preparatory division for the expanded school, and plans were unveiled for several areas of advanced work, including Normal [i.e., teacher training] and Indian departments. The school's purpose, according to McFarland, was "to meet the present and future needs of all classes of people" of the territory.[18]

Officials of the new home board of the reunited church, however, objected to this grand scheme. In December 1870 the corresponding secretary, Cyrus Dickson, advised McFarland that his effort was "unwise," that his primary responsibility was "preaching the gospel," and that the work of education "belonged to other departments of the church." The following spring McFarland wrote Sheldon Jackson that with home board support he could "firmly establish his school enterprize" and Presbyterian work in New Mexico could become self-sustaining. Such optimism faded, however, in the face of board resistance and the missionary's failing health, and in 1874 McFarland departed Santa Fe a defeated man. Thanks to continued support from the Ladies Board of Missions of New York, however, his school remained open throughout the 1870s, but certainly not on the grand scale he had envisioned.[19] Clearly the fate of McFarland's Santa Fe University and Miss Gaston's free school was not an auspicious beginning for the cause of Presbyterian mission schools in the Southwest.

Early Presbyterian school ventures in Las Vegas and Taos, New Mexico, experienced similar, though not as severe, difficulties. When John Annin arrived in Las Vegas in October 1869, he found dismal prospects for mission work among the town's non-Mexican population. The latter included "atheistic" German Jews and Anglo cowboys, who, Annin reported, were "living in sin and shame." The only people who seemed the least interested in his Protestant offerings were a group of native New Mexicans who had come under the influence of Jose Ynes Perea; heir to a wealthy New Mexico family, Perea had converted to Protestantism while in school in the East years before. Despite explicit board directions to the contrary, Annin, with the urging of Sheldon Jackson, established a church among this small group of New Mexicans in March 1870.[20]

Simultaneously Annin opened the doors of the San Miguel County Educational and Literary Institute. To the readers of the *Presbyterian,* he explained that "the only way to reach this native population is to begin with the young." While home board officials fumed about their insubordinate missionary, Annin's school received financial support from the Ladies Board of Missions of New York and the Ladies Union Mission School Association. Initially Annin taught alone, and in its first term his school had twelve "regular scholars," mostly young children from New Mexican families who required "very rudimentary instruction."[21]

In 1872 Annin's two daughters came to New Mexico and took over his school. They taught in Spanish, entertained their students with the piano and singing, and taught sewing to the women of the community. Most of the sixty to seventy students who attended the school by the mid-1870s were Catholic; some resisted the Annins' Protestant overtures, but Annin reported in 1873 that around forty students regularly joined in nonmandatory prayer and scripture reading. The pupils ranged from little children to nearly full-grown men, some of whom were apparently attracted to the school because of the comely Annin daughters. Since most of the students were from poor families, Annin decided not to charge tuition and provided most school supplies free. Soon the school was overcrowded. Despite persistent financial problems, Annin's school was recognized as "something of a power in the region."[22]

The beginnings of Presbyterian educational missions in Taos were even more uncertain than those in Santa Fe and Las Vegas. The Reverend James Roberts arrived in the northern New Mexico community in 1872 with intentions of working among the Taos Pueblos. Native intransigence and bitter opposition from Roman Catholic priests led Roberts to turn his attention to another native group that seemed more interested in his message. These were the followers of the late Padre Martinez, the priest who had fiercely defended traditional New Mexican culture and Catholicism against the criticisms of Archbishop Lamy. Roberts described this group as "a small minority who desire to have their children educated, and [who] are entirely dissatisfied with the priests." Like McFarland and Annin, Roberts encountered official home board resistance. Sheldon Jackson, however, encouraged Roberts to barge ahead and helped him secure financial support from the Ladies Board of Missions of New York.[23]

Roberts cautiously began a night school in January 1873 and four months later opened a day school with five pupils. The followers of Padre Martinez, who included a number of prominent families and several former penitentes, not only sent their children but also donated money for school furnishings. In addition they provided a large home, free of rent for a year, in which the Roberts lived and conducted their school. The Catholic hierarchy threatened to excommunicate any parent who sent a child to the Presbyterian school and refused sacraments to all who associated with the newcomers. These threats had little effect, however, apparently because most of the native families that patronized the Presbyterian school were already alienated from Catholicism. The Reverend and Mrs. Roberts suggested that the presence of their school also led the priests and nuns to upgrade their schools and discontinue charging tuition. Although the school operated by the Robertses never drew as many pupils as McFarland's or Annin's, it, too, paved the way for the Presbyterian advance north into southern Colorado, east toward Las Vegas, and south toward Santa Fe. By 1879 there were six Presbyterian schools with eight teachers and nearly 200 pupils in northern New Mexico and southern Colorado (see table 1 and map 2).[24]

The beginning of Presbyterian school work in Utah was as inauspicious as in New Mexico. Like McFarland in Santa Fe, the first Presbyterian missionaries in Utah began as traditional home missionaries intent on working among westward-moving Anglo Protestants. Yet even then, Presbyterians in Utah saw schools as critical to their work. Soon after arriving in the Gentile town of Corrine in the spring of 1870, Edward Bayliss wrote to Sheldon Jackson that a Presbyterian academy might win the local people to Presbyterianism. Several months later, he reported that he had secured several teachers and that the parents of Corrine were eager to have their children in school. By year's end the energetic Bayliss reported that he had been chosen chairman of the recently established board of directors of Utah Presbyterian College.[25] Home board officials did not respond kindly to Bayliss's scheme. In January 1871 Henry Kendall advised him, "Our advice is emphatic, *stick to your preaching* and let the university alone!" Bayliss complied with Kendall's directive but did not completely give up his scheming for a school. In September 1871 he opened an academy with hopes that

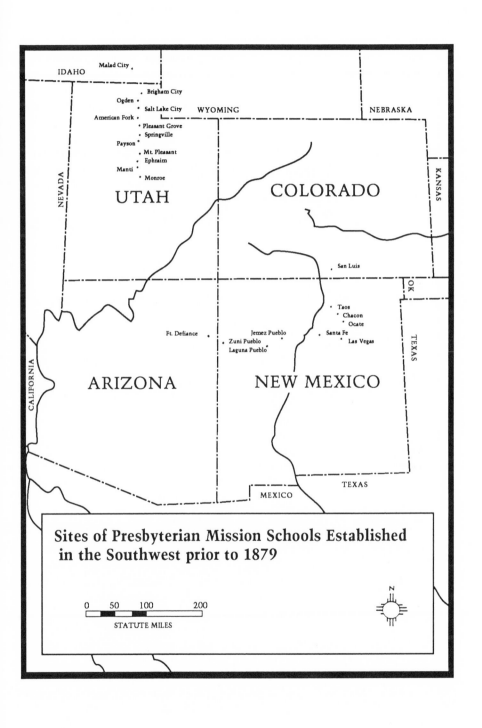

IDAHO

Malad City

Brigham City

Ogden
Salt Lake City   WYOMING   NEBRASKA
American Fork
Pleasant Grove
Springville
Payson
Mt. Pleasant
Ephraim
Manti
Monroe

NEVADA

UTAH   COLORADO   KANSAS

San Luis

OK

Taos
Chacon
Ocate
Ft. Defiance   Jemez Pueblo   Santa Fe
Zuni Pueblo   Las Vegas
Laguna Pueblo

TEXAS

CALIFORNIA

ARIZONA   NEW MEXICO

TEXAS
MEXICO

Sites of Presbyterian Mission Schools Established
in the Southwest prior to 1879

0   50   100   200

STATUTE MILES

Table 1. Presbyterian Mission Schools Established in the Southwest Prior to 1879

New Mexican Field		
Location	Opened	Closed
Santa Fe	1867	1958
Las Vegas	1870	1909
Taos	1872	1918
Chacon (El Rito)	1875	1958
Ocate	1878	1910
San Luis	1878	1896

Mormon Field		
Location	Opened	Closed
Salt Lake City	1875	*
Mt. Pleasant	1875	**
Springville	1877	1913
Ephraim	1877	1900
Monroe	1877	1929
Brigham City	1878	1909
American Fork	1878	1909
Payson	1878	1909
Manti	1878	1909
Pleasant Grove	1878	1889
Ogden	1878	1889
Malad City	1878	1908

Indian Field[1]		
Location/Tribe	Opened	Closed
Ft. Defiance (Navajo)***	1868	1883
Laguna (Pueblo)	1878	1902
Jemez (Pueblo)	1878	1894
Zuni (Pueblo)	1878	1897

* Present-day Westminster College.
** Present-day Wasatch Academy.
*** Presbyterians opened and closed schools at Ft. Defiance on several occasions. The 1883 closing marked the end of Presbyterian work at Ft. Defiance.

1. The Reverend Charles Cook served as a government teacher in the Pima-Papago field from 1870–78; however, his work was not affiliated with Presbyterians until 1881.

tuition revenues would cover its expenses. Apparently this did not happen, however, for his school closed in less than two months.[26]

Four years passed before another Presbyterian missionary attempted to establish a school in Utah. These years, however, were not inconsequential for the Presbyterian cause. The railroad and the discovery of rich mineral deposits brought in Anglo Protestants and weakened Mormonism's hold on Utah and its people. In May 1875 the *Rocky Mountain Presbyterian* reported that "thousands of Mormon parents are sufficiently shaken in their allegiance to the church to patronize Gentile schools."[27] Even if exaggerated, there was some truth to the Presbyterian claim. Indeed, just the month before, Presbyterian missionaries had opened schools in Salt Lake City and the Sanpete valley town of Mt. Pleasant.

Mt. Pleasant was widely recognized as a hotbed of Mormon apostacy. Consequently, when the Reverend Duncan McMillan came to Utah in the spring of 1875 "to restore his health," Sheldon Jackson and the missionaries already in the territory urged him to initiate work there. Despite this encouragement, McMillan arrived in Mt. Pleasant without official appointment or salary. Soon he made acquaintance with leading apostates in the town, who urged him to establish a school and offered to sell or rent to him their own Liberal Hall for a schoolhouse. Years later McMillan recalled that the apostates warned him that "we won't believe a damn word you say, for we are done with all religions." But, they assured him, "we will stand by you, if you will stand by us."[28]

Despite many setbacks and considerable Mormon resistance, McMillan opened his school in Liberal Hall six weeks after arriving in Mt. Pleasant. By early May he reported to Jackson that he had fifty-four scholars of all ages, including the mayor of Mt. Pleasant. McMillan humbly admitted that "his honor's" comment that this was "the best school in Utah" was "not saying much." The school, however, continued to grow and by July enrollment exceeded a hundred. L.D.S. authorities, however, could not ignore this success. In mid-July Brigham Young and a retinue of Mormon apostles visited Mt. Pleasant. Young denounced the local Mormon bishop and leaders for allowing the Presbyterian to establish his school and excoriated McMillan as an "imp of perdition, a minion of Satan, and a damn Presbyterian devil." When only two of his scholars showed up the following day, McMillan temporarily closed his school.[29]

The missionary took advantage, however, of the "indeterminate vacation" that resulted from Young's harangue. He spent the next several months traveling throughout the territory, enduring "intense heat," dust and bad water, and numerous "pestiverous creatures," to survey the field for the Presbyterian cause. One visit took him to the "hottest hole in the Mormon realm." When an L.D.S. bishop warned that preaching there might lead to the missionary's death, McMillan retorted that he "had fought under our flag and could preach wherever it could float." On other occasions McMillan responded to threats by brandishing a six-shooter of his own. By the fall of 1875 he returned to Mt. Pleasant, where he secured a "lady teacher" to conduct his school. Attendance quickly returned to what it had been before Young's visit, and McMillan soon reported that space was inadequate for all who wanted to attend.[30] Clearly his unauthorized educational venture had proven itself worthy of support.

The other Presbyterian school established in Utah in April 1875 took the name Salt Lake Collegiate Institute. The Reverend Josiah Welch had labored in the Mormon capital since 1871 and, despite much opposition and many setbacks, had managed to organize a church and erect a substantial building for it. By 1874, however, he concluded that the only hope of reaching Mormons lay in providing schools for their children. Consequently, he planned his new church building with thoughts of establishing a school in the basement and made known his interest in securing a teacher. In 1875 his prayers were answered in triplicate, in the persons of Dr. and Mrs. J. M. Coyner and their daughter Emma. Coyner, a former school superintendent in Indiana, had retired several years before but was forced to return to work after losing all of his savings in the Panic of 1873. He became acquainted with Welch in 1874, while en route to a teaching position in Idaho with the Presbyterian foreign board's mission among the Nez Perce Indians. The following year Coyner responded to Welch's plea and returned to Salt Lake City to open the Collegiate Institute. With the three Coyners serving as teachers, twenty-seven pupils showed up on the first day of classes. Within a few months enrollment exceeded 140, including many children from Mormon families. Like McMillan's Mt. Pleasant school, the Collegiate Institute had not been approved by the home board and relied upon tuition payments to meet its expenses.[31]

Thanks to donations from the East and "Godless men" (Coyner's label for Mormon apostates) in Salt Lake City, the school expanded its facilities in 1877. The next year enrollment neared 200, over one-half of whom received some financial assistance. Coyner suggested that if more funds were available, enrollment would increase further. In September 1878 he wrote to Jackson, "We must not give up the ship or run deeper in debt." By this time, however, Coyner appealed to Jackson and home board officials for a "more regular means of support." This, Coyner repeatedly asserted, was a small price to pay for an "opening wedge" into the empire of Brigham Young.[32]

The initial success of the Presbyterian schools in Mt. Pleasant and Salt Lake City spurred interest throughout Utah territory. A liberal leader in one community told Duncan McMillan in 1875 that if he could find a teacher "who would take his pay in pumpkins and wood" to "send him along." Two years later missionary Samuel Gillespie informed Jackson that disaffected Mormons in the model L.D.S. community of Brigham City were "willing to make every possible sacrifice to get free from Mormon influence" and were then busily raising money to establish a schoolhouse for Presbyterian teachers. Even as home board officials wrung their hands over these unauthorized developments, Presbyterian schools sprang up in Utah. By 1878 the twelve Presbyterian mission schools in the territory had sixteen teachers and more than 700 pupils (see table 1 and map 2).[33]

The Board of Foreign Missions initially conducted Presbyterian educational efforts among the southwestern Indians. This, of course, was in accord with traditional Presbyterian policy.[34] Whereas there was no precedent for schools among the New Mexicans and Mormons, the foreign boards had long considered schools essential to their Indian missions. Consequently, when the Old School's Board of Foreign Missions dispatched James Roberts to labor among the Navajos in 1868, it was expected that he would start a school. The following year Charity Ann Gaston joined Roberts, and soon after her arrival they opened a school with financial support from the Board of Foreign Missions (of the by then reunited Presbyterian Church, U.S.A.) and the New Mexico, Arizona, and Colorado Union Missionary Association (a forerunner of the Ladies Board of Missions of New York). In 1871 John Menaul, previously a missionary in Africa, joined the Navajo mission. Despite much hard work, the school accomplished little. The widely scattered Navajo population severely hampered the missionaries' efforts, and school attendance was erratic. In 1871 Roberts complained that planting, harvesting, and sheep herding took precedence over schoolwork and that his pupils were "seldom in school for more than 2–3 months at a time." Inadequate facilities and the language barrier further limited the missionaries' effectiveness. By the early 1870s, however, conflicts with the Navajo agent, military officials, and white civilians became the missions' most serious challenge. The failure of the Indian Office to delineate clearly the duties of agent and missionary produced tensions; the missionaries' puritanical expectations exacerbated the situation. By 1872 the school was closed. Menaul remained as agency physician, but after several years of continued feuding with the agent, he and Miss Gaston (whom he married in 1872) departed Ft. Defiance.[35]

With urging from the Presbytery of Santa Fe and Sheldon Jackson, the Board of Home Missions in the mid-1870s showed cautious interest in assuming the foreign board's duties in the Navajo field. After a number of delays, the Reverend Alexander Donaldson arrived at Ft. Defiance in November 1879 and soon thereafter reopened a day school. Although most of the old problems remained, Donaldson proved very resourceful. In a few months he made progress toward learning the difficult Navajo language and won the friendship of many Navajos with kindness and genuine concern. Unfortunately, he assumed additional responsibilities when he agreed to work among the nearby Hopis. Already in poor health and unaccustomed to the area's rigorous climate and the unhealthful conditions in which he lived, Donaldson overextended himself and died in April 1880. Thereafter Presbyterian work among the Navajos was temporarily discontinued.[36]

In 1872 the Presbytery of Santa Fe urged the foreign board to send missionaries to the Pueblos. By November of that year arrangements had been made for three Presbyterian schools in that field. However, at San Felipe and Santo Domingo pueblos threats by Catholic priests that Indians who sent their children to the Presbyterian schools would suffer "pains and penalties, both temporal and eternal" prevented classes from ever being conducted. At Taos Pueblo James Roberts, recently arrived from the Navajo field, faced similar opposition. In a letter to his benefactors of the Ladies Union Mission School Association in February 1873, Roberts reported that Catholic opposition and influence was so strong that he could not even secure a school room. "I go each fine day," he wrote, "and sit on the ground, Indian like, on the sunny side of the old church [Roman Catholic], and sing hymns and songs until the young men and boys collect around me, and then I cease singing and teach them." With "no roof . . . but the canopy above, no floor but that furnished by mother earth, no place, nor wood, for fire," Roberts conducted classes. After several months with little encouragement, however, he gave up teaching in Taos Pueblo and initiated work among the New Mexicans in the nearby village of the same name.[37]

When government teachers were withdrawn from Laguna Pueblo in 1875 because of federal budgetary woes, Presbyterians, with support from the Ladies Union Mission School Association, initiated what became their most fruitful educational effort among the Pueblos. Two factors explain Presbyterian success at Laguna: the circumstances of the pueblo itself and the talented man who labored as missionary there from 1875 to 1889. Laguna was always more progressive than other New Mexico pueblos. For several centuries the Laguna people had had amiable relations with Spaniards, Mexicans, and Americans. In the 1850s a Baptist missionary labored in the village, and after the Civil War two Anglo-Protestant brothers, Walter and Robert Marmon, settled in the pueblo, married native women, and developed a significant influence.

The other key ingredient for Presbyterian success at Laguna was John Menaul. After leaving the Navajo field, the Irish-born Menaul worked briefly among the Apaches before assuming the Laguna position. Dedicated, energetic, and practical, Menaul was able to take advantage of the circumstances that made Laguna so well suited to his work and creatively devised means to overcome many obstacles that remained in his way. He learned the Keres language and struggled to put it into written form. By 1882 he had translated *McGuffey's First Eclectic Reader* and the *Shorter Catechism* into the Laguna language. He and his career missionary wife, the former Miss Gaston, conducted a day school with relative success. In the early years attendance averaged thirty to forty-five students, but later, when his more advanced students transferred to boarding schools in Albuquerque and Carlisle, Pennsylvania, attendance dropped. Menaul knew that educating the Lagunas meant more than just teaching the three Rs. He also instructed them in such practical areas as agriculture, carpentry, weaving, and sewing and introduced fruit trees and vegetables to improve the native food supply. Fellow churchmen, government officials, and even individuals who generally opposed the Protestant missionary cause roundly praised Menaul.[38]

In no other pueblo did Presbyterians find the combination that made their mission at Laguna so successful. With urging from Sheldon Jackson, the home board sent missionaries to Zuni Pueblo in 1877 and Jemez Pueblo the following year. At Zuni Dr. and Mrs. H. K. Palmer found conditions far more difficult than they had known as longtime missionaries for the foreign board in India. Geographical isolation, harsh weather, inadequate funding, and native indifference and intransigence hampered their efforts. Their school never managed to attract more than a few pupils, and then only occasionally. The drafty, poorly ventilated mission facilities (several rooms in the Indians' multistoried communal dwelling) ruined Dr. Palmer's health, and less than a year after his arrival he departed Zuni "a very ill man." At Jemez Pueblo Dr. J. M. Shields and family faced similar obstacles, but they were less fortunate than the Palmers. After several months in the "damp and filthy" mission quarters at Jemez, Mrs. Shields became ill and died, leaving her husband to raise two young sons and conduct a mission school alone. In addition, intense opposition from Catholic priests assured Shields of relatively few pupils and otherwise made his work very difficult.[39] (For the locations of the four mission schools Presbyterians established among southwestern Indians prior to 1878, see table 1 and map 2.)

The tragedies that befell Donaldson, Dr. Palmer, and Mrs. Shields reflected a general crisis of Presbyterian home missions in the Southwest that became increasingly apparent as the decade of the 1870s advanced. Inroads had been made in each of the three fields, but many problems plagued the cause. Not only was financial support uncertain and inadequate, but missionaries lived and taught in miserable facilities with meager supplies. They were often overworked and faced native resistance and occasionally life-threatening hostility. The disdain of other Anglos, who shared neither their religious views nor their concern for the southwestern natives, further hindered their cause.

Missionaries in the field attributed many of their difficulties to their church's reluctance to support their cause. For example, in 1874 the Presbytery of Santa Fe endorsed and distributed for publication in church papers a letter that castigated Presbyterians for not supporting their missionaries among Indians and New Mexicans. Several years later J. M. Shields at Jemez Pueblo charged his church with complacency: "While the Home Board sleeps," he asserted, "the battle is raging in New Mexico . . . [and] Hell itself is being moved for the final struggle."[40] Missionary entreaties from Utah were even more fervent. In 1878 Duncan McMillan complained to Jackson that his clothes were worn and patched and that he had to support much of his work from his own insufficient salary. "It looks to me," he concluded, "that the board regards our services worthless and are [sic] trying to starve us out."[41]

There was some truth in the missionaries' observations. Through the early 1870s conservative sentiment continued to hold sway at home mission headquarters. Still committed to the traditional Presbyterian definition of "home" missions and chagrined at Jackson's frequent disregard for their authority, the board refused to give official sanction to the mission school effort. Furthermore, because of budget woes that resulted from a nationwide economic crisis, conservative board members advocated strict fiscal policies. This, of course, dampened enthusiasm for expansion into new fields and particularly for projects like the mission schools that required relatively large initial investments with no certainty of success.[42] Finally, the contributions from women's missionary societies that had compensated for this lack of official support proved increasingly inadequate as the mission schools increased in the 1870s.

For all their sense of crisis, the southwestern missionaries questioned neither the necessity nor the desirability of making the exceptional populations less exceptional. Similarly, they never once questioned that mission schools were the best means to this end. Indeed, experience reinforced their optimism. What had initially been a spontaneous response to a peculiarly different home mission field became by the late 1870s the essential ingredient in the missionaries' strategy for the Southwest. A Presbyterian-nominated Indian agent in New Mexico suggested in 1877 that the mission school was "the most efficient, if not the only means that can be employed, in the civilizing of these tribes." The next year a missionary among the New Mexicans wrote the ladies board that one "might as well come here and go to sleep as to try to work without a school." In 1879 the Utah Presbytery reported that "the work of evangelization in Utah is the work of education," and the Salt Lake City minister R. G. McNiece wrote a leading Presbyterian woman that "it would be suicidal to abandon" the schools. Other observers suggested even more ominous consequences. "The Mormon problem," wrote one Presbyterian, "will be solved either by schools or the sword."[43]

Despite the despair that hovered over their work, Presbyterian missionaries in the Southwest believed they had made great strides toward fulfilling their Christian duty. God, they were sure, had always been on their side. Their church's traditional emphasis on education and the relative absence of public schools in the Southwest had led them to what was nothing less than a panacea for the ills of the exceptional populations. Only the reluctance of their church to embrace and support fully this mission school effort stood in the way of a glorious victory.

Notes

1. Jackson's recollections are recorded in *HMM* 23 (September 1909): 264. Missionaries in the field expressed similar sentiments to Jackson. See, for example, J. M. Roberts to S. Jackson, January 1, 1878, SJCC.

2. Howard Miller, *The Revolutionary College: American Presbyterian Higher Education, 1707–1837* (New York: New York University Press, 1976); John H. Fisher, "Primary and Secondary Education in the Presbyterian Church, U.S.A.," *Journal of Presbyterian Historical Society* 24 (January 1946): 13–43.

3. Miller examines Presbyterian concern with inculcating virtue through education in *The Revolutionary College*, 82–88.

4. Miller, *The Revolutionary College*, 146; Goodykoontz, *Home Missions on the American Frontier*, chap. 12; T. Scott Miyakawa, *Pioneers and Protestants: Individualism and Conformity on the American Frontier* (Chicago: University of Chicago Press, 1964), 21–32, 99–103; Carl F. Kaestle, *Pillars of the Republic: Common Schools and American Society, 1780–1860* (New York: Hill and Wang, 1983). William B. Kennedy, *The Shaping of Protestant Education: An Interpretation of the Sunday School and the Development of Protestant Educational Strategy in the United States, 1789–1860* (New York: Association Press, 1966), and Anne M. Boylan, *Sunday School: The Formation of an American Institution, 1790–1880* (New Haven: Yale University Press, 1988), examine the general Protestant support for Sunday- and charity schools.

5. Robert Berkhofer, Jr., *Salvation and the Savage: An Analysis of Protestant Missions and American Indian Response, 1787–1860* (Lexington: University of Kentucky Press, 1965), and "Model Zions for the American Indian," *American Quarterly* 15 (Summer 1963): 176–90; Dorothy C. Bass, "Gideon Blackburn's Mission to the Indians: Christianization and Civilization," *Journal of Presbyterian History* 52 (Fall 1974): 203–26. Clifton Jackson Phillips examines the work of the ABCFM (*Protestant America and the Pagan World: The First One-Half Century of the American Board of Commissioners of Foreign Missions, 1810–1860*, Harvard East Asian Monographs, 32 [Cambridge: Harvard University Press, 1969]). Cole-

man, *Presbyterian Missionary Attitudes,* examines the Indian work of the Old School's Board of Foreign Missions.

6. The Old School's parochial school movement is thoroughly analyzed by Lewis J. Sherrill, *Presbyterian Parochial Schools, 1846–1870,* Yale Studies in Religious Education, 4 (New Haven: Yale University Press, 1932; reprint, New York: Arno Press, 1969).

7. Dianna Everett, "The Public School Debate in New Mexico," *Arizona and the West* 26 (Summer 1984): 107–10; Jane Atkins, "Who Will Educate? The Schooling Question in New Mexico, 1846–1911" (Ph.D. diss., University of New Mexico, 1982); Robert W. Larson, *New Mexico's Quest for Statehood, 1846–1912* (Albuquerque: University of New Mexico Press, 1968), 20–22, 124–25; Lamar, *The Far Southwest,* 89, 167. For information on New Mexico's Catholic parochial schools, see Horgan, *Lamy of Santa Fe,* 317–19; and Frederick G. Bohme, "A History of the Italians in New Mexico" (Ph.D. diss., University of New Mexico, 1958).

8. O'Dea, *The Mormons,* 148, and Arrington and Bitton, *The Mormon Experience,* 304–6, examine the discrepancy between the Mormon educational ideal and actuality in early Utah. Three insightful studies of early education in Utah are Fred S. Buchanan, "Education among the Mormons: Brigham Young and the Schools of Utah," *History of Education Quarterly* 22 (Winter 1982): 435–59; Merrill Hough, "Two School Systems in Conflict: 1867–1890," *Utah Historical Quarterly* 28 (April 1960): 112–28; and S. S. Ivins, "Free Schools Come to Utah," ibid. 22 (July 1954): 321–42.

9. Spicer, *Cycles of Conquest,* 152–69, 186–97, 210–13, 218–32, 288–333; Marc Simmons, "History of Spanish-Pueblo Relations to 1821," 181–93; Warner, "Protestant . . . Navajos," 26–41; Russell, *The Pima Indians,* 26–34.

10. American Protestant mission school work among Indians before the Civil War is examined by Phillips, *Protestant America and the Pagan World,* 57–76; Berkhofer, *Salvation and the Savage;* Coleman, *Presbyterian Missionary Attitudes,* 16–20, 91–92, 152–55. Warner, "Protestant . . . Navajos," 42–46, and Ernest Stapleton, "The History of Baptist Missions in New Mexico, 1846–1860" (M.A. thesis, University of New Mexico, 1954), examine early Baptist efforts among the southwestern Indians.

11. Margaret Connell-Szasz, *Education and the American Indians,* 8–15; and Prucha, *Americanizing the American Indians, 1880–1900* (Lincoln: University of Nebraska Press, 1973), 191–292, examine Indian education during this period. Simmons, "History of the Pueblos since 1821," 214–21; Warner, "Protestants . . . Navajos," 112–50; John M. Hamilton, "A History of Presbyterian Work among the Pima and Papago Indians" (M.A. thesis, University of Arizona, 1948), 18–30, examine Protestant educational missions in the Southwest during this period.

12. Drury, *Presbyterian Panorama,* 199; Bailey, "Strategy of Sheldon Jackson," 208–12.

13. Inez Moore Parker, *The Rise and Decline of the Program of Education for Black Presbyterians of the United Presbyterian Church, USA, 1865–1970,* Presbyterian Historical Society Publications Series, 16 (San Antonio: Trinity University

Press, 1977); Andrew Murray, *Presbyterians and the Negro: A History,* Presbyterian Historical Society Publications Series, 7 (Philadelphia: Presbyterian Historical Society, 1966), 170–77.

14. David Tyack, "The Kingdom of God and the Common School: Protestant Ministers and the Educational Awakening of the West," *Harvard Educational Review* 36 (Fall 1966): 462–63.

15. Jackson's promotional efforts and frequent run-ins with missions officials are examined in Bailey, "Sheldon Jackson's Strategy," 326–54. The role of women in support of mission school effort in the Southwest is examined in detail herein in chap. 4.

16. The general information about the Santa Fe mission in this and the following paragraphs is drawn from the following sources: "Santa Fe Mission, 1867–68," PHS, RG 101, Box 5, F-9; "Historical Sketch of Presbyteries, Churches, and Mission Work of the Synod of Colorado," SJCC; D. F. McFarland, "Historical Narrative of the Presbytery of Santa Fe," *RMP* 1 (May 1872); Barber and Agnew, *Sowers Went Forth,* 9–15; T. D. Allen, *Not Ordered by Men* (Santa Fe: Rydal Press, 1967), 1–48.

17. Minutes, Presbytery of Santa Fe, December 19, 1868, 1:21; Report from John N. Schulze, Chaplain of 38th Infantry, U.S.A., to the *Presbyterian,* December 25, 1868, SJS 53:16; 3d Annual Report of New Mexico, Arizona, and Colorado Union Missionary Association, 1871, SJS 53:118.

18. Circular announcing the opening of Santa Fe University, SJS 55:95; D. F. McFarland, "To Churches and Christians in the U.S.," SJS 53:32–33.

19. Minutes, Presbytery of Santa Fe, March 8, 1871, 1:59–65 (excerpts from Dickson's December 27, 1870, letter to McFarland are included in these minutes); D. F. McFarland to S. Jackson, March 23, 1871, SJCC.

20. "From N.M.," clipping dated 1871, SJS 53:81; John Annin, "N.M., Vol. 14," *Presbyterian,* 1870, in SJS 53:28–29. The Presbyterian cause in Las Vegas is the subject of J. A. Schufle's *Preparing the Way: History of the First 100 Years of the Las Vegas Presbyterian Church* (Las Vegas, N.M.: First Presbyterian Church, 1970). Also see Barber and Agnew, *Sowers Went Forth,* 17–22. The career of Perea, the first Hispanic to become an ordained minister in the Presbyterian church, is examined by Banker, "Missionary to His Own People: Jose Ynes Perea and Hispanic Presbyterianism in New Mexico," in *Religion and Society in the American West,* ed. Carl Guarnari (Lanham, Md.: University Press of America, 1987).

21. J. Annin, "New Mexico, No. 10," SJS 53:23–24; 2d Annual Report of Ladies Union Mission School Association, 1872, SJS 53:141.

22. First-hand accounts of the Las Vegas school are numerous. This description is compiled from the following: annual reports of Ladies Union Mission School Association, 1872 and 1873, SJS 53:78–79, 142; William B. Truax, "From Chicago to Santa Fe," clipping dated November 25, 1872, SJS 53:65–66; "Letter from Laura Annin," *RMP* 2 (November 1873); "The Work at Las Vegas," *RMP* 2 (November 1873); and "New Mexico: Mission Stations and Missionaries," SJS 53:38.

23. See James Roberts to S. Jackson, February 24, July 14, and July 16, 1873; Mrs. Roberts to S. Jackson, July 2, 1874; and S. Jackson to Roberts, July 9, 1873,

all in SJCC. Also see "History of Church of Taos, N.M.," 1877, SJS 54:129; and Barber and Agnew, *Sowers Went Forth,* 23–27.

24. Annual Report, Board of Home Missions, 1879, 101.

25. Bayliss to Jackson, May 17, December 5, 1870, January 3, 1871, all in SJCC; Rev. E. E. Bayliss, "Utah Opening to the Gospel," August 4, 1870, SJS 59:101–2; Carl Wankier, "History of Presbyterian Schools in Utah" (M.S. thesis, University of Utah, 1968), 16–18; George K. Davies, "A History of the Presbyterian Church in Utah," *Journal of Presbyterian Historical Society* 23 (December 1945): 243–44.

26. First-hand accounts of Bayliss's educational venture are found in articles from the *Corrine Reporter,* April 14, August 18, August 22, August 23, and September 2, 1871, all cited by Wankier, "History of Presbyterian Schools," 16–18.

27. "Monthly Concert for May — Special Prayer Is Asked in Behalf of Utah," *RMP* 3 (May 1875).

28. Pierce Historical Hall at Wasatch Academy in Mt. Pleasant, Utah, holds many records from the early years of Presbyterian work in that town and related to the career of Duncan McMillan. The quote is from an undated address given by McMillan entitled "Early Beginnings of Wasatch," which is filled with many colorful anecdotes and much factual information. The Pierce collection has many other similar documents, including "Stories of Dr. McMillan" and "Wasatch-Logan Academy Outline Talk" by Dr. McMillan. Other accounts of McMillan's early work in Mt. Pleasant are found in Arthur V. Boand, "The Timber of a Man's Soul," *HMM* 38 (December 1923): 40–41; McMillan, "Pioneer Bearers of the Cross," *HMM* 35 (December 1920): 29–32; Hans P. Freece, "Are You That Damned Presbyterian Devil?" *Presbyterian Magazine* (October 1931), copy in Utah Historical Society.

29. McMillan to Jackson, March 31, April 21, May 1, August 16, and November 6, 1875, SJCC; Sheldon Jackson, "Persecutions on the Home Missions Field," *RMP* 5 (April 1876). The Young quote is from McMillan's own recollection of Young's visit to Mt. Pleasant recorded in "Early Beginnings of Wasatch," Pierce Historical Hall, Wasatch Academy. Though he does not specifically comment on Young's visit to Mt. Pleasant, T. Edgar Lyon suggests that Presbyterians exaggerated Mormon hostility toward them ("Evangelical Protestant Missionary Activity in Mormon-dominated Areas, 1865–1900"). This writer does not disagree with this assertion. There is evidence (such as that cited in note 28) that McMillan, in particular, was prone to exaggeration.

30. McMillan to Jackson, September 15, November 6 and 19, 1875, SJCC; McMillan, "Who Will Furnish a Bell for Utah? — Progress at Mt. Pleasant," 1875, SJS 60:12; Freece, "Are You That Damned Presbyterian Devil?"

31. See Welch to S. Jackson, May 3, June 14, and September 1, 1875, SJCC; and "Salt Lake Collegiate Institute," *RMP* 4 (September 1875). The Collegiate Institute was the forerunner of the present-day Westminster College in Salt Lake City. The William Mitchell Paden Collection of the college's archives is a gold mine of materials on the history of Utah Presbyterianism and of the Collegiate Institute/College in particular. Coyner's own account, "History of Salt Lake Col-

legiate Institute from Its Organization, April 12, 1875, to May 5, 1885," written December 16, 1897, provides a detailed picture of the early days of the school.

32. Coyner to Jackson, December 22, 1876, SJCC. Coyner regularly reported on his school in the *RMP*. See, for example, "Salt Lake Collegiate Institute," *RMP* 4 (September 1875); "Utah Educational Matters," *RMP* 4 (October 1875); "Salt Lake Collegiate Institute," *RMP* 6 (April 1977).

33. See McMillan to Jackson, September 15, 1875, March 8, 1879, and Gillespie to Jackson, August 29, 1877, all in SJCC; "Presbyterianism in Utah," *RMP* 7 (December 1878).

34. Prior to the 1869 reunion the Old School conducted Indian missions through its own foreign board. The New School, on the other hand, initially supported Indian missions conducted by the interdenominational American Board of Commissioners for Foreign Missions. When this arrangement proved unsatisfactory in 1861, the New School placed its Indian work under its own Home Missions Committee. This precedent ultimately influenced those in the reunited church who believed Indian missions should be considered home, rather than foreign, work.

35. Minutes, Presbytery of Santa Fe, April 16, 1872, 91–92; "Report from James M. Roberts, July 11, 1871," *The Field Is the World,* SJS 53:31; 3d Annual Report of the New Mexico, Arizona, and Colorado Union Missionary Association, 1871, SJS 53:118–120; Warner, "Protestant . . . Navajos," 112–50.

36. See Donaldson to Jackson, December 24, 1879, January 4, 1880, to Mrs. F. E. H. Haines, February 13, 1880, Mrs. Donaldson to Jackson, April, April 29, and May 21, 1880, SJCC. Also see Warner, "Protestant . . . Navajos," 151–73.

37. William B. Truax, "Letter from New Mexico," *RMP* 2 (June 1873); Roberts to Ladies Union Mission School Association, February 3, 1873, reprinted in Annual Report of Ladies . . . Association, 1873, SJS 53:75–76; "History of Church of Taos, N.M.," 1877, SJS 54:128–29.

38. Banker, "Presbyterian Missionary Activity," 56–58.

39. S. Jackson, "An Appeal for Pueblo Missions," *RMP* 7 (October 1878); untitled, undated clipping appealing for donations to construct mission stations among the Pueblos, SJS 54:94, 99; Banker, "Presbyterians and Pueblos," 33–34. At this time Presbyterians did not yet conduct missions or schools among the Pimas and Papagos. However, Charles H. Cook, who was supported in part by the Presbyterian Ladies Board of Missions of New York and who became the foremost Presbyterian missionary among these people after Presbyterians assumed official responsibility for this work in 1881, had been working among the southern Arizona tribes as a government teacher since 1870. During the 1870s Cook experienced problems very similar to those of Presbyterian missionaries among Navajos and Pueblos. He became so discouraged that he resigned from his job as government teacher in 1878 to work for a local trader. See Hamilton, "A History of Presbyterian Work among the Pima and Papago Indians," 18–30.

40. "To Churches and Christians in the U.S.: An Appeal from the Presbytery of Santa Fe, March 1871," SJS 53:32–33; Minutes, Presbytery of Santa Fe, November 17, 1874; J. M. Shields to S. Jackson, February 10, 1880, SJCC.

41. Duncan McMillan to S. Jackson, May 2, 1878, SJCC. Similar appeals were made in both private letters and articles in church papers. See, for example, the following letters from the SJCC: R. G. McNiece to Jackson, March 12, March 25, 1879; Gallagher to Jackson, February 17, 1879. Also see Gallagher, "Home Missions among the Mormons," November 1878, SJS 60:28–29; "Desperate," 1879, SJS 60:20; "An Appeal from the Presbytery of Utah to the Officers and Ministers of Presbyterian Churches," SJS 60:34–35; "What Is to Be Done for Utah?" *RMP* 8 (March 1879).

42. Thomas S. Goslin, II, "Henry Kendall: Missionary Statesman," *Journal of Presbyterian Historical Society* 27 (June 1949): 70–73, 27 (September 1949): 169.

43. John E. Pyle to S. Jackson, September 26, 1877, SJCC; Annual Report, Ladies Board of Missions of New York, 1878, SJS 54:140; Minutes, Utah Presbytery, March 14, 1879, 88–89; R. G. McNiece to Mrs. F. E. H. Haines, December 4, 1879, PHS, RG 105, Box 10, F-4; "Mormonism," *RMP* 8 (April 1879).

4

The Women Take Charge

No less than a general preparing for battle, Sheldon Jackson was aware that support from behind the lines was essential for victory at the front. Consequently, even as the missionaries in the Southwest endured unanticipated hardships and complained bitterly about the indifference of their fellow Presbyterians, Jackson sought support for their cause.

By the mid-1870s Henry Kendall and many of his former New School colleagues on the Board of Home Missions joined Jackson in support of a new and broadened vision of home missions. With Kendall at board headquarters in New York City and Jackson dividing time between his vast field and promotional tours in the East, the cause of the southwestern missions was kept prominently before Presbyterian eyes. In the face of nationwide economic woes and resulting budget shortfalls, Kendall, Jackson, and their supporters pressed fellow Presbyterians to endorse and expand the mission schools in the Southwest. In this effort their strongest foes were the more traditional-minded members of their own Board of Home Missions.[1]

Division in the home board became readily apparent in the fall of 1876 when a $500 check designated "for support of teachers in Utah" arrived at board headquarters. Both supporters and opponents of the schools recognized that acceptance of the check might be taken as official home board recognition of the school work. After much debate the board voted to accept the gift with the understanding that this action did not obligate it to further commitment to the schools.

The issue, however, would not go away. Several months later Utah Presbytery (with encouragement from Jackson and his friends) directed an overture to the 1877 General Assembly calling for the home board to commission "lady teachers and Bible readers" to labor among the exceptional populations.[2] Kendall and supporters of the schools managed to express their view in the home board's seventh annual report, issued just before the

General Assembly convened. Referring to the recent arrival of railroads among the exceptional populations as "providential intimations that ought to be sufficient for those that are accustomed to follow where God leads the way," the report emphasized that there "was no element ready to be organized into Presbyterian churches" among the southwestern peoples and that, indeed, "they do not welcome us and many are hostile to us." Under these circumstances, the report continued, the work in the Southwest must be conducted "like that in Persia or India." Mission schools had to be established "as auxiliary and preparatory to the preaching of the gospel." In conclusion, the report asked the General Assembly "to authorize, advise, or at least recognize in way of approval" this new departure in home missions.[3]

Effective lobbying from Sheldon Jackson and a rousing address from Henry Kendall swayed the General Assembly to endorse the Utah overture. The victory, however, was less than complete. Home board conservatives and others opposed to the school work managed to attach an important and intentionally limiting proviso: "Funds for such schools," the General Assembly advised, "[would] be raised by the ladies mainly." Seven months later the home board emphasized that Presbyterians would initiate schools only among peoples who could not be reached by churches and conventional home missions methods and only in states and territories without adequate public school laws. Most importantly, they reaffirmed that "so far as possible, the financial support for this school work shall be committed to the women of our church."[4] There can be little doubt that those who opposed the school work believed these provisions would stifle and ultimately subvert Jackson's mission school scheme. Those individuals, however, sorely underestimated Sheldon Jackson and the power of Presbyterian women.

The 1877 call for Presbyterian women to support the southwestern mission schools was hardly surprising. Women had for several years unofficially provided financial support for the schools already in existence. Moreover, this support was not unique. American Protestant women had played increasingly important roles in the missionary work of their churches since the early 1800s. Initially, women met spontaneously in small local groups and prepared boxes of clothing, sewing materials, medicines, and other goods for missionary families. They also contributed small sums for support of missionaries, seminary students, and other charitable causes. Usually these monies were channeled through denominational and interdenominational boards for support of existing projects and personnel established and administered by the male-controlled boards. But by mid-century some women banded together in interdenominational missionary societies of their own.[5]

Developments during the Civil War era accelerated women's involvement in missionary causes. Participation in the abolitionist and early women's rights movements before the war broadened women's experiences and heightened their expectations. During the war, involvement in the Red Cross, the Christian Commission, and other charitable organizations prepared women for a greater role in missionary activities. Furthermore, after Appomattox northern Protestant women shared the optimism and millennial hopes of many of their male counterparts. Consequently they were eager to "labor for the master" in new fields and in new and more responsible roles.[6]

Prevailing social proscriptions, of course, still sharply limited the types of activities women could support. For example, because it was deemed improper for women to oversee work performed by or directed primarily toward males, women's societies assumed support for missionary wives and families and work directed toward destitute women and children as their special responsibility. Nurturing activities such as education and health care became widely recognized as particularly well suited for women's support. Direct female involvement in the mission fields was initially limited to missionary wives, but by mid-century several missions agencies, including the Presbyterian Board of Foreign Missions, commissioned single women to teach in overseas mission schools.[7]

The initiation of Presbyterian women's work in the Southwest was part of this broader trend. In 1866 — eleven years before the General Assembly officially designated the southwestern schools women's work — Cornelia W. Martin shared letters from her daughter, who was married to an army officer stationed in Santa Fe, with the members of her Auburn (New York) Female Bible Society. The daughter's description of the physical and spiritual destitution of that territory's native populations and the problems besetting the Reverend David McFarland's recently established mission in Santa Fe so moved the women that they organized the Santa Fe Association for the purpose of supporting McFarland's mission. Within a few months, they sent McFarland a $500 check for support of a teacher for a free school.[8]

Because the Auburn benefactors soon recognized even greater needs in the Southwest, in 1868 Martin traveled to New York City, where she visited Julia Graham, a close personal friend and leader in the interdenominational Women's Union Missionary Society of New York City. As a result of this meeting the New Mexico, Arizona, and Colorado Union Missionary Association was formed for the purpose of assisting missionaries and supporting Bible readers and teachers in the "new territories." Following Presbyterian reunion in 1869, this group reorganized into the purely Presbyterian Ladies Board of Missions of New York. As an auxiliary to both the foreign and home missions boards, the ladies' board supported missions in Santa Fe and Las Vegas, New Mexico, and among the Navajo and Pima Indians, in addition to several overseas mission projects. At the same time, other regional groups of Presbyterian women were being organized to coordinate the work of local missionary auxiliaries. In addition, some Presbyterians continued working through interdenominational organizations, such as the Ladies Union Mission School Association.[9]

Despite individual differences these organizations shared much in common. Although they were not officially recognized agencies of the Presbyterian church, all of the groups were committed to supplementing the work of that church's more formally constituted boards. In this effort the various groups engaged in similar work: preparation of missionary boxes and securing of monies for support of missionaries, teachers, and mission schools. The missions in the Southwest made up only a small part of the work that these groups supported. Indeed, their greatest concern was foreign missions. Until this period the home board neither commissioned missionary wives nor (officially) conducted mission schools; consequently, Presbyterians considered foreign missions more appropriate for women's support. For many Presbyterians in the early 1870s, however, the missions in the Southwest seemed like foreign work. Thus they became an acceptable object for feminine sympathies. By 1875 the various women's groups were the primary supporters for four schools among the New Mexicans, two schools in Utah, and two schools among the southwestern Indians.[10]

As the number of schools increased and the educational work proved more complex and costly than originally assumed, shortcomings in the existing arrangement for conducting the schools became increasingly apparent. Not surprisingly, Sheldon Jackson was one of the first to recognize that, with support divided between several different regional missionary societies, systematic control of the southwestern schools would be impossible and funding would be uncertain and inadequate. As a remedy Jackson proposed the establishment of a national Presbyterian women's organization devoted exclusively to home missions. According to Jackson's good friend and biographer, Robert Laird Stewart, that proposal earned Jackson more "misapprehension, reproach, and determined opposition" than any other cause of his long and controversial career. Though Stewart was occasionally guilty of exaggeration, this observation was probably correct.[11]

Jackson's critics opposed his efforts to establish a centralized, separate women's home missions society on many grounds. All of them shared a concern that Jackson's scheme would divide Presbyterian women and consequently weaken their influence in the church. Members of the Board of Foreign Missions and the existing regionally organized women's missions societies charged that he was attempting to subvert their influence. Julia Graham of the influential Ladies Board of New York, which by the 1870s was the most important single supporter of the southwestern schools, was particularly chagrined. Finally and most significantly, the more cautious and conservative members of Jackson's own home board objected to what they considered yet another case of unauthorized scheming by their Rocky Mountain superintendent.[12]

Jackson was characteristically undaunted by this opposition. By the mid-1870s he and friends promoted with equal enthusiasm a national women's society for home missions and the southwestern mission schools. This move, of course, was not mere coincidence. Jackson recognized that support for the one justified support for the other. To traditional-minded individuals who questioned women's involvement in home missions, Jackson pointed to the great need for the mission schools (an undeniably proper field for feminine support) to regenerate the exceptional populations. Conversely, when asked how the already financially strapped home board could afford to engage in such relatively expensive work as the mission schools, Jackson pointed to the women of his church, eager to increase their support for missions. Thus he justified his appeal for a more centralized agency for women's home missions support. Like two strands of a rope, Jackson's two objectives intertwined and reinforced each other. Proponents of one became proponents of the other, and by 1877 the logic of Jackson's appeals became increasingly convincing to many of his fellow Presbyterians. But Jackson was also very much aware that the action of the General Assembly of that year approving the southwestern mission schools and designating that the "ladies mainly" were expected to provide the financial support for that effort represented only a partial victory. As field general for the Presbyterian advance into the Southwest, Jackson knew that a more centralized and reliable source of support for the mission schools was absolutely necessary. And this, he maintained must come from a *single national* women's home missions organization.

For the next year and a half, Jackson and his followers dedicated themselves to accomplishing their second goal. Appeals in each issue of the *Rocky Mountain Presbyterian* for women not to fail in their new responsibilities for the school work were invariably followed by distressing news from the Southwest. As noted in the previous chapter, missionaries in the field faced native hostility and intransigence and suffered many hardships, which they and their superintendent attributed to the lack of full support from their church. And activities at board headquarters gave credence to these suspicions. The conservatives had been set back but not defeated. Guidelines for the school work (devised after the 1877 General Assembly officially endorsed that work) stated clearly that funding of the schools would come from women's contributions and not from the regular Home Missionary fund. Consequently, in the absence of large contributions from the women, Corresponding Secretary Dickson and the conservatives refused to expand or strengthen the existing mission school effort. In March 1878 Kendall wrote

Jackson that he would support no more appointments to the school work until "Dr. Dickson and the Board will assure them against starvation." Several months later he wrote disparagingly of Dickson: "I don't believe another teacher would be appointed if we waited for him to nominate and push them."[13]

Under these circumstances Jackson accelerated his efforts in behalf of a central women's home missions organization. Upon the urging of Kendall and several friends, including Faith E. H. Haines, leader of the women's organization in the New Jersey Synod and a longtime friend of both home and foreign missions, Jackson in January and February 1878 made an eighteen-day tour throughout New Jersey and Pennsylvania in which he spoke on "Home Missions and What Women Can Do for Them." Following Jackson's address before the women of the Synod of New Jersey, Haines wrote ecstatically, "You have given us facts as to the destitutions in our own country that cannot be forgotten." In a second, more personal, note written on the same day, she informed Jackson that she had seldom seen such enthusiasm "among our staid Presbyterian women."[14]

In May, just weeks before the General Assembly of 1878, Jackson wrote the leaders of all synod-level women's missionary societies and proposed that a woman's home missions board be organized at the upcoming General Assembly. To sweeten his proposition, Jackson offered each of the women a position as vice president in the envisioned organization. Although seven of ten responses expressed cautious approval of the plan, four turned down Jackson's offer of a position in any new board, and none formally accepted such. Three respondents expressed strong opposition to the plan. One writer objected that Jackson's proposal would multiply work and concluded her letter with a prayer: "From more societies and meetings and organizations and machinery, Good Lord deliver us."[15]

With the leaders of the synodical missionary societies unwilling to endorse his plan and board conservatives continuing to block his efforts, Jackson on his own called for a women's meeting to coincide with the meeting of the 1878 General Assembly in Pittsburgh. He later described the meeting that resulted "a grand rally of ladies in behalf of woman's work for women in this country." Another participant, Mrs. S. F. Scovel, more modestly reported that attendance was small and that few of those who attended "were aware of the object of the meeting." According to Mrs. Scovel, most of the women in attendance were sympathetic with the cause of home missions, but they were reluctant to endorse Jackson's proposed "radical course." Instead they concluded that the already existing Ladies Board of Missions of New York was well suited to overseeing an enlarged home missions effort. Consequently, a committee of eleven women, headed by Faith Haines of the Synod of New Jersey (and a vice president of the New York society) was appointed to propose that the ladies board drop its responsibilities in the foreign field and devote its entire attention to home missions.[16]

At a tense but courteous meeting on July 11, 1878, in New York City, Julia Graham announced that her Ladies Board of New York would not relinquish their foreign missions obligations and thus could not assume added home missions responsibilities. Thereafter, Faith Haines's committee appealed to the Board of Home Missions for "guidance and counsel." Several months later a committee of the home board suggested that Haines's group organize synod-level committees for home missions and further advised that representatives of each synodical committee join to create a "central executive committee" as an "organ of communication" with the home board. In accord with this recommendation, a number of Presbyterian women gathered at the Bible House in New York City on December 12, 1878, to organize formally the Woman's Executive Committee of Home Missions.[17] Sheldon Jackson's long-awaited national women's home missions society was finally born. Characteristically, Jackson's *Rocky Mountain Presbyterian* pronounced that this marked "a new era in home missions." The women themselves, however, were not so certain. The day after Christmas Haines wrote to Jackson: "You do not know how weak we feel about this." Two months later Scovel echoed these sentiments: "The six months preceding the birth of the Executive Committee may never be fully comprehended," she wrote to Jackson, "but I know my hair is whiter and my work basket heavier for the thought and time devoted to it."[18]

Uncertainty and caution did not immediately disappear following the establishment of the Woman's Executive Committee. For example, after their first formal meeting in January 1879, the members conceded that they "never felt [their] own incompetence more than now." Twenty years later one of the early leaders of the committee described how they went to work in "a dingy little 7' × 9' room" in the building occupied by the home board. "Those first months," she recalled, "seemed like working in the dark . . . , [and] the responsibilities of foundation laying seemed almost overwhelming." Long-accepted attitudes about women's "proper" place made matters more difficult. For example, Haines, the committee's first corresponding secretary, found speaking before male audiences a "severe strain." Yet another early problem was continued tensions among several of the regionally organized women's groups, particularly Graham's Ladies Board of New York.[19]

In spite of these early difficulties, most Presbyterians by the mid-1880s recognized the Woman's Executive Committee as an important cog in the machinery of their church missions. By 1883 the regional organizations of women's missions unified their home missions efforts with those of the Woman's Executive Committee. Simultaneously the church and home board broadened the work and responsibilities of the women. With his trailblazing work in the Rocky Mountain West seemingly completed, Sheldon Jackson turned to Alaska and urged his church, particularly its women, to expand their efforts to that distant field; they did not disappoint him. The General Assembly in 1884 urged the auxiliaries under the Woman's Executive Committee to contribute monies for the support of schools conducted by the Board of Freedmen in the South; two years later the term *exceptional populations* was further broadened to include "mountaineers," poor whites in the southern Appalachian mountain region. By 1890 the women were conducting 118 schools with 368 teachers and nearly 7,500 pupils in the West, Alaska, and the South. They also proved very effective fund-raisers. Each year of the 1880s their giving surpassed that of the preceding year, and by 1890 their annual receipts exceeded those of their male counterparts on the Board of Home Missions by $40,000.[20]

Several factors contributed to the success of the Woman's Executive Committee during its first decade. Leadership, of course, was essential. The real power in the early years was Corresponding Secretary Faith E. H. Haines. The wife of a wealthy businessman, Haines devoted long hours toward establishing procedures and policies, securing mission school teachers, and providing them and their supporters in local auxiliaries with encouragement through thousands of personal letters. Perhaps Haines's greatest asset was that she filled this role without appearing to vacate the accepted women's sphere. One of her co-workers recalled years later that Haines was "a rare type of woman, combining in her nature: force, strength, and great sweetness and sympathy." After Haines's death in 1886, Mrs. Darwin R. (Mary E.) James became the dominant figure on the committee and served as its president until 1909. The wife of a member of the U.S. House of Representatives, James had keen political and business sense and was personally acquainted with many prominent people of the era. On four different occasions, she visited with U.S. presidents to discuss matters of concern for Presbyterian home missions.[21]

A second key to the early accomplishments of the Woman's Executive Committee was effective organization. At their New York headquarters the women worked closely with home missions officials, particularly Henry Kendall and Sheldon Jackson. The women recognized and accepted their role as junior partners in the mission school enterprise. Their recommendations to the home board regarding the filling of teaching positions, construction of mission facilities, and other concerns were considered in light of the broader needs and status of the home missions budget and were usually followed. An 1885 article in the *Presbyterian Home Missionary* concluded, "The church enjoys the benefit of the noble impulses and best judgement of a dozen wise and practical women and the long experience and business knowledge of the Board of Home Missions."[22]

The Woman's Executive Committee was also effectively organized throughout the multitiered structure of the Presbyterian church. By 1888 more than 450,000 Presbyterian women participated in 3,500 local home missions auxiliaries affiliated with the Woman's Executive Committee. The latter groups chose representatives to 170 presbyterial and 27 synodical societies that provided effective links to the New York City headquarters. The executive committee consisted of the presidents and secretaries of the synodical committees and annually selected officers, including a president, four vice presidents, two corresponding secretaries, a recording secretary, and a treasurer. Provision was made for one annual meeting of the full executive committee and regular monthly meetings of the officers and other members who could attend. Guidelines were clearly established for communications regarding activities at headquarters and in the field to the full membership of the organization at the grassroots level.[23] This typically Presbyterian bureaucratic structure did not dampen the women's enthusiasm — a third major reason for their success. Even during difficult economic times, such as the mid-1890s, Presbyterian women were undaunted. Without their support and enthusiasm, the work in the Southwest most assuredly would have withered and been forgotten. By 1890 the Woman's Executive Committee conducted seventy-six schools with nearly 4,400 students among southwestern Indians, New Mexicans, and Mormons (see table 2).

Table 2. School Statistics, 1880 and 1890

Year	Field	Schools	Teachers	Pupils
1880	Mormon	15	22	754
	New Mexican	8	10	193
	Indian*	2	3	92
Total		25	35	1039
1890	Mormon	38	95	2420
	New Mexican	32	60	1552
	Indian	6	27	421
Total		76	182	4393

* No statitics provided for schools at Laguna Pueblo and Ft. Defiance (Navajos).

Source: School Department Statistics, 10th Annual Report (1880) and 20th Annual Report (1890), Board of Home Missions.

The women's contributions to the conduct of the school work fell into two broad areas: publicity and fund-raising, and oversight of the schools.

As befitted Sheldon Jackson's support for "woman's work," he reserved page three of the *Rocky Mountain Presbyterian* as the official organ for the regional women's missionary societies that initially supported the work in the Southwest. Following the establishment of the Woman's Executive Committee in 1878, this arrangement continued. When Jackson turned the paper over to the home board in 1882 and as it passed through several name changes, it continued to carry regular articles from the Woman's Executive Committee. Finally, in November 1886 the women established a magazine of their own, *Home Mission Monthly*. Each issue of this magazine had articles about the committee's responsibilities and reports and photographs from the field. It also offered hints to local auxiliaries about fund-raising, conducting meetings, and other matters. By the 1900s *Home Missions Monthly* had a circulation in excess of 40,000 and proved very effective in publicizing women's efforts in behalf of home missions.[24]

The Presbyterian fund-raisers surprised even themselves with their prowess. During its first full fiscal year (May 1879 to May 1880), the Woman's Executive Committee raised $11,467. In 1884 and 1885 the women's contributions reached $128,500, an increase of more than eleven times. By the 1890 fiscal year the canvassers more than doubled their 1885 receipts and raised almost $338,000. Except for several years in the mid-1890s, when nationwide economic woes prohibited the women from reaching projected giving goals, the committee stayed out of debt.

Small contributions from Presbyterian donors channeled through their local auxiliary societies represented the single largest source for the committee's funds. For example, of the nearly $335,700 raised in 1893–94, $181,500 (54 percent) came from local auxiliaries. Other sources of the committee's receipts were Sunday schools and young peoples' groups, legacies (memorial funds), personal gifts, and interest from their permanent funds. Until the mid-1890s the federal government contracted with the home board for the conduct of schools among several Indian tribes. In 1893 and 1894 the women received through this arrangement more than $58,000, exceeding 17 percent of their budget for that year. Also in the 1890s they instituted a tuition policy in their mission schools; this policy was intended more as a means of instilling a spirit of self-help than for defraying expenses. Most families could contribute only small amounts for the support of their children in the schools, but by the mid-1890s the total raised from tuition at all schools was $24,500.[25]

The Woman's Executive Committee conducted special fund-raising campaigns for building projects and devised means to increase personal interest and support for the school work. The most popular of these was the scholarship system, under which local auxiliaries, young peoples' groups, and individuals contributed funds for support of specially designated students or teachers. The annual scholarship amount varied from $75 to $125 per pupil at the boarding schools to $15 to $30 at the day schools; these monies usually covered books and school supplies and defrayed costs for school furnishings and teachers' salaries. Some auxiliary groups assumed responsibility for the full salary for a designated teacher, an amount that averaged $400 to $500 per year. In the fiscal year 1890–91 societies and individuals contributed $61,000 for support of 139 teachers (out of 368 employed) and $31,000 for scholarships for 600 pupils (out of 7,478 enrolled in the schools).[26]

Benefactors and recipients of their charity were expected to correspond with one another. Teachers made regular reports to scholarship providers about the work of the student(s) assigned to them. Sponsors often sent gifts to their pupils, particularly at Christmas. Contributors of scholarships to Indian schools had the added privilege of giving an English name to the beneficiary of their gift. At the Albuquerque Indian School in the early 1880s, Pueblo students were renamed Abraham Lincoln, Henry Kendall, and Sheldon Jackson. One lad was given the name Lafayette Park, after a Presbyterian church in St. Louis that supported him.[27]

The scholarship system was not without its disadvantages. Teachers had to be reminded not to solicit donations for their work without approval of mission officials. Frequent turnover in students receiving scholarships created record-keeping difficulties. There was also much concern that the system would "injure parental feelings and create jealousies among the pupils." Finally the burden of correspondence became overwhelming, particularly for mission teachers. In 1890 a teacher at Zuni Pueblo complained that the leader of a Brooklyn Sunday school group that supported several Zuni pupils was "one of those dear souls who have the best of intentions but no comprehension of the situation." The benefactor expected long reports from the students her group supported, but "not one" of the Zuni children could "write even a short letter."[28]

The Woman's Executive Committee also coordinated the preparation and distribution of boxes to missionary families, teachers, and mission school children. Although this practice was already in decline at the time the committee was organized and declined further as the decade of the 1880s advanced, it still was recognized as an important aspect of woman's work. Guidelines from headquarters for those who continued to prepare boxes became increasingly precise. An article in *Home Mission Monthly* in 1892 indicated that secondhand clothing was not wanted, that sewing material should be of good quality, and that sewing societies should prepare only plain, neat clothing that would "serve as a positive object lesson" for mission school children. The same article also gave specific directions for coordination of the box work with committee headquarters so that proper sizes and specific needs could be met and problems related to shipping could be avoided.[29] The old days of spontaneous and unsupervised women's support for missions had passed.

The emphasis on greater systematization was equally present in the oversight of the mission schools. When the board, and later the Woman's Executive Committee, assumed responsibility for the mission schools, each school operated independently, and administration was haphazard. This problem is apparent in a 1878 letter informing Jackson of recent board approval of "regulations for teachers and missionaries." These guidelines consisted of three statements: that the board would only pay authorized expenses, that the matter of tuition would be left to the teachers (but that they "were expected to make them as large as possible"), and that in "*ALL* schools the Bible was to be read and the Assembly's catechism taught." Otherwise, teachers were left on their own. In the months after the establishment of the Woman's Executive Committee simple administrative policies were gradually devised. While the home board was ultimately responsible for the schools, it gave the women and local officials oversight of the details related to that work.[30]

The most important and immediate responsibility for the Woman's Executive Committee was the recruitment and selection of teachers. Early efforts to staff the schools had been haphazard, creating numerous headaches for home missions officials. For example, in March 1879, just a few months after the woman's committee was formed, Kendall complained to Jackson, "We cannot and will not be perplexed as we were last year; [with] applications from strangers dropping in all winter." The new committee quickly took charge of this matter. Within a year criteria for hiring teachers had been developed, and Haines reported to Jackson that she had "excellent applications on hand" for teaching positions.[31]

By the early 1880s the executive committee designated four essential qualities for its mission school teachers. Applicants had to provide a statement of good health from an accredited physician. Secondly, applicants were expected to have training, and preferably experience, in teaching, certified by a statement from the training institution or school board under which they had been employed. The committee emphasized that "thorough rudimentary education was essential, that normal school training was desirable, and knowledge of music and good voice [was] almost indispensable." The third requisite was ability, which the women defined as "practical common sense, the power of overcoming obstacles, of being strong without being strong-minded." Finally the executive committee looked for evidence of piety in its applicants. They warned that "gushing enthusiasm [and] fiery zeal" were not adequate and that "there must be a deep love for the Redeemer, a self-sacrificing spirit, a consecration of life . . . chastened temper, the wisdom of meekness, the sweetness of peace and joy." Knowledge of the Bible was important, but the women advised that their teachers should be "less committed to theory and more to obedience to its teachings." Statements from the applicant's home church and Presbytery certifying his or her piety were to be included in the application.[32]

Missionaries in the field frequently advised home missions officials about the traits necessary for those seeking to join their ranks. Most missionaries agreed that those who would join them in the Southwest had to be practical. For example, John Menaul at Laguna Pueblo emphasized that missionaries need not be clergymen and that, indeed, "without certain faculties that do not come from books, the best of men are well-nigh useless out here." Missionaries also frequently commented on the preferred age for missionary teachers. One minister among the New Mexicans of southern Colorado wrote to Jackson, "We do not need old maids here, but young women who are willing to be superintended in the work and capable of molding themselves to it." A Utah missionary more subtly suggested that teachers "should not be under 25 or over 35." The former, he asserted, lacked "judgment, experience, and stability" and the latter ("with a few exceptions") were "not so adaptable." Most missionaries also agreed that teachers needed sufficient musical talent "to play the organ and lead the singing of Moody and Sankey hymns."[33]

Some missionaries were even more exclusive about admitting newcomers to their ranks. While on an eastern tour in the spring of 1881, the Utah superintendent of schools, Duncan McMillan, interviewed five teaching applicants. He unenthusiastically recommended that one of them be hired but urged Haines to reject the others for a variety of reasons: one was "a Methodist," another was "too young," another "too pretty," and the fifth one, "a slender reed," whom he feared too fragile. From Jemez Pueblo, J. M. Shields was even more caustic. In 1880 he suggested that Jackson should determine whether applicants were interested in the work "for health or a nice trip, or whether they meant business and understood they were to be missionaries of the cross to help conquer this dark land for Jesus." Even missionaries who were not so abrupt often had unrealistic expectations of teaching applicants and of the home board officials who hired them. For example, the Reverend G. W. Martin of Manti, Utah, wrote Haines in 1881 that he needed for his school "one who knows *how* to do things when needed—one who can *draw,* one who has *force and magnetism* and *executive ability* as well as piety." "We *can* wait a few weeks, or even months for the *right* one," he assured Mrs. Haines. Such demands irritated even the saintly Haines, and she occasionally reminded missionaries that the task of selecting and assigning teachers was more difficult than it appeared.[34]

While Haines and other home missions officials were sorting through the numerous requests and recommendations from the field, they also reviewed applications from those seeking to join the Presbyterian army in the Southwest. The humble message Haines received from Ella McDonald in 1881 was typical: "I am ready to say here I am, send me. I love the Lord; I have given myself (just now I have nothing else to give) and now I am ready to go where He sends me and so do the work He gives me to do."[35] To their credit, missions officials did not take advantage of the unrealistic expectations of many of the applicants and strove to make them aware of the hardships and discouragements of missionary life. For example, in 1884 Haines wrote a youthful Alice Hyson about to embark on a long career in Taos, New Mexico: "The work is not merely to teach but to be as truly a missionary as if you were to go to China or Africa." The federal officials who cooperated with missions officials in appointing teachers to contract Indian schools were equally straightforward in describing the work to prospective teachers. An 1887 letter from the commissioner of Indian affairs, informing J. R. Douglas that the Presbyterians had recommended that he be hired to teach among the Papagos, warned that he "must be prepared to forego many of the pleasant associations of civilization, and be content to live among a people just emerging from barbarism."[36]

It is impossible to determine from remaining records how many applications for teaching positions the Woman's Executive Committee received, or what percentage of the applicants were hired and went to work in the home missions field. One can, however, piece together from scattered information an imprecise composite of the teachers actually hired and their backgrounds.[37] The most apparent characteristic of the southwestern teacher corps is the large percentage of females, particularly single women. Of the thirty-five teachers commissioned by the Woman's Executive Committee in 1880, thirty (86 percent) were women; of these women, eighteen (51 percent) were identified as "Miss." Several of the twelve who were designated "Mrs." were wives of missionaries or of local men, but a larger number of them were widows. By 1890 the percentage of "lady teachers" increased further. Of the 185 teachers commissioned for the southwestern schools in that year, twenty-two (12 percent) were males, twenty-four (13 percent) were either married or widowed females, and 139 (75 percent) were single women (see table 3).[38] The few men who were commissioned to work in the mission schools were usually married and served in traditionally male positions. These included superintendents of the larger boarding schools (although several of these schools initially had female heads) and teachers of industrial courses, such as agriculture and woodworking.

This reliance on women in the school work is not surprising. The first Presbyterian teacher in the Southwest, Charity Ann Gaston, was a woman. Moreover, a number of churchmen by the early 1870s considered educational missions a particularly suitable sphere for Christian women. In the South-

Table 3. Sex and Marital Status of Mission School Teachers, 1880 and 1890

Year	Field	Men	Married Women	Single Women
1880	Mormon	4 (18%)	5 (23%)	13 (59%)
	New Mexican	1 (10%)	5 (50%)	4 (40%)
	Indian	0	2 (67%)	1 (33%)
Total		5 (14%)	12 (34%)	18 (51%)
1890	Mormon	3 (3%)	12 (12%)	82 (85%)
	New Mexican	10 (17%)	7 (12%)	42 (71%)
	Indian	6 (22%)	3 (11%)	18 (67%)
Total		19 (10%)	22 (12%)	142 (78%)

Source: School Department Statistics, 10th Annual Report (1880) and 20th Annual Report (1890), Board of Home Missions.

west Duncan McMillan and Sheldon Jackson were the most vocal advocates of enlisting women into the mission teacher corps. Years later McMillan recalled that he had "steadfastly maintained that women were braver, more dependable than men, more willing to endure privation." He and Jackson repeatedly emphasized that only women could reach and minister to the women and children of the exceptional populations. Yet other reasons were offered for the preference for "lady teachers." Julia Graham of the Ladies Board of New York suggested in 1878 that many of the men that her board had sent into the mission field were unable "to come down to an elementary school . . . to which a lady is better adapted." Furthermore, the very attributes that the executive committee looked for in its teachers—submissiveness, patience, love, willingness to sacrifice—were widely recognized in the late nineteenth century as feminine traits.[39] Finally, evidence suggests that men were less eager than women to engage in the school work. For example, upon receiving word that the home board had approved him as missionary teacher and physician to Jemez Pueblo, Dr. J. M. Shields wrote to Sheldon Jackson, "If I go, I must leave property, friends, social enjoyments, educational advantages for my family, and I must leave a practice and home which makes my family comfortable and happy." Shields accepted the offer and went to Jemez, but it appears likely that many other men, facing the same choice, decided to forego work in the mission schools.[40]

Of course, Presbyterian reliance on "lady teachers" mirrored developments in the broader society. As the nineteenth century advanced, women constituted an increasingly larger percentage of the American Protestant missionary force, both in domestic and overseas missions. By 1890 women made up slightly more than 60 percent of all active missionaries. Similarly the teaching profession in general became increasingly identified as a "woman's field" during this period. By 1900 more than 70 percent of all teachers in the United States were female. The parallels did not stop there. Presbyterian policies that gave preference for males in administrative positions and paid higher salaries for male teachers mirrored trends in the public schools. Finally, the large number of single women who entered the Presbyterian teaching ranks was part of a broader trend in which American women began to challenge the long-accustomed view that members of their sex could only be wives and mothers.[41]

Discerning the mission teachers' backgrounds is far more difficult. General studies suggest that most Protestant missionaries of the period were from small towns in the North and Midwest and were products of the then widespread small denominational colleges. One important study asserts that a large number of female missionaries were daughters of ministers or women's society leaders.[42] The scanty evidence from the Presbyterian missions in the Southwest largely substantiates these contentions.

An 1887 article in *Home Mission Monthly* reported that mission teachers were "daughters of loving households" and that many of them were from "homes of wealth and culture." The same article emphasized that many of the teachers were well educated. Nine years earlier, an article about the fifteen teachers then serving in the Utah field reported that "they have all had the advantages of superior education obtained in some of the nation's best schools." Although the educational attainments of Presbyterian teachers probably surpassed those of most public school teachers of the era, the majority of the mission school teachers in the early years probably had no more than a normal school education. By late in the century, however, an increasingly large number of the teachers had college training. Perusal of missions literature reveals that many of the teachers (and the male missionaries as well) graduated from (or at least attended) small Presbyterian colleges, including Lafayette and Westminster in Pennsylvania, Tusculum and Maryville in Tennessee, Hanover in Indiana, and Muskingum in Ohio.[43]

It is impossible to determine definitively the geographic origins of the mission teachers, but remaining evidence suggests a pattern. Of sixteen teachers employed in the Utah field in 1880, four were from Iowa, four from Pennsylvania, three from Illinois, and Tennessee, New Jersey, Ohio, New York, and Indiana each had one representative. Records of the Albuquerque Indian School, open from 1881 to 1889, give the home states for eighteen teachers employed during that period. Pennsylvania, Tennessee, and Kansas each sent three teachers; two teachers hailed from New York, and the other seven came from Virginia, Wisconsin, Indiana, Illinois, New Jersey, Massachusetts, and the District of Columbia. Though inconclusive, these records suggest that the majority of the teachers came from traditional

Presbyterian strongholds in the East, Midwest, and upper South, areas that were very homogeneous, culturally and religiously.[44]

Another source for teachers was the Southwest. Presbyterians very early recognized that utilization of native teachers would greatly enhance their effort to reach the exceptional populations.[45] Consequently, by the mid-1880s they offered more advanced course work in several schools in each field to prepare one generation of students to be teachers for the next generation. Results fell far short of this goal, but progress was made. In 1883 five (out of fifty-five) teachers in the Utah field were mission school products. Seven years later seven (out of sixty-two) New Mexico teachers were natives of the region. Interestingly, six of these seven were males. The Presbytery of Santa Fe devised an arrangement that enabled young New Mexican men to teach in the mission schools as they studied and prepared to become evangelists and ministers; a number of the early native leaders in the church, including Jose Ynes Perea, J. J. Vigil, and Gabino Rendon, were products of this system. A few Indian "helpers" took advantage of similar arrangements. Many factors, however, undermined Presbyterian intentions to utilize native teachers. The latter were frequently paid less than regular teachers and were often assigned to isolated regions, where other teachers would not serve. Most seriously, many of the eastern missionaries doubted the abilities and competence of the native workers.[46]

Another notable characteristic of the Presbyterian teacher corps is the large number of families that sent more than one member to the Southwest. For example, in Utah in 1890 mother-daughter and sister teams were responsible for six schools. Some families did even better. For example, a brother and niece joined John Menaul and his missionary wife, the former Charity Ann Gaston, in New Mexico in the 1880s, and in the 1890s Bessie Menaul (John's daughter) served in the Indian and New Mexican fields. The Gilchrist family was more impressive. Within a decade of the Reverend J. J. Gilchrist's arrival in southern Colorado, his older brother, two sisters, two sisters-in-law, and a widowed cousin joined him in the New Mexico field. However, having relatives in the mission field was not always an advantage. Dr. J. M. Shields of Jemez Pueblo and his cousin, Lora Shields, teacher at the Albuquerque Indian School, were frequently at odds with one another.[47]

Beyond these general characteristics, the only generalization that can be made about the missionaries' backgrounds is that they were incredibly diverse. Included in the missionary ranks were immigrants, Civil War veterans, successful businessmen and doctors, and even one former member of an Arctic expedition. Some teachers were experienced missionaries; others began missionary careers in the Southwest and transferred to other mission fields. Many of the mission teachers were young, and for some the work in the Southwest was a first job. Other teachers were advanced in age and came with years of classroom experience; many in this latter group were able to enter mission work only after the death of a parent or the removal of other responsibilities at home. The one trait the mission teachers shared in common was a commitment to use their talents for the cultural and spiritual regeneration of the exceptional populations.

Once teachers were in the field, the home board and the Woman's Executive Committee delegated much of the responsibility for oversight of the mission schools to the presbyteries and synods where the schools were located. Distance and communication difficulties made this necessary, but the arrangement was also in accord with traditional Presbyterian preference for control by local officials. In the late 1870s the presbyteries of Utah and Santa Fe appointed Duncan McMillan and Sheldon Jackson respectively as "Superintendents for School Work" within their bounds. No official description of their duties remains, but existing records indicate that these two men and their successors advised the executive committee in selecting teachers and assigning them to their positions and were the teacher's most immediate supervisors. Later presbyterial and synodical missionaries assumed many of the duties of the school superintendents.[48]

Despite this arrangement there was always some confusion about the relative responsibilities of the local judicatories and national missions officials for the school work. This confusion was partly the result of Corresponding Secretary Haines's belief that the Woman's Executive Committee should keep in regular contact with teachers in the field. She justified this practice by asserting that since most of the teachers were women "there should be more free exchange of opinion . . . and more intelligent sympathy" between her office and the teachers than might occur in their more formal communications with local male officials and the home board. Indeed, Haines and her successors carried on a voluminous correspondence with mission teachers. Haines's letters were so filled with encouragement, warmhearted suggestions, and personal notes that they read more like exchanges between mother and daughter than the correspondence of supervisor and employee.[49]

The most surprising aspect of the communications between home missions headquarters, the school superintendents, and teachers in the field during the early years of the mission schools is the almost total absence of details about teachers' classroom duties and academic matters. While instructions from New York detailed policies regarding matters such as pay, vacations, and monthly reports, no guidelines for the conduct of classes and nothing resembling a recommended course of study was provided. Other than an occasional suggestion that students be exposed to "more than mere book learning," Haines's correspondence rarely touched upon classroom duties. Instead she instructed teachers to consult with their school superintendent about textbooks and methods of instruction.[50] The remaining records of the presbyteries and superintendents, however, are equally obscure and shed little light on actions taken regarding academic matters. For example, though Jackson's voluminous correspondence collection contains many letters from New Mexico and Arizona teachers during the period he was superintendent of schools for that field, most of them deal with problems related to inadequate facilities and native hostility. The closest they come to addressing what might be considered academic matters is when they complained about the lack of teaching supplies, textbooks, and classroom articles.

While this apparent inattention to details about academic matters might appear curious in light of traditional Presbyterian commitment to education and the central role of the schools in the Presbyterian strategy for the Southwest, it is not really that surprising. First, it should be recognized that when the schools were established practically all of the work was at the primary level. Since most of the teachers hired had at least some normal school training and many were experienced in the classroom, missions officials probably assumed that little supervision was necessary. This conclusion is more plausible when one considers that the supervisors had little classroom experience. Haines never taught school, and Sheldon Jackson considered his few years as teacher among the Choctaws in the 1850s one of the most miserable periods of his life. Only Duncan McMillan (of the earliest supervisors) had appreciable teaching experience, and he clearly preferred preaching and administration to classroom duties.[51]

More importantly, instructions from board headquarters and publicity in missionary magazines indicate that the primary objective of the Presbyterian schools was not *formal* education. Teachers, of course, taught the three Rs. However, they could not fail to understand that these were a means to a greater end. A fourth R was more important. Above all else, the mission schools were established to *regenerate* spiritually and culturally the youth of the exceptional populations and through them their entire peoples.[52] In obvious contrast to the absence of guidelines about classroom duties, teachers received detailed instructions about their religious responsibilities and "broader duties." These guidelines instructed teachers to open school daily with prayers and singing, to use the Bible regularly as a textbook, and to observe the Sabbath. Because the schools were "intended as a means for the entrance of the gospel," teachers were expected to become acquainted with the people of their communities and "make their influence for good felt in every way." Directives from headquarters instructed teachers to conduct Sunday schools (and Sunday services if a minister was not available) and offer evening classes in reading, sewing, singing, and other activities that would uplift the community. Finally, missions officials frequently reminded teachers that they must be good role models, not only in their personal habits but also in their dress and housekeeping. As one home missions official later recalled, the mission school teacher carried "along with her Bible and spelling book, the needle and soap and all the arts of home."[53]

By the early 1880s the Presbyterian mission school effort in the Southwest appeared to be on the verge of a new phase of growth and vitality. The establishment and effective organization of the Woman's Executive Committee of Home Missions provided the financial backing, administrative support, and personnel necessary to enlarge the effort to regenerate the exceptional populations. With this behind-the-lines victory achieved, triumph in the more important battle at the front appeared certain and imminent.

Notes

1. Thomas S. Goslin, II, "Henry Kendall: Missionary Statesman," *Journal of the Presbyterian Historical Society* 27 (June 1949): 71. The attitude of the former New Schoolers is not surprising; their faction of the church had always taken a larger view of home missions than their Old School counterparts.

2. "Historical Notes," *HMM* 1 (January 1887): 54. In Presbyterian parlance an overture is a petition to a higher level of authority (judicatory) in the church's multitiered governmental structure. The General Assembly, composed of ministers and laypersons, meets annually in the spring; it is the church's national judicatory and the ultimate source of authority in the church.

3. Seventh Annual Report, Board of Home Missions, 1877, 7–10.

4. Henry Kendall and Cyrus Dickson, "Appeal," undated document held in the library of the Presbyterian Historical Society, Philadelphia.

5. A great deal has been written about women's involvement in and support for missionary work. Good general treatments are R. Pierce Beaver, *American Protestant Women in World Missions: History of the First Feminist Movement in North America* (Grand Rapids, Mich.: Eerdmans Publishing Co., 1984); Barbara Welter, " 'She Hath Done What She Could': Protestant Women's Missionary Careers in Nineteenth-Century America," in *Women in American Religion,* ed. Janet Wilson Jones (Philadelphia: University of Pennsylvania Press, 1980), 110–25; Rosemary Skinner Keller, "Lay Women in the Protestant Tradition," in *Women and Religion in America,* vol. 1, *The Nineteenth-Century,* ed. Rosemary Radford Ruether and Rosemary Skinner Keller (San Francisco: Harper and Row, 1981), 242–53. A number of studies examine the activities of Presbyterian women. See, for example, Hayes, *Daughters of Dorcas;* Lois Boyd and Douglas Brackenridge, *Presbyterian Women in America: Two Centuries of a Quest for Status,* Presbyterian Historical Society Publications Series, 9 (Westport, Conn.: Greenwood Press, 1983); Elizabeth Howell Verdesi, *In but Still Out: Women in the Church* (Philadelphia: Westminster Press, 1975); Janet Harbison Penfield, "Women in the Presbyterian

Church: An Historical Overview," *Journal of Presbyterian History* 55 (Summer 1977): 107–24.

6. Anne Firor Scott, "What, Then, Is the American: This New Woman," *Journal of American History* 65 (December 1978): 679; Verdesi, *In but Still Out*, 40–41; Boyd and Brackenridge, *Presbyterian Women in America*, 13–14.

7. Welter, "She Hath Done What She Could," 112–18; Beaver, *American Protestant Women*, chap. 3; Boyd and Brackenridge, *Presbyterian Women in America*, 10–12; Bailey, "Strategy of Sheldon Jackson," 389.

8. First-hand accounts of the organization of the Santa Fe Association are found in Cornelia W. Martin to S. Jackson, June 9, 1883, SJCC; and *The Ladies Board of Home Missions of N.Y.*, undated pamphlet, SJS 54:26. Also see Verdesi, *In but Still Out*, 45–46; Hayes, *Daughters of Dorcas*, 54–56.

9. Verdesi, *In but Still Out*, 46–47; Hayes, *Daughters of Dorcas*, 56; Boyd and Brackenridge, *Presbyterian Women in America*, 17.

10. Boyd and Brackenridge, *Presbyterian Women in America*, 18; Bailey, "The Strategy of Sheldon Jackson," 380–81.

11. Bailey, "The Strategy of Sheldon Jackson," 382–86; Stewart, *Sheldon Jackson: Pathfinder and Prospector of the Missionary Vanguard in the Rocky Mountains and Alaska* (New York: Fleming H. Revell Co., 1908), 262–63.

12. Bailey, "The Strategy of Sheldon Jackson," 384–85; Stewart, *Sheldon Jackson*, 265; Hayes, *Daughters of Dorcas*, 60–63.

13. Henry Kendall to S. Jackson, March 4, 1878, July 23, 1878, SJCC. Similar sentiments are expressed in S. S. Gillespie to S. Jackson, January 22, 1877, SJCC.

14. Mrs. F. E. H. Haines to S. Jackson, December 31, 1877, February 23, 1878. Not all Presbyterians were so enthralled, however. See, for example: "Circular Sent by Frank F. Ellinwood, D.D., a Secretary of the Board of Foreign Missions, to Woman's Foreign Missionary Societies," January 1, 1878, Mrs. E. J. Paxton to S. Jackson, February 4, 1878, H. Kendall to S. Jackson, March 4, 1878, SJCC.

15. Cautiously positive responses to Jackson's proposal are found in the following letters to Jackson in the SJCC: Mrs. J. P. E. Kunler, May 1878; Mrs. J. F. Young, May 6, 1878; Mrs. J. A. Blanchard, May 7, 1878; Mrs. H. F. Waite, May 9, 1878; Mrs. Arch McClure, May 9, 1878; Mrs. Henry Childs, May 11, 1878; Mrs. C. J. McClung, May 14, 1876. The quote is from Julia P. Kendall's letter to Jackson, May 16, 1878, SJCC. Other negative responses are found in Melissa P. Dodge to Mrs. Paxton, May 15, 1878, and N. McK. Lewis to Jackson, June 4, 1878, SJCC.

16. "Home Missions: The Woman's Society," SJS 53:372–73; Mrs. S. F. Scovel, "Woman's Executive Committee of Home Missions: History of Its Organization," *RMP* 8 (June 1879). Mrs. Scovel's article is one of the most informative and objective of several first-hand accounts of these developments. Good secondary accounts are found in Boyd and Brackenridge, *Presbyterian Women in America*, 25–29; Stewart, *Sheldon Jackson*, 272–75; Hayes, *Daughters of Dorcas*, 73–78.

17. Evidence of the tensions present at the July 11 meeting is found in H. Kendall to S. Jackson, July 11, 1878, and Mrs. L. M. Dickson to Jackson, September 6, 1878, SJCC. "Woman's Work and Board of Home Missions," *RMP* 7 (November

1878); *RMP* 8 (February 1879), describes the actual organization of the woman's executive committee. The use of the singular *woman's* in the organization's official name was in accord with prevailing standards of the time.

18. F. E. H. Haines to S. Jackson, December 26, 1878, Mrs. S. F. Scovel to S. Jackson, March 6, 1879, SJCC.

19. "First Circular, Woman's Executive Committee of Home Missions of the Presbyterian Church," copy held in the library of the Presbyterian Historical Society; "After Twenty Years," *HMM* 14 (May 1900): 149–52; "Reminiscences of a Vice President," *HMM* 14 (May 1900): 155. Also see F. E. H. Haines to S. Jackson, May 3, 1879, SJCC.

20. "Brief History of Women's Home Missionary Societies of the Presbyterian Church," *PHMy* 15 (August 1885): 178. A review of the gradual expansion of women's responsibilities into new fields is found in the 30th Annual Report, Women's Board of Home Missions, 1910, 70. Hayes, *Daughters of Dorcas,* 97, 112, and Drury, *Presbyterian Panorama,* 204–5, both comment on the women's fundraising abilities.

21. Verdesi, *In but Still Out,* 58; "Mrs. F. E. H. Haines," *PHMy* 15 (December 1886): 268; "After Twenty Years," *HMM* 14 (May 1900): 150; Boyd and Brackenridge, *Presbyterian Women in America,* 37–39.

22. "First Circular, Woman's Executive Committee"; "Brief History of Women's Home Missionary Societies of the Presbyterian Church."

23. "First Circular, Woman's Executive Committee"; "Diagram of the Plan of Work of the Woman's Executive Committee," *HMM* 2 (February 1888): 88–89.

24. Report of Woman's Executive Committee of Home Missions, 9th Annual Report, Board of Home Missions, 1879, 106–7; "Address of the Executive Committee to the Women of the Presbyterian Church," *RMP* 8 (March 1879); "Our Magazine," *HMM* 1 (November 1886): 1; Drury, *Presbyterian Panorama,* 208–9.

25. "Summary of Two Decades," *HMM* 14 (May 1900): 149; "Our Sources of Revenue," *HMM* 10 (October 1896): 272–73; 14th Annual Report, Board of Home Missions, 1894.

26. "Our Work for the Present Year," *RMP* 9 (September 1880); Mrs. F. E. H. Haines to Miss N. J. Hall, November 2, 1882, PHS, RG 105, Box 2, F-8; Haines to Maxwell Phillips, January 6, 1881, PHS, RG 105, Box 2, F-12; "Scholarships," *PHMy* 14 (December 1885): 282; Report of Woman's Executive Committee of Home Missions, 20th Annual Report, Board of Home Missions, 1890, 150–51.

27. "A Brief History of Women's Home Missions Societies of the Presbyterian Church," *PHMy* 14 (August 1885): 179; R. W. D. Bryan to Friends of Home Missions, February 17, 1883, SJS 57:43; "The Indian Idea," *Chicago Inter-Ocean,* April 13, 1883, clipping, SJS 55:123.

28. "A Brief History of Women's Home Missionary Societies"; Mrs. Haines to Fellow Workers, July 4, 1884, PHS, RG 51, Box-1, F-5; Mrs. Haines to Miss N. J. Hall, November 2, 1882; Mary E. Dissette to Mrs. D. E. Finks, November 17, 1890, PHS, RG 51, Box 1, F-25.

29. "A Brief History of Women's Home Missionary Societies"; "Boxes for Mission Schools," *HMM* 6 (September 1892): 257.

30. Kendall and Dickson to Jackson, December 12, 1878, SJCC; "First Circular, Woman's Executive Committee"; "To Our Missionary Teacher," undated policy statement probably written by Mrs. Haines, PHS, RG 51, Box 1, F-5; "Brief History of Women's Home Missionary Society."

31. Henry Kendall to S. Jackson, March 1879; F. E. H. Haines to S. Jackson, December 24, 1881; both in SJCC.

32. "To Our Missionary Teachers," undated rough draft of manual probably prepared by Mrs. Haines, PHS, RG 51, Box 1, F-5; "The Qualifications of a Teacher," *PHMy* 13 (December 1884): 282.

33. Menaul, quoted in "Gen. Armstrong among the Indians of New Mexico and Arizona," *New York Evangelist,* September 12, 1883, clipping, SJS 56:73; W. W. Morton to S. Jackson, December 8, 1880, SJCC; "Qualifications for Teaching in Utah, by a Home Missionary," *PHMy* 12 (August 1883): 186.

34. D. McMillan to Mrs. Haines, May 18, 1881, PHS, RG 105, Box 1, F-7; J. M. Shields to S. Jackson, November 12, 1880, SJCC; G. W. Martin to Mrs. Haines, PHS, RG 105, Box 1, F-7. Mrs. Haines to Rev. T. F. Day, May 12, 1884, PHS, RG 105.

35. Miss Ella McDonald to Mrs. F. E. H. Haines, June 27, 1881, PHS, RG 105, Box 5, F-6.

36. Mrs. Haines to Alice Hyson, March 18, 1884, PHS, RG 105, Box 2, F-10; J. D. C. Atkins to J. R. Douglas, September 21, 1887, NA, RG 75, Education Division: Letters Sent, 10:346.

37. Many of the records of the woman's executive committee, including most of those related to personnel, no longer exist. The composite presented here is drawn from those records that remain (held by the Presbyterian Historical Society), records of the Board of Home Missions, the women's magazines, and other records pertinent to each of the three fields.

38. The figures presented here reflect only individuals commissioned by the woman's executive committee for the school work. The home board also commissioned a number of ministers and evangelists (all males) to serve in churches among the southwestern population. In 1880 twenty-seven men were commissioned for the southwestern field and in 1890 forty-four. Some of these men (for example, John Menaul at Laguna and Charles Cook, who worked among Pimas and Papagos) engaged in the school work along with their ministerial duties. One occasionally finds minor discrepancies in the statistics provided here and elsewhere in this study. The statistics are taken directly from Presbyterian sources, and sometimes even in a single source one finds conflicting figures. However, the statistics provide reliable, *approximate* information.

39. Mrs. A. G. Rullifson to S. Jackson, March 2, 1871, SJCC; D. J. McMillan, "Pioneer Bearers of the Cross," *HMM* 35 (December 1920): 30; "Address to the Ladies by S. Jackson: Wonderful Revelations as to the Degradation of Women on the Frontier," SJS 54:77; Julia Graham to S. Jackson, August 5, 1878, SJCC.

40. J. M. Shields to S. Jackson, February 6, 8, 1878, SJCC. Several months after Shields accepted the Jemez post, a candidate refused the vacant position at Zuni Pueblo, stating that he had "no intention of taking my family there to endure

the trials" experienced by the previous missionaries to Zuni (M. Fitch Williams to Jackson, July 16, 1878, SJCC).

41. Welter, "She Hath Done What She Could," 119; David Tyack, *The One Best System* (Cambridge: Harvard University Press, 1974), 61–63. Chap. 3 of Sarah Deutsch, *No Separate Refuge: Culture, Class, and Gender on an Anglo-Hispanic Frontier in the American Southwest,* examines the motivations and experiences of women mission teachers in New Mexico, with special emphasis on Presbyterians (New York: Oxford University Press, 1987).

42. John C. B. Webster, Introduction to "American Presbyterians in India and Pakistan," special issue of *Journal of Presbyterian History* 62 (Fall 1984): 193–94; Keller, "Lay Women in the Protestant Tradition," 247.

43. "Monthly Concert: Our Missionaries and Mission Teacher," *HMM* 2 (November 1887): 8; "Presbyterianism in Utah," dated September 12, 1878, SJS 60:69–70; "An Influence in New Mexico," *HMM* 37 (January 1923): 69.

44. Minutes, Presbytery of Utah, August 20, 1880, 1:140; Albuquerque Indian School File, Menaul School Archives, Box 1, Menaul Historical Library.

45. See, for example, J. M. Coyner, "The Utah Column," *RMP* 9 (May 1880); Minutes, Presbytery of Santa Fe, September 17, 1881, 2:89; 14th Annual Report, Board of Home Missions, 1884, 17–19.

46. There have been several studies of mission school graduates and other natives who became active participants in the Presbyterian cause. See, for example, Gabino Rendon's autobiography as told to Edith Agnew, *Hand on My Shoulder* (New York: Board of National Missions, 1953); Banker, "Missionary to His Own People: Jose Ynes Perea and Hispanic Presbyterianism in New Mexico," in *Religion and Society in the American West,* ed. Carl Guarnari (Lanham, Md.: University Press of America, 1987). Also see "Out of Mormonism," *HMM* 30 (January 1916): 61; Minutes, Presbytery of Utah, March 1883, 1:267; 20th Annual Report, Board of Home Missions, 1890), 138–41; 21st Annual Report, Board of Home Missions, 1891, 158. A longtime New Mexico teacher, Matilda Allison, wrote near the end of her career that experience with native teachers made her feel "that it will be a long time before our mission schools can dispense with American teachers" (PHS, RG 101, Box 9, F-2).

47. 20th Annual Report, Board of Home Missions, 1890, 138–41; Banker, "Presbyterian Missionary Activity in the Southwest: The Careers of John and James Menaul," *Journal of the West* 23 (January 1984): 55–61; "Notes on Gilchrist Family History," Gilchrist Papers, Menaul Historical Library. One of the many disputes involving the two members of the Shields family is apparent in J. M.'s letter to Lora, January 31, 1881, SJCC.

48. Jackson was responsible for both Indian and New Mexican schools within Santa Fe Presbytery, which at the time included New Mexico and Arizona.

49. "To Our Missionary Teachers." See, for example, Mrs. Haines's detailed letter to new teachers describing clothing and furnishings needed in the missions field (July 4, 1881, PHS, RG 105, Box 2, F-7).

50. Mrs. Haines to Dear Worker, July 4, 1884, and "To Our Missionary Teachers"; Haines to Maxwell Phillips, 1881, PHS, RG 105, Box 2, F-9.

51. Stewart, *Sheldon Jackson,* 40–50, examines Jackson's experiences as teacher among the Choctaws. McMillan's disregard for classroom work is seemingly apparent in his decision to secure a teacher for his Mt. Pleasant school soon after it was opened.

52. This emphasis on education as a means to uplift and homogenize less fortunate and disparate peoples was not unique to Presbyterians. Historians of American education recognize that these very considerations were a major motive for the public school movement in the nineteenth century. See, for example, David Tyack, "Onward Christian Soldiers: Religion in the American Common School," in *History of Education,* ed. Paul Nash (New York: Random House, 1970), 212–55; idem, "The Kingdom of God and the Common School: Protestant Ministers and the Educational Awakening of the West," *Harvard Education Review* 36 (1966): 447–69; Robert Carlson, *The Quest for Conformity: Americanization through Education* (New York: John Wiley and Sons, 1975), 70–76, 79–83.

53. Mrs. Haines to Fellow Workers, July 4, 1884, and "To Our Missionary Teachers"; E. G. Pierson, "Need of the Work of the Woman's Board," *HMM* 13 (May 1899): 148.

5

"Making Haste Slowly"

As expected, the Presbyterian mission school effort in the Southwest expanded rapidly in the years after the establishment of the Woman's Executive Committee. Between 1879 and 1895 Presbyterians added seventy-two new schools to the twenty-two schools they had earlier established in the region (see table 4 and maps 3 and 4). Although a number of these schools remained open only briefly, in 1890 Presbyterians conducted a record seventy-five mission schools in the Southwest: thirty-seven in Utah, thirty-two in New Mexico, and six among southwestern Indians. A number of other Protestant denominations—most notably Methodists, Congregationalists, Baptists, and Episcopalians—established mission schools in the Southwest during this same era, and Roman Catholics operated a number of schools for southwestern Indians. No other denomination, however, emphasized education as strongly as the Presbyterians nor matched the systematic Presbyterians' approach to the three southwestern peoples combined.[1]

Even during this period of their greatest advance into the Southwest, however, Presbyterian missionaries found the challenge of southwestern pluralism far more formidable than they and church officials had assumed. Many of the problems that plagued the earlier spontaneous mission school effort persisted, and new and unexpected difficulties appeared. These prolonged problems did not defeat the Presbyterian cause, but they disheartened individual missionaries and gradually sobered Presbyterian expectations. By the 1890s many Presbyterians in both the Southwest and the East were beginning to recognize the truth in John Menaul's early observation from Laguna Pueblo. "It is well," Menaul had explained to his eastern supporters in 1877, "to make haste slowly."[2]

The most immediate problems for the enlarged Presbyterian force that arrived in the Southwest in the 1880s were loneliness and physical deprivation. The isolation of many mission stations, irregular postal services, and

Table 4. Presbyterian Mission Schools Established in the Southwest, 1879–95

New Mexican Field		
Location	Opened	Closed
Corrales	1879	1886
Fernando de Taos	1880	1903
Cenicerro	1880	1881
Conejos	1881	1882
Glorieta	1881	1891
Jemez Hot Springs	1881	1906
Mora (boarding school)	1881	1889
Ocazi	1881	1882
Antonito	1882	1908
Holman (Agua Negra)	1882	1958
La Costilla	1882	1903
Los Lentes	1883	1904
Pajarito	1884	1907
Ranchos de Taos	1884	1958
El Prado de Taos	1884	1927
Salazar	1884	1901
Agua Caliente	1885	1904
Copper City	1885	1887
Llano	1885	1900
Penasco	1885	1909
Wallace	1885	1886
Las Vegas	1886	1895
Capulin	1887	1889
Dixon (Embudo)	1887	1958
Raton	1887	1911
Alamosa Canon	1888	1908
Buena Vista	1888	1897
El Moro	1888	1892
Golondrinas	1888	1890
Las Cordovas	1888	1890
Los Alamos	1888	1891
Rociada	1888	1894
Agua de Lobo	1888	1893
Chaperito	1889	1904
El Aguila	1889	1901
Mora (day school)	1890	1905
Archuleta	1891	1892
Los Valles	1891	1892
Arroyo Seco	1891	1903
Pena Blanca	1891	1893
San Pablo	1891	1916

Table 4. Continued

New Mexican Field		
Location	Opened	Closed
Del Norte	1892	1900*
La Florida	1892	1896
Ignacio	1893	1906
Placitas	1893	1900
Albuquerque	1895	**
Arroyo Hondo	1895	1910
Canon Bonito	1895	1898
San Jan	1895	1922

Mormon Field		
Location	Opened	Closed
Franklin	1879	1884
Logan	1879	1934
Nephi	1879	1909
Cedar City	1880	1885
Richfield	1880	1908
St. George	1880	1912
Parowan	1880	1908
Silver Reef	1880	1889
Toquerville	1880	1890
Spanish Fork	1881	1905
Fillmore	1881	1890
Gunnison	1881	1908
Hyrum	1881	1908
Kaysville	1881	1909
Smithfield	1881	1909
Wellsville	1881	1907
Fairview	1881	1910
Millville	1881	1889
Scipio	1882	1896
Marysvale	1883	1893
Richmond	1883	1907
Mendon	1884	1910
Salina	1884	1918
Samaria	1884	1905
Paris	1884	1908
Montpelier	1884	1898
Benjamin	1885	1901
Ferron	1895	1924

Table 4. Continued

	Indian Field	
Location/Tribe	Opened	Closed
Hopis	1880	1882
Isleta (Pueblo)	1888	1893
Albuquerque***	1881	1889
San Xavier (Papago)	1884	1888
Tucson (Pima-Papago)	1886	1959

* College of the Southwest.

** Present-day Menaul School.

*** The Albuquerque School was originally established as a government contract school for Pueblos. Utes, Apaches, and Pimas also attended. In 1886 the government assumed full control of the school, and the Presbyterians moved to another Albuquerque site and conducted an Indian school of their own until 1889.

local coolness combined to leave many missionaries homesick and discouraged. Ella McDonald spoke for many of her colleagues when she wrote to mission officials after several months at her isolated station in northern Utah: "I am trying to do all in my power to show the beauty of the Christian life but I feel how small and helpless I am." The board's practice of assigning single teachers to schools many miles distant from other missionaries exacerbated this sense of loneliness. Of the thirty-five teachers commissioned in 1880, fifteen (43 percent) served alone.[3]

The condition of mission facilities further dampened missionary enthusiasm. Missionaries among the Pueblos lived in small, dark rooms in the multistoried communal pueblo buildings; teachers in New Mexican villages set up housekeeping in crumbling adobe houses with dirt floors and leaky roofs; and early teachers in Utah made their homes in log huts that were infested with vermin.[4] School rooms were equally miserable. From Zuni Pueblo Mary Ealy reported that she taught in a "dark, filthy, [and] uninhabitable" room; spending six hours daily in it, she observed, would mean "almost certain death" to "a delicate person." Several years later, another missionary lamented that she was "always cold" after teaching in her "dark, cellar like" school room at Isleta Pueblo. From the New Mexico field, the Reverend James Roberts commented in 1879 that the mission schools in the Taos area were "little corner rooms . . . with no ventilation [and] scarcely light enough to see at mid-day." His wife added that all of the rooms had dirt floors and that the movement of pupils filled the air with dust. Another New Mexico teacher reported that the dirt floor of her school room became "a pool of mud and water" when it rained. Conditions in the Utah field were little better. In Springville, Anna Noble taught thirty-eight pupils in

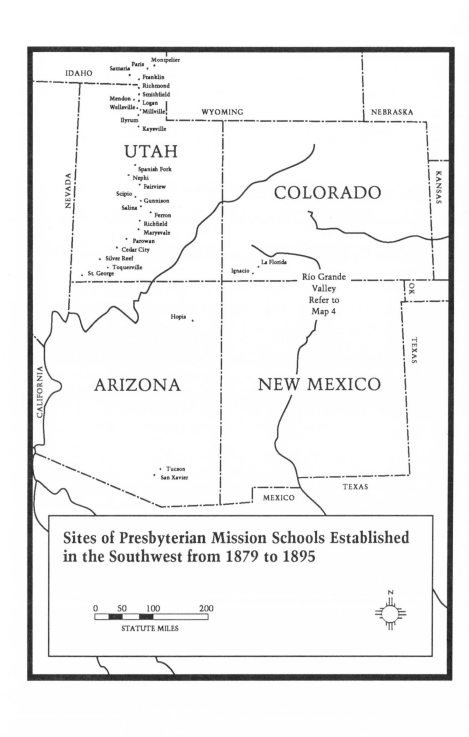

IDAHO

Montpelier
Paris
Samaria
Franklin
Richmond
Smithfield
Mendon
Wellsville
Logan
Millville
Ilyrum
Kaysville

UTAH

NEVADA

Spanish Fork
Nephi
Fairview
Scipio
Gunnison
Salina
Ferron
Richfield
Marysvale
Parowan
Cedar City
Silver Reef
Toquerville
St. George

WYOMING

NEBRASKA

KANSAS

COLORADO

La Florida
Ignacio

Rio Grande
Valley
Refer to
Map 4

OK

Hopis

CALIFORNIA

ARIZONA

NEW MEXICO

TEXAS

Tucson
San Xavier

TEXAS

MEXICO

Sites of Presbyterian Mission Schools Established in the Southwest from 1879 to 1895

```
0    50   100        200
STATUTE MILES
```

N

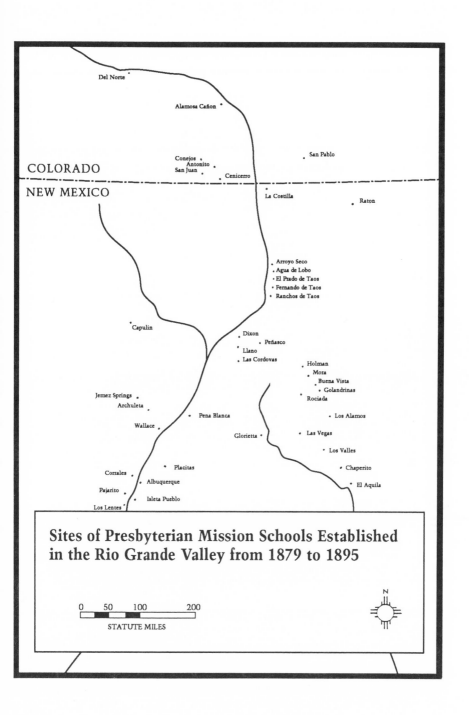

Del Norte

Alamosa Cañon

San Pablo

Conejos
Antonito
San Juan
Cenicerro

COLORADO

— —

NEW MEXICO

La Costilla

Raton

Arroyo Seco
Agua de Lobo
El Prado de Taos
Fernando de Taos
Ranchos de Taos

Capulin

Dixon
Peñasco
Llano
Las Cordovas

Holman
Mora
Buena Vista
Golandrinas
Rociada

Jemez Springs
Archuleta

Pena Blanca

Los Alamos

Wallace

Glorietta

Las Vegas

Los Valles

Placitas

Chaperito

Corrales
Albuquerque
Pajarito
Isleta Pueblo
Los Lentes

El Aquila

Sites of Presbyterian Mission Schools Established in the Rio Grande Valley from 1879 to 1895

0   50   100   200

STATUTE MILES

N

a twelve-by-twenty-four-foot "low, dark, dingy, leaky adobe house" that was "bug infested and poorly ventilated." A visitor described the mission school at Moroni, Utah, as "far from an inviting place, with its rough walls, low ceiling, and rude benches."[5]

The harsh conditions in which missionaries lived and worked took their toll. At least four missionaries from the Indian field died between 1878 and 1886, and several mission teachers died in the New Mexico and Utah fields during the 1880s. While records are not always clear about the causes of these deaths, the difficult conditions in which the teachers lived undoubtedly were a contributing factor.[6] Missionary families proved even more vulnerable. Between 1880 and 1882 four infant missionary children died at Indian and New Mexican stations. For missionary wives overwork plus the danger of childbearing often contributed to ill health and untimely deaths. The missionary father and husband felt particularly helpless at such times. In 1880 Charles A. Taylor contrasted his "dark and uninviting field" among the Hopis with his wife's "bright and comfortable home" in Princeton, New Jersey, and concluded: "I cannot restrain a tear in her behalf." He also lamented that "our little babe, too, must grow up with little knowledge of the nobler world." That child, along with Taylor's idealism, became a victim of the harsh realities of missionary life. Naturally, the passing of loved ones left survivors distraught. After losing a second infant in less than a year, the Charles Taylors departed their mission stations among the Hopis. Following the death of a son at Zuni Pueblo in 1880, the Taylor F. Ealys did likewise. Several months after his wife's death, J. M. Shields lamented to Sheldon Jackson that his young sons "missed their mother greatly" and that "we are lonely indeed but doing the best we can."[7]

Primitive conditions in the mission stations posed more than physical hardships. Permanent dwellings, schools, and churches were necessary to convince native southwesterners that the Presbyterian presence was more than temporary. The people of Corrales, New Mexico, for example, complained to missionary Jose Ynes Perea that he was not living among them "as one who intends to stay" and that they wanted "to see him build a good school room with a bell" before they would send their children to his classes.[8]

Communication presented another obstacle for many missionaries. The unwritten Indian languages proved particularly difficult to master. Initially missionaries used interpreters who translated their messages from English to Spanish and then to the native tongues. This arrangement proved unsatisfactory, however, and missionaries often surmised that their Hispanic Catholic translators modified and misconstrued the message.[9] Under these circumstances missionaries recognized that they had to learn the native tongues, but even the most dedicated missionaries quickly discovered that this was a formidable challenge. John Menaul reported that the Keresan language of the Lagunas had no articles, prepositions, conjunctions, or relative pronouns and that it lacked abstract words essential to the Christian message such as "spirit," "soul," "virtue," and "vice." An early missionary wrote that the Pima language consisted of "nine words, 10,000 grunts, and innumerable signs." Some missionaries attempted shortcuts in learning the native tongues; for example, T. F. Ealy at Zuni Pueblo reported in 1879 that he was using a book entitled *Introduction to the Study of the Indian Language.* Not surprisingly, this proved of little aid. When Ealy left his station two years later, he was still unable to communicate in the Zuni dialect.[10] Federal policies that prohibited the use of the vernacular in all contract Indian schools exacerbated the communication problem. A mission teacher at Isleta Pueblo, who used only English in her instruction, confessed that "indeed very little of anything is taught in my school."[11]

Missionaries among the New Mexicans and Mormons also faced language barriers. Only a few workers came to the New Mexico field able to communicate with the territory's Spanish-speaking natives. Despite one missionary's optimistic observation that "nineteen days of school teaching among Mexicans, accompanied by study of a Spanish textbook, will give any cultivated person a good headway in knowledge of Spanish," most missionaries to New Mexico spent considerably more time than that before they were able to communicate with the people they came to serve.[12] Because Mormons recruited heavily in Europe, even the missionaries in Utah faced communication barriers. In 1887 a teacher in Spring City conceded that she could not really comment on the impact of her work since she could not communicate with the predominantly Danish population of that town.[13]

Native resistance posed a more serious obstacle for the Presbyterians. Generally speaking, the peoples of each of the three fields met the missionaries with kindness and curiosity. However, when the Presbyterians' reasons for coming to the Southwest became clear, many of the locals turned indifferent, and a few were even hostile. Missionaries blamed native religious leaders — the Indian shamans and medicine men, Catholic priests in Indian and New Mexican villages, and Mormon officials — for fomenting these responses. According to Presbyterian accounts, Catholic priests told their Pueblo and New Mexican parishioners that the missionaries were "veritable devils" and "corrupt and wicked heretics" and denied the sacraments to those parents who sent their children to the mission schools and associated with the missionaries.[14] Missionaries among Mormons reported even more serious harassment. The Presbytery of Utah in 1880 charged that "Mormon hoodlums" frequently cursed mission teachers, threw rocks through their windows, or sang and hooted around their doors late at night. Missionaries also charged that L.D.S. officials persuaded Mormons not to rent rooms or sell food and other goods to them, and one L.D.S. bishop reportedly cut off irrigation water to families who failed to obey his orders not to send their children to Presbyterian schools.[15]

Extant records report only two incidents of physical violence against missionaries. In 1885 the Presbytery of Utah complained that "two drunken hoodlums" had assaulted a teacher in Mendon. A decade later a "stranger known to be a gambler" attacked and robbed a longtime mission teacher in Penasco, New Mexico. Two other reports, one from Utah and the other from New Mexico, describe assaults on natives who converted to Presbyterianism. Although the victim in New Mexico died from his wounds, Presbyterians apparently could not prove that his conversion to Protestantism was the major cause of the incident. Consequently, they made little of it. There were also occasional reports that Indian tribal leaders publicly whipped students from mission schools for wearing western clothes and embracing other aspects of white culture. Clearly Presbyterian influence exacerbated tensions in societies already straining from rapid and traumatic change.[16]

Native religious leaders usually found more subtle ways to counter the Presbyterian challenge. For example, Catholic priests in New Mexico and Mormon officials in Utah established schools of their own and upgraded those that already existed. In response to the opening of Presbyterian Sunday schools, New Mexico Catholic priests initiated their own Sabbath schools, and Mormon officials expanded their Youth Mutual Benefit Societies. Occasionally native leaders were even more innovative. For example, in 1888 a Taos, New Mexico, priest acquired a billiard table that won the loyalty of many boys, or so several chagrined Presbyterians believed.[17]

Native religious leaders were not alone in hindering Presbyterian efforts. Missionaries complained frequently and bitterly about "fellow Americans" who seemed determined to undermine mission interests. Missionaries among Indians, for example, found many flaws in the much celebrated cooperative arrangement between the churches and federal government for civilizing the Indians. In 1882 one missionary suggested that "the government does not select the *wisest* or *best* men as their agents," while another surmised that many Indian agents "love the missionary about as much as a New York City pickpocket does a policeman." Not even agents that Presbyterian officials recommended to the government in accord with the Grant Peace Policy escaped missionary criticism. In the midst of a bitter quarrel with the Hopi agent, whom the Presbyterians had nominated, Charles Taylor wrote to Jackson: "I have witnessed so much hypocrisy, deceit, and intrigue in the last few years . . . that I have almost lost confidence in humanity generally and in territorial humanity in particular but in Indian Bureau humanity emphatically." For their part, agents found the missionaries meddlesome, self-righteous, and unwilling to comply with government policies.

Even Pueblo agent B. M. Thomas, a Presbyterian whom Jackson and home missions officials widely respected, complained on occasion about the missionaries the board assigned to his field.[18]

Federal agents represented only one obstacle to Presbyterian Indian missions. Missionaries also complained regularly about corrupt traders, who sold whiskey on the Sabbath, and land hungry settlers, who cheated Indians. Howard Billman, superintendent of the Tucson school for the Pimas and Papagos, worried in the late 1880s that "depraved white men will undo our work almost as fast as it is done." Several Anglos, who later became well-known public figures, were particularly obnoxious to the missionaries. These included the early ethnographer Frank Cushing, who lived among the Zunis, and the California journalist Charles F. Lummis, who spent several years at Isleta Pueblo.[19]

Missionaries in Utah and New Mexico took a similarly dim view of much of the Gentile and Anglo populations of those territories. A missionary in Brigham City, Utah, observed that many of that town's non-Mormon prospectors and miners did not keep the Sabbath and were devoted to "billiards, cardplaying, whiskey, and obscene singing." Mormon apostates proved even less helpful to the Presbyterian cause, although their children often attended the mission schools. One child in the Monroe, Utah, mission school refused to read from the Bible because his father said it was "all trash and he don't believe it."[20] New Mexico missionaries often complained about the Anglo cowboys and Jewish merchants who preceded them there, and the Presbytery of Santa Fe frequently commented on the harmful influence of incoming Anglos, particularly their disregard for the Sabbath. In the late 1870s the renowned Lincoln County War impeded Presbyterian efforts to extend their missions into southeastern New Mexico. After dodging bullets and rubbing elbows with such fellow Anglos as Billy the Kid, Taylor F. Ealy and family were glad to transfer to remote and inhospitable Zuni Pueblo.[21]

Foes of the Presbyterian cause included more than desperadoes and "vile and profane men." Missionaries from other Protestant churches competed (sometimes aggressively) with the Presbyterians for the souls of the exceptional populations. Despite talk of "Christian cooperation," Presbyterians and Methodists were often at odds in the New Mexico field, and Methodists, Episcopalians, and Congregationalists all competed with the Presbyterians in Utah. In the mid-1890s a Utah missionary reported the loss of several recent converts to the Seventh-Day Adventists and conceded "we need superhuman wisdom to know what to do."[22]

Native resistance and indifference from other Americans impeded the work of the Presbyterian mission schools, but they rarely succeeded in stopping it altogether. Presbyterian teachers, however, faced formidable obstacles in their efforts to introduce southwestern youths to the three Rs and the values of Christian civilization. Their most immediate problem involved luring students into their classrooms. Because each of the three southwestern peoples depended heavily on agriculture, students were often removed from classes to work alongside parents in the fields. In 1880 a southern Colorado missionary reported that many of his students worked on ranches and tended sheep and that they "vamos the school early in the spring and are late coming back in the fall." A teacher in Spring City, Utah, reported that she opened school in autumn 1886 with only ten pupils because adults expected "even the children" to help in "such work as 'pickin up taters.' "[23] Attendance was most erratic at the Indian schools, where both parents and pupils exhibited indifference toward the "white man's education." In 1880 the teacher at Zuni Pueblo explained her failure to report enrollment in her school: "I cannot possibly tell how many there will be [because] there is nothing more uncertain than the Zuni mind."[24]

In the Indian and New Mexican fields, missionaries reported particular difficulties in attracting and retaining girls in their schools. In 1878 a teacher at Zuni Pueblo reported that she opened classes with twenty-one boys and no girls. The latter, she commented, were "timid and busy" and already engaged at a "tender age" in "their life of drudgery." Several New Mexico teachers reported that many girls in their schools married at a young age and thus rarely completed their educations. New Mexican parents, Matilda Allison reported, "could not understand our interest in [their daughters]."[25]

Poverty apparently also contributed to attendance problems. Parents often withdrew older children from school to work, and consequently many of them received only a partial education. Furthermore, several teachers reported that attendance dropped during the coldest months because many of their pupils did not have adequate clothing to keep warm. Other teachers worried that expecting students to pay for books and tuition would drive them from the mission schools. Rather than do this, missionary teachers often accepted token payment in kind in lieu thereof. For example, in 1880 Elizabeth Smith at Corrales, New Mexico, reported that she had received "some sheepskins, three chickens, two eggs, some beef and $1.50 cash" in payment for tuition.[26]

Teachers used a variety of "carrots" to entice pupils to their schools. In 1878 J. M. Shields explained that "it takes a good many presents . . . to win these little Aztecs [Jemez Pueblos] and secure their confidence." Less than a month later James Roberts at Taos suggested, "I think we can get many more pupils if we can do something at clothing the very poor." T. F. Ealy at Zuni Pueblo was even more inventive. Upon concluding that many Zuni girls were grinding grain by hand when they should be attending his school, he introduced a small, wind-powered mill and offered to grind corn for those who would send their daughters to his school.[27]

More surprisingly, some missionaries de-emphasized formal religious instruction to keep students whose parents objected to Presbyterian teachings. In 1878 John Annin of Las Vegas, one of the staunchest Presbyterians in the New Mexico field, explained that he did not require students to participate in religious activities because it "would have subverted" his school. In Manti, Utah, Mrs. Joseph McMillan opened and closed her school with prayer and scripture reading, but she "did not think it expedient" to make study of the Bible part of her course of study. To secure room and board in a Utah town in 1882, another Presbyterian teacher had to promise not to preach or teach religion in her school. Several years later a teacher at Zuni Pueblo suggested that "what ever religious training is brought to bear must be slow [and] silent."[28]

The attendance problem was, of course, only the first of many challenges to the mission teacher. The earliest classrooms rarely provided a suitable atmosphere for learning, and teachers had little or no teaching materials and supplies. Throughout the 1880s teachers in all three fields pleaded frantically for desks, blackboards, maps, globes, slates, pencils, chalk, and erasers. Textbooks were in short supply, and teachers often asked pupils to bring books from home. They were dismayed to find that many families owned no books. At Corrales, New Mexico, Susan Perea was appalled when her students brought to her Protestant school the Catholic prayer books they had previously used in the public schools.[29]

The incredibly diverse array of students who attended the mission schools posed another problem for teachers. The twenty-seven pupils enrolled on the first day of classes at the Salt Lake Collegiate Institute were "as great a variety of classification as any teacher had to handle." Elizabeth Craig's first pupils at El Prado de Taos, New Mexico, in 1888 were "all sizes and ages . . . little tots and young men and women and all ages in between." Whole families occasionally enrolled in the Tucson Indian School, and parents and children sometimes studied in the same classroom. The problem was most severe in the small, one-room schools in isolated areas, where single teachers labored alone. A teacher in the Pajarito, New Mexico, school in 1886 had so many levels of pupils that she "was compelled to hear sixty-four lessons per day."[30]

Many students came to the mission schools totally unprepared for school-work. For example, students arrived at J. M. Shields's Jemez Pueblo school barely clothed and carrying bows, arrows, and knives. A Santa Fe teacher reported that several of her boys were very ill behaved and brought "revolvers and great knives" to her school. When a group of Ute students arrived at the Albuquerque Indian school in 1883, a teacher reported that "they had been taken right out of tents from the wildest kind of life" and that several of the young men were former warriors who had recently engaged in depredations on white settlers. Five years later the superintendent of the Tucson Indian School wrote that "the average Indian child who comes to us knows almost nothing as he should know it." Teachers among the Indians also complained that their pupils frequently brought baby brothers and sisters to school along with them, to the almost constant distraction of the schoolwork. Of course, the mission school students also engaged in a normal amount of horseplay. A visitor to the Albuquerque Indian school noted that students threw spitballs and occasionally quarreled with one another. He also observed a Comanche boy "engaged in the interesting anatomical experiment of determining how far his slate pencil [would] go in the ear of the meek looking Laguna boy next to him."[31]

Once students had been secured for the mission schools, emergencies and unexpected events occasionally posed problems. Outbreaks of smallpox, measles, typhoid, and diphtheria were reported from all three fields. Pupils and teachers occasionally died, and, of course, schools then had to be temporarily closed. The destruction by fire of a nearly completed two-story building filled with furnishings and supplies was a major reason for the home board's decision to close the Albuquerque Indian School in 1889. Heavy rains and flooding also occasionally posed problems. Of course, native religious leaders were quick to attribute such difficulties to divine displeasure with parents who sent their children to the Presbyterian schools.[32]

Success in combating the above obstacles occasionally created another problem — overcrowding. By the late 1880s several teachers from all three fields reported that their energies and facilities were overtaxed and that pupils had to be turned away. The Pajarito, New Mexico, teacher who heard sixty-four lessons daily probably expressed the sentiments of many of her mission teacher colleagues when she confessed to home board officials that she hoped no more students would come. Turning children and parents away, she lamented, irreparably harmed all that she had worked so hard to accomplish.[33]

Finally, some of the mission school problems were of the Presbyterians' own making. Although most missionaries were virtuous and honestly strove to meet the high expectations of their church and mission board, a few did not. Federal Indian officials fired at least two Presbyterian-appointed male teachers. One was charged with public drunkenness and selling whiskey to the Indians. The other was accused of multiple offenses, including conducting personal business when he was supposed to be in the classroom; his "business" included renting houses to prostitutes. The home board and southwestern presbyteries also occasionally dismissed unsatisfactory teachers from their positions. In 1884 Mrs. Haines expressed concern about rumors that a Moroni, Utah, teacher "danced and played cards in the presence of Mormons." Eight years later Utah synodical missionary Samuel Wishard wrote a scathing letter to board headquarters reporting that one of his young teachers had engaged in similar activities and had recently married a Mormon.[34]

Petty rivalries, jealousies, and un-Christianlike dissension also occasionally plagued work at a number of the early schools. Sometimes the chief source of tension lay in the feeling that one's efforts were not appreciated. A missionary couple in Ocate, New Mexico, frequently charged that Taos missionary James Roberts (their immediate supervisor in the field) "had never been interested" in their work. From Utah Duncan McMillan complained to Jackson in 1880 that Salt Lake City missionary J. M. Coyner "never mention[ed] the work in the San Pete Valley" in his articles in Jackson's paper. Perhaps the most heated animosities occurred between the Hopi missionary Charles Taylor and Mr. and Mrs. J. D. Perkins, who labored nearby among the Navajos. The Perkinses often complained to Jackson that Taylor did not fulfill his duties. In turn, Taylor wrote of Mrs. Perkins: "I have met many wicked men, deep evil schemers in this far west, but I have never met anyone, anywhere who I believe to be more wicked." Taylor likened his adversary's hypocrisy and deceitfulness to that of presidential assassin Charles Guitteau. Similar problems led Utah Presbytery in 1890 to direct that "all discussion of grievances shall cease in the homes of the people and on the street."[35]

Confusion about responsibility for the mission schools sometimes exacerbated problems in the field. Missionaries in the early years often attributed this confusion to Sheldon Jackson's peripatetic leadership. A southern Colorado missionary whom board officials reprimanded in 1880 for establishing schools without proper authority blamed Jackson for his "interminable tangle." In the same year Utah Presbytery unanimously requested that the Board of Home Missions divide the territory under Jackson's authority since "he [had] not been in Utah in two years." Other missionaries chided Jackson for his lack of interest and communication with them and complained bitterly when his ambitious eyes turned northward to Alaska.[36]

More serious problems resulted from the church's failure to clearly define responsibility for the unprecedented mission school work. In 1883 the Utah superintendent of schools, Duncan McMillan, refused to follow instructions from the Utah Presbytery that he dismiss a teacher. When he asserted that the home board had full responsibility over the schools and that the local judicatories had only advisory power, the presbytery charged him with "lack of harmony" and did not reappoint him to his position. Eight years later the same presbytery charged that the home board's long-standing interference with the Utah work violated the "fundamental principles of the presbyterian form of government." For its part the Presbytery of Santa Fe was slightly less hostile. In 1886 it labeled its relationship with the home board on the school question "abnormal" and suggested means of "increasing the efficiency of the schools and minimizing conflict."[37]

From all three fields teachers complained of overwork. J. M. Shields of Jemez Pueblo wrote in 1881, "I have to preach, teach, doctor, and look after everything." Several months later his cousin, Lora Shields, at the Albuquerque Indian school, commented that the teachers there were "all too enthusiastic not to put heart and soul into [their] work." But, she added, "we cannot do double duty long." From Utah a teacher lamented that she needed "more power, more hands, more bodies to be in more places." Another Utah teacher was more philosophical. "I have been busy," she wrote, "so busy I have not had time to think whether I am contented or not."[38]

Inadequate and irregular missionary salaries also created dissent in mission ranks. While still a missionary among the Navajos, John Menaul wrote bluntly to mission officials: "It is about time that the Church and board accept the truth, that missionaries are men, not angels, or even prophets fed by ravens." Erratic pay schedules caused many hardships and occasionally forced missionaries to borrow money, which one Utah teacher indicated "goes against every fibre of my nature." Difficult economic times, like those in the mid-1880s, worsened these problems.[39]

Perhaps nothing proved more counterproductive for the Presbyterian cause than missionary inflexibility. Certain aspects of the culture of the exceptional populations so repulsed some missionaries that they could not even meet their subjects halfway. For example, Charles A. Taylor was so appalled with the "filth and vermin" of the Hopi's mesa-top villages that he could not bring himself to establish his school there, even when he conceded that he could never reach those people from "down below." Other missionaries were so attached to eastern standards of doing things that the unique southwestern environment rendered them completely ineffective. A telling example came from a missionary at Zuni Pueblo in the early 1880s. He waited to build a badly needed fence until he could get "good cedar posts." "I would not use any other," he observed, even though the eastern cedar that he sought did not grow anywhere near his isolated station. When he left his position soon thereafter, he had not built his fence. Neither had he made any measurable impact on the Zunis.[40]

The wide gap between the missionaries' lofty expectations and the reality of their experience in the Southwest left many of them disheartened. In 1881, after five years at Laguna Pueblo, John Menaul glumly wrote to Sheldon Jackson: "There is really little to be said about our work now. The Indians seem determined not to have our religion and only as little of our civilization as they can help." Writing to Jackson only a few days after

Menaul, a southern Colorado missionary offered a long list of reasons to justify his resignation from his duties. These included the constant poor health of his family, excessive responsibilities, and missionary quarreling. He was particularly dismayed that the effort to reach the New Mexicans required preaching "against Catholicism" rather than the "preaching of Christ." In 1893 another New Mexico teacher bluntly commented: "I get weary watching and waiting for some of my pupils to give themselves to Christ." Missionaries in Utah experienced even deeper despair. Their letters commented regularly on the persistence of Mormon opposition and their inability to win converts. One Utah teacher likened Presbyterian missions in Utah to attacking "the Rock of Gibraltar with a little hammer."[41]

Although mission officials were unusually tight-lipped about the matter, it is clear that the attrition rate for southwestern missionaries was high. One-third of the twenty-seven men whom the home board commissioned as ministers and evangelists for the southwestern fields in 1880 served less than five years, and slightly more than a quarter (seven, or 27 percent) served three years or less (see table 5). The attrition rate for teachers was

Table 5. Service in Southwest of Twenty-seven Ministers and Evangelists Commissioned by Board of Home Missions in 1880

	Years Served	Number of Missionaries	Percent of Missionaries
	1	1	4
	2	5	19
	3	1	4
	5	2	7
Total Serving 1–5 Years		9	34
	6	1	4
	7	1	4
	8	1	4
	9	1	4
	10	3	11
Total Serving 6–10 Years		7	27
	14	2	7
	17	2	7
Total Serving 10–20 Years		4	14
Total Serving 20–30 Years		4	15
Total Serving More Than 30 Years		3	11

even greater. Of the thirty-five teachers commissioned in 1880, only thirteen (37 percent) served more than five years, and seventeen (49 percent) served three years or less (see table 6).[42] This frequent turnover of personnel, of course, reflected and exacerbated the other difficulties that beset the Presbyterian effort in the Southwest.

In spite of these many difficulties, the Presbyterian mission school effort in the Southwest persisted and even expanded in the decade and a half after the establishment of the Woman's Executive Committee. While a number of schools remained open only briefly and many teachers left the Southwest after serving relatively short tenures, the number of pupils increased annually. In 1893 and 1894 an all-time high of 4,941 southwestern youths enrolled in Presbyterian mission schools.[43]

More significantly, those missionaries who persevered beyond the first five or so trying years often served for considerably longer tenures. For example, twenty-two (35 percent) of the sixty-two ministers and teachers

Table 6. Service in Southwest of Thirty-five Missionary Teachers Commissioned by Woman's Executive Committee of Home Missions in 1880

	Years Served	Number of Teachers	Percent of Teachers
	1	1	3
	2	3	9
	3	13	37
	4	1	3
	5	4	11
Total Serving 1–5 Years		22	63
	6	1	3
	7	0	0
	8	3	9
	9	1	3
	10	1	3
Total Serving 6–10 Years		6	18
	13	1	3
	15	1	3
	16	2	6
Total Serving 10–20 Years		4	12
	25	2	6
	26	1	3
Total Serving More Than 20 Years		3	9

commissioned to work in the Southwest in 1880 served ten years or longer, and fifteen (24 percent) served more than fifteen years. Some missionaries did considerably better. For example, Charles Cook, the Apostle to the Pimas, and New Mexico teachers Elizabeth Craig and Alice Blake each remained in the Southwest for more than forty years. John and Charity (Gaston) Menaul served more than thirty years in several different southwestern assignments; Alice Hyson worked thirty-one years at Ranchos de Taos, New Mexico; and George W. Martin served thirty years at Manti, Utah. A number of other missionaries made careers of more than twenty years in the Southwest. They included Anna Noble, Josie Curtis, and Samuel Gillespie in the Utah field; R. W. and Sadie Hall, Matilda Allison, Vicente Romero, Ronaldo Montoya, and Jose Ynes Perea in New Mexico.[44]

Deep religious faith sustained these long-timers through many challenges. God, they repeatedly observed, had not forsaken them. J. M. Shields concluded an otherwise bleak report from Jemez Pueblo in 1880 with the observation that "the things that are impossible with man are possible with God." Three years later a Utah teacher observed: "One thing is certain; the word of God will not fail—missionary work well done will succeed." Another Utah teacher concluded a report the following year: "This work would be terribly difficult were it our own. Thank God it is not, but *His* own; in His strength we go forward."[45]

The missionaries who persevered and remained in the Southwest for considerable periods of time were not, however, Pollyannas. Indeed, firsthand experience taught them that their work was not easy and that the victory once considered imminent was elusive. While few missionaries questioned the goal of "regenerating the exceptional populations," experience led some of them to gradually recognize that this effort required far more time and effort than Sheldon Jackson and other early proponents of Presbyterian missions for the region had assumed. For example, veteran New Mexico missionary John Annin repeatedly advised new teachers to have "realistic expectations." "It will take years of living, working, and praying," a Utah missionary wrote in 1882, "to make much impression on this stronghold of Mormonism." The year before, a missionary from the Pima-Papago field wrote: "I think we make a mistake in expecting the Indians to adopt our habits in a day." John Menaul at Laguna Pueblo was perhaps the most perceptive Presbyterian commentator on the tenacity of southwestern pluralism. Throughout his long career among both Indians and New Mexicans, he urged Presbyterians "to make haste slowly" and to exhibit patience in their southwestern missionary endeavors. His blunt advice to the idealistic friends of Indian missions in 1880 that "it won't help the Indian if we pretend he is what he is not" reflected an understanding uncommon for the time.[46]

These observations from veteran missionaries in the field gradually influenced the outlook of mission officials in the East on the work in the Southwest. While the home board's annual reports continued on a hopeful note, they used words like "slow," "difficult," "costly," and "discouraging" to describe the southwestern missions. The 1887 report went a step further and conceded that the educational missions to the native southwesterners were "capable of indefinite expansion."[47] Presbyterians had discovered that the challenge of southwestern pluralism was indeed formidable.

Notes

1. In territorial Utah (1850–96) the Methodists established twenty-six schools, and the Congregationalists twenty-eight schools. The same two churches were also active in the New Mexico field, establishing twelve and eight schools respectively. Episcopalians and Baptists operated schools on a smaller scale in both fields. A number of Protestant denominations as well as the Roman Catholics established schools among southwestern Indians.

2. John Menaul, 1877 Annual Report to the Ladies Union Missionary Association, reprinted in *RMP* 6 (October 1877). Presbyterian-nominated Pueblo agent B. M. Thomas used the same phrase in a letter to Sheldon Jackson, January 21, 1879, SJCC.

3. Ella McDonald to Mrs. Haines, December 30, 1881, PHS, RG 105, Box 1, F-7. Other particularly vivid accounts of missionary homesickness and loneliness are found in O.E.B., "Utah," *PHM* 11 (January 1882); Matilda Allison, "Mission Work in N.M.," *HMM* 1 (September 1887): 252; *HMM* 4 (February 1890): 73.

4. For descriptions of early missionary homes see the following letters from the SJCC: Charles Taylor (missionary to the Hopis), July 22, November 4, 1880; Mrs. T. F. Ealy (from Zuni Pueblo), November 18, 1878; Alice Hyson, "Words from Workers — N.M.," *HMM* 1 (December 1886): 14; "Letters from Missionary Teachers in Utah," PHS, RG 105, Box 1, F-5.

5. "News from Western Fields — N.M.," *RMP* 9 (January 1880); anonymous, undated teacher's report from Isleta Pueblo, PHS, RG 51, Box 1, F-7; James M. Roberts, "From Fernando de Taos, N.M.," SJS 54:61; Mrs. Roberts, "Fernandez [*sic*] de Taos, N.M.," SJS 54:109; "Extracts of Letters from N.M.," SJS 56:3; Matilda Allison, "Santa Fe Boarding and Industrial School for Mexican Girls," *La Aurora* 3 (November 6, 1902): 21; Rev. George W. Leonard, "An Appeal for Springville," SJS 60:61; "Our Schools in Utah," October 11, 1883, PHS, RG 105, Box 1, F-1.

6. See the following letters to Sheldon Jackson from the SJCC: Mrs. F. D. Palmer, April 17, 1878; John Menaul, April 18, 1878; Mrs. A. H. Donaldson, June 29, 1880; J. M. Shields, December 3, December 9, 1878. Also see J. H. Willson, "Words from Workers," *HMM* 2 (January 1888): 58.

7. See the following letters from the SJCC: Charles A. Taylor, January 19, July 21, and July 22, 1882; Jose Ynes Perea, January 9, 1880; J. M. Shields, December

9, 1878. Norman J. Bender, ed. *Missionaries, Outlaws, and Indians: Taylor F. Ealy at Lincoln and Zuni, 1878–1881* (Albuquerque: University of New Mexico Press, 1984), 138–39. Cheryl J. Foote, " 'Let Her Works Praise Her' " (Ph.D. diss., University of New Mexico, 1986), 47–83, and Barbara Welter, "She Hath Done What She Could," 113–17, examine the particular plight of missionary wives.

8. Jose Ynes Perea to S. Jackson, April 9, 1880, SJCC. Similar sentiments are expressed in R. W. Hall to S. Jackson, April 20, 1880, SJCC; and J. M. Roberts, "Northern New Mexico," *RMP* 9 (February 1880).

9. Rev. J. M. Shields, "From Jemez, N.M.," *SJS* 57:27; H. K. Palmer, "A Zuni Experience," *RMP* 7 (October 1878); John Menaul, "Laguna Pueblo," *SJS* 55:105; S. A. Bentley to S. Jackson, November 5, 1881, SJCC; Mrs. Haines to Miss Lora Shields, October 27, 1881, PHS, RG 105, Box 2, F-7.

10. John Menaul to S. Jackson, March 6, 1879, SJCC; J. Menaul, 2d Annual Report, Laguna Mission, 1877, SJS 53:340–41, 3d Annual Report, 1878–79, SJS 55:118. The quote about the Pima tongue is from *PHM* 10 (May 1881): 274. T. F. Ealy to S. Jackson, September 24, 1879, SJCC.

11. A. B. Upshaw to H. Kendall, July 16, 1887; J. D. C. Atkins to Kendall, February 11, 1888, NA, RG 75, Education Division — Letters Sent, 9:485 and 12:57; anonymous undated teacher's report from Isleta Pueblo, PHS, RG 51, Box 1, F-7.

12. Alexander Darley, "The Secondary Languages of the United States," *SJS* 54:11; Miss Celia Morgan, "Words from Workers — N.M.," *HMM* 1 (January 1887): 62; Mollie Clements, "A Service of Joy," *HMM* 31 (November 1916): 6.

13. Miss A. M. Whitehead, "Words from Workers — Utah," *HMM* 1 (February 1887): 86.

14. Jose Ynes Perea to S. Jackson, December 8, 1879, SJCC; Miss E. M. Fenton, "Words from Workers — N.M.," *HMM* 2 (April 1888): 133; "How Domingo Was Converted," *HMM* 4 (February 1890): 99–100. A federal Indian inspector, C. H. Howard, commented on Catholic opposition to the Albuquerque Indian School in his report to the commissioner of Indian affairs, H. M. Tellet, February 2, 1883, Reports of Inspections of the Field Jurisdictions of the Office of Indian Affairs, NA, microfilms, roll 41.

15. Minutes, Presbytery of Utah, March 15, 1880, 1:133–34; George W. Gallagher to S. Jackson, December 28, 1878, SJCC; R. G. McNiece, "Utah: Spring Meeting of Presbytery of Utah," *PHM* 11 (June 1882): 134; "Historical Notes," *HMM* 1 (January 1887): 77; Rev. W. M. Cort, "Home Mission Work in Southern Utah," *PHM* 11 (October 1882): 225; "Religious Persecutions in the U.S.: Reports of Teachers in Utah," *PHM* 11 (August 1882): 187.

16. Minutes, Presbytery of Utah, March 30, 1885, 2:110. The assault on the New Mexico teacher is reported in *HMM* 9 (February 1895): 75. "Words from Workers — Mormon," *HMM* 8 (January 1894): 64–65; "A Martyred Mexican Boy," *PHMy* 13 (February 1884): 43; *HMM* 5 (December 1890): 25.

17. "News from the Western Fields — Utah," *RMP* 9 (January 1880); R. G. McNiece to Mrs. Haines, July 23, 1880, PHS, RG 105, Box 1, F-4; Mrs. C. R. Winters to Board of Home Missions, undated, PHS, RG 51, Box 1, F-7; C. M. Parks to S. Jackson, May 12, 1879; Anna Ross to S. Jackson, January 26, 1882, SJCC; "Words from Workers — N.M.," *HMM* 2 (July 1888): 210.

18. See the following letters to Jackson from the SJCC: J. M. Shields, July 28, 1879, February 3 and March 24, 1882, March 16, 1883; Thomas Thompson, June 14, 1882; Taylor, December 1, 1881; Thomas, January 31, 1881; Charles Cook to Jackson, December 6, 1882, SJS 57:58. Reba Benge, "Benjamin M. Thomas, Career in the Southwest, 1870–1892" (Ph.D. diss., University of New Mexico, 1979), examines Thomas's career as Pueblo agent.

19. Rev. Howard Billman to Mrs. Paterson, undated, Records of Tucson Indian Training School, Arizona Historical Society. Miss Jennie Hammaker complained to Jackson about Cushing's influence on the Zunis in a letter of June 16, 1881, SJCC. An anonymous, undated teacher's report from Isleta Pueblo, PHS, RG 51, Box 1, F-7, made a similar observation about Lummis.

20. George Bird, "Heathenism at Home," SJS 60:13; "Words from Workers — Utah," HMM 2 (August 1888): 230. Missionary comments about Mormon apostates are numerous. See, for example, J. Welch, "Utah" and "Affairs in Utah," SJS 61:78, 104–5; Minutes of Utah Presbytery, March 15, 1879, 1:98; J. M. Coyner, "Utah Column," SJS 60:54; "Words from Workers — Utah," HMM 4 (November 1889): 14.

21. John Annin, "From N.M.," SJS 53:81; Minutes, Presbytery of Santa Fe, September 4, 1880, 1:60. Norman J. Bender, ed., *Missionaries, Outlaws, and Indians,* skillfully presents the Ealys' dilemmas at Lincoln.

22. Minutes, Presbytery of Santa Fe, April 1890, 3:108. Randi Walker, "Protestantism in the Sangre de Cristos," 203–7, examines Presbyterian-Methodist rivalries in New Mexico. The quote about Seventh-Day Adventism in Utah is in "From Our Missionaries," HMM 10 (June 1896): 180. Presbyterian concern about other missionaries in Utah is evident in George W. Gallagher to S. Jackson, March 7, 10, 1879, SJCC; Minutes, Presbytery of Utah, March 31, 1886, 2:205–6; and Mr. J. F. Millspaugh, "Present Condition and Future Prospects of Salt Lake Collegiate Institute," PHMy 14 (December 1885): 281.

23. J. J. Gilchrist to S. Jackson, January 7, 1880, SJCC; Miss A. M. Whitehead, "Words from Workers — Utah," HMM 1 (February 1887): 85. Missionaries to Indians faced similar difficulties. See, for example, Rev. Howard Billman to Mrs. Lauretta Maxwell, April 19, 1889, Records of Tucson Indian Training School; James H. Willson to S. Jackson, April 12, 1883, SJCC; and Mary Dissette to Dear Friends, April 7, 1894, NA, RG 75, B.I.A. Special Cases/SC 143 NM.

24. See Floretta Shields to Mrs. D. E. Finks, November 1886, and to Mary E. Dissette, September 29, 1890, PHS, RG 51, Box 1, F-19 and F-25; J. H. Willson, "Words from Workers — N.M.," HMM 2 (January 1888): 58; Leila Butler, "Albuquerque, N.M.," SJS 57:37. The reports of government inspectors confirm Presbyterian reports about irregular school attendance. See, for example, Report of Zuni Inspection by Inspector Howard, July 1882, and Report by Inspector Junkin on Pueblo Agency Schools, March 4, 1891, 4, from Reports of Inspectors of Field Jurisdiction, Office of Indian Affairs, Pueblo and Jicarilla Agency, microfilm roll 41.

25. Comments on the problems of attracting girls to the Zuni mission school are found in RMP 7 (December 1878) and 9 (April 1880); M. Allison, "Santa Fe

Mission Boarding School," *HMM* 7 (November 1893): 10; Mollie Clements, "A Service of Joy," *HMM* 31 (November 1916): 6.

26. "Topic for the Month — The Mexicans," *HMM* 7 (November 1893): 6–8; Report of Miss Elizabeth B. Smith, Corrales, N.M., Mission School, Fall 1880, PHS, RG 105, Box 1, F-7; Lila Morton to Mrs. Allen, October 23, 188?, SJS 60:93. Also see Mrs. J. D. Perkins, "Santa Fe, N.M.," *RMP* 9 (March 1880); S. V. Dilley, "Words from Workers — N.M.," *HMM* 2 (July 1888): 210; Mrs. G. W. Gallagher to S. Jackson, August 19, 1879, SJS 60:11; "Our Schools in Utah," PHS, RG 105, Box 1, F-4; Miss Anna F. Hubbard, "Words from Workers — Mormon," *HMM* 9 (December 1894): 42.

27. See the following letters to Jackson from the SJCC: Shields, June 22, 1878; J. M. Roberts, July 23, 1878; and J. S. Shearer, February 2, 1881. *RMP* 9 (April 1880).

28. J. Annin, "To Our Teachers," SJS 54:56; "From Mrs. McMillan at Manti," *RMP* 7 (May 1878); "A Missionary Teacher in Utah," *PHM* 11 (March 1882): 67; "Words from Workers — N.M.," *HMM* 4 (December 1889): 37.

29. Teachers' requests for supplies were so common that one can only cite a few of the most fervent pleas. Examples from the New Mexico field are Elizabeth B. Smith to S. Jackson, November 5, 1880, Maxwell Phillips to S. Jackson, October 24, 1881, SJCC. From the Utah field: George W. Gallagher, "The Wants of the Mission Schools of Utah," SJS 60:82; Miss Clemmie Brown to Dear Friends, November 24, 1880, PHS, RG 105, Box 1, F-4. From the Indian field: Mrs. T. F. Ealy to S. Jackson, November 18, 1878, Miss Mary Perry to S. Jackson, September 13, 1880, SJCC.

30. J. M. Coyner, "History of Salt Lake Collegiate Institute," written December 16, 1897, copy in Paden Collection, Westminster College Archives; Elizabeth W. Craig, "Thirty Years in New Mexico," *HMM* 28 (November 1913): 10; Mrs. C. E. Walker to Rev. T. C. Kirkwood, November 13, 1886, PHS, RG 105, Box 2, F-12; Howard Billman to Mrs. H. L. Kneass, October 26, 1891, PHS, RG 51, Box 2, F-2. Also see Mrs. John Annin to Mrs. S. Jackson, January 23, 1878, SJCC; "Perplexed but Not in Despair," 8 (May 1884): 110; Miss Mary L. Stright, "Words from Workers — Mexican," *HMM* 5 (May 1891): 158; Miss M. Beekman, "Words from Workers — Mexican," *HMM* 6 (May 1892): 179.

31. J. M. Shields, "Home Missions Letter to Children — Pueblo of Jemez," *RMP* 7 (September 1878); Mrs. J. M. Sharon, "New Mexico," *RMP* 8 (August 1879); Letter from Lila Butler, May 23, 1883, SJS 57:49; Rev. Howard Billman to Mrs. C. E. Walker, November 25, 1888, records of Tucson Indian Training School. Complaints about Indian babies in the classroom are found in Jennie Hammaker to Mrs. McMurray, January 10, 1880, reprinted in *RMP* 9 (August 1880); anonymous, undated teacher's report from Isleta Pueblo, and Floretta Shields to Mrs. D. E. Finks, December 27, 1886, PHS, RG 51, Box 1, F-7 and F-19. "Sons of Savages," SJS 55:120.

32. Problems related to epidemic diseases are reported in "Zuni Mission, New Mexico," February 8, 1878, SJS 58:136; "N.M. — Albuquerque," *PHMy* 13 (July 1884): 149; Miss Burnham, "New Mexico," *RMP* 7 (May 1878); Anna Ross, "New

Mexico — La Costilla," Spring 1883, SJS 54:119–20; M. Allison, "Words from Workers — Mexican," *HMM* 6 (November 1891): 12; "Review of Our Schools among the Mormons," *HMM* 7 (May 1893): 153. The fire at the Albuquerque Indian School and its consequences are described in "Words from Workers — N.M.," *HMM* 2 (September 1888): 253–54. Miss Delia Hills reported that flood waters had set back her school work in Salazar, New Mexico, "for an indefinite period" ("Words from Workers — N.M.," *HMM* 1 [January 1887]: 63).

33. Comments on problems related to overcrowding appear frequently in missionary correspondence and reports. See, for example, Rev. James Fraser, "New Mexico: Our Schools among the Mexicans," *PHMy* 14 (February 1885): 40; "Words from Workers — New Mexico," *HMM* 3 (February 1889): 83; Rev. Howard Billman, "Words from Workers — Arizona," *HMM* 3 (October 1889): 277; Coyner, "History of the Salt Lake Collegiate Institute." Miss Winters commented on overcrowding of her Pajarito school in an undated letter (probably written in late 1880s) to the Board of Home Missions, PHS, RG 51, Box 1, F-7.

34. J. D. C. Atkins to Rev. H. Kendall, December 16, 1887, January 17, 1888, NA, RG 75, Education Division: Letters Sent, 11:304, 425; Report of Inspector Gardner on Pueblo Agency, April 27, 1885, Reports of Inspections of Field Jurisdictions, Office of Indian Affairs, NA, microfilm roll 41; Mrs. C. E. Walker to Mrs. J. R. Hawley, November 30, 1886; Mrs. Haines to Sadie L. Brown, March 27, 1884, PHS, RG 105, Box 2, F-12 and F-10; C. M. Parks to S. Jackson, March 1879, SJCC; J. Duncan Brite, "History of Presbyterian Churches and Schools in Cache Valley," unpublished manuscript, Pierce Historical Hall, Wasatch Academy, Mt. Pleasant, Utah, 4; Minutes, Presbytery of Santa Fe, October 20, 1887, 2:330; J. S. Shearer to Mrs. F. E. H. Haines, October 14, 1881, PHS, RG 105, Box 1, F-6; Samuel Wishard to executive committee of woman's board, January 21, 1892, PHS, RG 51, Box 2, F-3.

35. Problems at Albuquerque Indian School are aired in J. S. Shearer to Mrs. Haines, December 8, 1881, PHS, RG 105, Box 1, F-6, and Shearer to Jackson, April 7, April 11, 1882, SJCC. The Presbytery of Santa Fe discussed problems at the Mora mission school in its meeting of May 8, 1888, Minutes, 3:32. D. McMillan to S. Jackson, April 22, 1880, SJCC. For several years Jackson must have felt barraged with letters from the Perkinses and Taylor. See, for example, Mrs. Perkins to Jackson, November 3, 1881, and January 16, 1882, SJCC. Taylor's description of Mrs. Perkins is from his letter to Jackson of February 1, 1883, SJCC. Minutes, Presbytery of Utah, August 28, 1890, 3:197.

36. See the following letters from the SJCC: R. W. and Sadie Hall, December 15, 1879; W. W. Morton, December 8, 1880; Jennie Hammaker, June 16, 1881; Charles Taylor, April 25, 1882; Robert McNiece, February 14, 1879. Minutes, Presbytery of Utah, August 22, 1880, 1:145. A Montana missionary made a similar complaint about Jackson in 1876. See Goslin, "Henry Kendall," *Journal of Presbyterian Historical Society* 27 (June 1949): 78–79.

37. Minutes, Presbytery of Utah, August 22, 1883, 2:22–23, 38, and March 26, 1891, 3:229; Minutes, Presbytery of Santa Fe, April 9, 1886, 2:259–62.

38. See the following letters from PHS, RG 105, Box 1: J. M. Shields to Mrs.

Haines, January 25, 1881, F-5; Lora B. Shields to Mrs. Haines, April 24, 1881, F-4; Miss Clemmie Brown to Dear Friends, November 24, 1880, F-4. "Words from Workers — Utah," *HMM* 1 (December 1886): 14. These are only a few typical examples of missionary comments about their heavy duties. Many others are found in the SJCC, the missionary magazines, and the PHS correspondence files.

39. John Menaul to John Lowrie, May 20, 1873, American Indian Correspondence, Box M, vol. 1, letter 139, quoted by Foote, " 'Let Her Works Praise Her,' " 60; Miss Carrie Nutting to Mrs. F. E. H. Haines, October 23, 1882, PHS, RG 105, Box 1, F-4. Missionary records are filled with other comments on the matter of salaries. The impact of the financial woes of the mid-1880s are discussed in "Reduction of Work and Appropriations," *PHMy* 14 (July 1885): 146, and 15th Annual Report, Board of Home Missions, 1885, 11–13.

40. Charles A. Taylor to S. Jackson, February 25, 1881; S. A. Bentley to S. Jackson, November 5, 1881, SJCC.

41. John Menaul to S. Jackson, January 12, 1881; W. W. Morton to S. Jackson, January 17, 1881, SJCC; "Topic for the Month: The Mexicans," *HMM* 7 (November 1893): 8; Miss Osbourne, "Words from Workers — Mormon," *HMM* 6 (September 1892): 234.

42. Not all teachers, of course, resigned because of discouragement. Records suggest that a number of female teachers married after arriving in the Southwest and that with few exceptions they resigned from their teaching duties soon thereafter. See "Rev. Dr. Roberts' Address," *PHM* 11 (July 1882): 151. Some teachers also apparently resigned from their work in the Southwest to fulfill family obligations in the East. For example, Miss Lockwood explained her resignation because "a feeble mother needs me elsewhere" ("Words from Workers — Utah," *HMM* 1 [October 1887]: 272). Inadequate records for the 1880s make it difficult to compile more thorough statistics on missionary attrition, particularly for teachers. For several years in the late 1870s and early 1880s, the home board included lists of teachers in the appendices of their annual reports. This practice was discontinued, however, for several years in the mid-1880s. Consequently, the statistics on teachers presented in Tables 5 and 6 had to be drawn from a number of different sources. After 1890 the home board maintained more consistent records on the teachers that were commissioned.

43. According to the home board's 1894 annual report, Presbyterians in 1893 and 1894 conducted 31 schools in Utah with 90 teachers and 2,368 pupils; 33 schools in New Mexico with 51 teachers and 2,214 pupils; and 4 schools among southwestern Indians with 24 teachers and 359 pupils. Although the woman's executive committee expanded its mission school work in other areas (particularly Alaska and the South) during the period from 1879 to 1894, the Southwest continued to be the principal area of Presbyterian concern. Of the 123 Presbyterian mission schools conducted nationwide in 1894, 55 percent (68) were in the Southwest (24th Annual Report, Board of Home Missions [1894]: 171, 179).

44. Historians have examined the careers of several of these missionary long-timers. See, for example, Minnie Cook's biography of her grandfather, Charles Cook, *Apostle to the Pima Indians* (Tiburon, Calif.: Omega Books, 1976); Cheryl

Foote, "Alice Blake of Trementina: Mission Teacher in the Southwest," *Journal of Presbyterian History* 60 (Fall 1982): 228–43; Banker, "Presbyterian Missionary Activity in the Southwest: The Careers of John and James Menaul," *Journal of the West* 23 (January 1984): 55–61; Banker, "Missionary to His Own People: Jose Ynes Perea and Hispanic Presbyterianism in New Mexico," in *Religion and Society in the American West*, ed. Carl Guarneri (Lanham, Md.: University Press of America, forthcoming).

45. J.M.S., "Jemez Pueblo," *RMP* 9 (September 1880): 138; "The New Work in Utah," *PHMy* 12 (September 1883): 195. Similar expressions of faith are found in Duncan McMillan to S. Jackson, December 21, 1878, SJCC; "Reports from Teachers," *PHMy* 12 (November 183): 8; "Utah," *PHMy* 13 (January 1884): 17; Miss Ella McDonald to Mrs. Haines, December 30, 1881, PHS, RG 105, Box 1, F-7. Such faith, of course, was not unique to Presbyterians. Charles W. Forman comments on the general nineteenth-century missionary confidence that victory would be theirs ("A History of Foreign Mission Theory in America," in *American Missions in Bicentennial Perspective*, ed. Beaver (South Pasadena, Calif.: William Carey Library, 1977), 75–76.

46. J. Annin, "To Our Teachers," ca. 1879, SJS 54:55–56; Rev. William C. Cort, "Home Mission Work in Southern Utah," *PHM* 11 (October 1882): 225; William Meyer to S. Jackson, May 11, 1881, SJCC; J. Menaul, "1877 Annual Report," *RMP* 6 (October 1877); J. Menaul, "Laguna Pueblo: Annual Report," *PHM* 10 (January 1881): 219. After retiring from Laguna, Menaul on several occasions elaborated on this theme. See his comments in *HMM* 6 (February 1892): 73, 80. Other indications that the experience in the Southwest sobered Presbyterian expectations are found in Miss P. J. Hart, "Words from Workers — Utah," *HMM* 1 (September 1887): 254; Howard Billman to Mrs. C. E. Walker, November 25, 1888, Records of Tucson Indian Training School; James Willson, "New Mexico — Zuni Pueblo," *PHMy* 12 (June 1883): 136–37.

47. See the annual reports for the 1880s; Report of Standing Committee of Home Missions to 1887 General Assembly, 17th Annual Report, Board of Home Missions, 1887, 130.

6

"Signs of Promise"

When the southwestern natives were not drawn irresistibly to the Presbyterians' vaunted Christian civilization as Sheldon Jackson and other early Presbyterians in the region had predicted, missionaries in the field and mission officials in the East recognized that they must make changes in their mission strategy. These adjustments, however, did not represent a conscious retreat from the Presbyterians' earlier goal of "regenerating the exceptional populations." Indeed, the mission school remained central to the Presbyterian strategy for the Southwest, and mission officials implemented a number of changes intended to enhance the transforming power of the schools. At the same time, however, other more subtle developments quietly eroded some of the missionaries' most extreme criticisms of the native southwesterners and their cultures. Ethnocentrism persisted, to be sure, but by 1900 the Presbyterian view of the southwestern peoples had changed significantly. Like other newcomers to the Southwest before them, Presbyterian missionaries who remained in the region for extended periods of time found themselves being changed even as they were changing the Southwest.

Many missionaries and mission officials believed that the chaotic conduct of the mission school program was the major impediment to its success. While the Woman's Executive Committee did a masterful job of promoting, and securing teachers for, the mission cause, the administration of that work left much to be desired. Consequently, in the 1880s mission officials in the Southwest and the East strove to place the school work on a more systematic basis. Toward this end the Board of Home Missions asserted greater control over the mission school work. The 1888 General Assembly informed local ministers and presbyteries that they could advise the board in the conduct of the schools but that ultimate authority belonged in the hands of the board and its appointees. The Presbytery of Utah, in particular, resisted this action. However, the recalcitrant presbytery never managed to subvert the home board's authority and gradually accepted it.[1]

Several years later the board, on the recommendation of the Woman's Executive Committee, created the position of superintendent of educational work. The first appointee to this position, the Reverend George McAfee, had previously been superintendent of a mission school among the Sioux Indians. McAfee commented that the appointment came from the "two great powers of the world" ("God and the women") and immediately began to institute reforms that strengthened the school work and the board's control over it. Several years later a board official reported that the school superintendent was "the essential link between laborers in the field and the officers" at missions headquarters. The superintendent corresponded daily with principals, teachers, and synodical missionaries; discussed the needs of the schools with representatives of the Woman's Executive Committee; oversaw the purchasing of supplies; and regularly visited the far-flung network of mission schools.[2]

Improving teacher performance and the schools in general became the Presbyterians' most important goal. For example, efforts were made to ameliorate the conditions that contributed to the high attrition rate of missionaries. The Woman's Executive Committee established special building funds and regularly reminded Presbyterians of the harsh conditions in which their southwestern missionaries lived. Gradually improvements were made in mission residences and schools, although they often remained primitive by eastern standards. In 1888 the Presbytery of Utah expressed concern about the "breaking health" of a number of missionaries within its bounds and "earnestly advised" teachers and missionaries to "take at least six weeks absolute rest away from their fields every year." In a similar spirit, the home board strove to reduce the number of teachers assigned alone to isolated mission stations. By 1890 only twenty-one of the 171 teachers in the Southwest (12 percent) served without at least one companion.[3]

Similarly, the home board, with advice from the local judicatories, made efforts to put the school work on a more systematic basis. In 1884 the Presbytery of Utah issued a plan of school work that proposed guidelines for a school system consisting of primary day schools and academies topped by a four-year college. The plan proposed courses of study and uniform textbooks for each level and called for more systematic supervision of teachers. By 1888 three Utah schools had added academy-level course work. Progress was slower in the New Mexico and Indian fields. Although a New Mexico teacher reported in 1895 that the work there was much better organized than a decade before, a detailed course of study for that field was not developed until 1899; even then, it provided for only six years of instruction.[4]

The academic programs devised for the mission schools followed closely the standard educational offerings of the day. For example, the courses of study for primary-level students prescribed classes in reading, orthography, penmanship, geography, arithmetic, grammar, and history. Mission officials, however, emphasized that mission teachers should educate more than the minds of their pupils. Courses in elementary hygiene and physical culture (i.e., simple calisthenics and exercise) were mandatory. Bible study, of course, was another principal element in the mission school curriculum. Finally, mission teachers were expected to instill patriotism in their pupils. In 1894 teachers in Utah taught their pupils stories from American history to combat the "lack of patriotism and loyalty" among the Mormons. The following year New Mexico synodical missionary James Menaul urged all mission teachers to acquire American flags "so that all our mission schools may be able to float the stars and stripes, and . . . teach patriotism to the rising generation."[5]

Annual teachers' conventions were another innovation to strengthen teachers' performances and systematize the mission school work. Again Utah Presbytery led the way in this effort. Forty-seven teachers representing twenty-nine schools among the Mormons attended that first session in 1883 and listened to lectures and presentations on a variety of topics, including Character Building, Music in Mission Schools, Elocution, and The Mission Teacher Out of School. The convention proved so successful that it became an annual affair, scheduled in conjunction with the regular fall meetings of Utah Presbytery. Significant efforts to improve teacher performance in the Indian and New Mexican fields were not made until the 1890s. In September 1893 the Synod of New Mexico commented bluntly that some teachers "need help that they cannot get in any other way." Teachers in both New Mexican and Indian schools from throughout the New Mexico synod (Arizona and New Mexico) attended the first convention in Santa Fe in September 1894. The topics on the agenda were similar to those presented in the Utah teachers' conventions. As in Utah the teachers' institutes in New Mexico proved very popular and became annual affairs. After the 1895 teachers' institute New Mexico synodical missionary James Menaul proclaimed that it had given teachers in his field "renewed determination."[6]

The most significant development in the Presbyterian mission school program in the 1880s was the establishment of boarding schools in each of the three southwestern fields. Early mission teachers in the Southwest had occasionally taken in boarders when native parents were unable to care for their children or when families lived too far from their schools. This, however, was not considered part of the official mission school program, and mission officials did not encourage such practices.[7]

By the late 1870s, however, many southwestern missionaries began to suggest that large-scale boarding programs could benefit their beleaguered cause. In 1879 a missionary to the Pimas observed that "the only way to . . . improve the Indians mentally and morally is . . . by taking [the children] entirely from their parents and the dens they dignify by calling 'home.' " J. M. Shields at Jemez Pueblo was equally blunt. "If we just had these children away from this sink of abomination and iniquity," he wrote in 1880, "we might soon see them clothed and in their right mind sitting at the feet of Jesus." After three frustrating years teaching in the New Mexico field, Matilda Allison observed in 1886: "The *best* way to permanently benefit these people is to take their children away from the demoralizing influence of their homes, surround them with Christian influence [and] teach them *how* to live." These arguments, along with the record of Richard Henry Pratt's acclaimed Carlisle Indian Industrial Training School (in Pennsylvania), persuaded Presbyterian officials by the early 1880s of the need for boarding schools for the youths of the exceptional populations.[8]

In cooperation with the federal government, Presbyterians opened contract boarding schools for Pueblo Indian children in Albuquerque in 1881 and another for Pima and Papago youths in Tucson in 1888. At the Mora school in the New Mexico field, Presbyterian missionaries established a boarding department in 1882. Four years later they opened a co-ed boarding school in Las Vegas and a boarding school for girls in Santa Fe. In Utah the schools that offered academy-level work (Salt Lake City, Mt. Pleasant, Springville, and Logan) gradually added boarding departments to their programs. The Presbyterians initially had no set policies for boarding schools, and many differences existed in those that they established. For example, the Indian schools in Albuquerque and Tucson operated entirely on a boarding basis. On the other hand, the New Mexico and Utah schools continued to serve day as well as boarding pupils. In fact, day students far exceeded boarders in the Utah boarding schools for many years.

The levels of academic work offered in the different boarding schools also varied. In Utah boarding scholars usually studied at the academy level (grades seven to eleven). On the other hand, Indian students at Albuquerque and Tucson often started with basic primary instruction. The boarding schools in New Mexico fell somewhere between these two extremes. Missionaries envisioned that the boarding schools would offer advanced work to students who completed primary studies in the plaza day schools and prepare them to be leaders in the church. In the early years, however, many students in the Mora, Las Vegas, and Santa Fe boarding schools studied at the primary level. Secondary-level course work was not offered in the New

Mexico boarding schools on a regular basis until the early years of the twentieth century.[9]

The early boarding schools encountered many of the same problems that plagued the broader mission school effort. Because the Indian schools were initially contract schools with the federal government, they suffered from the vicissitudes of federal policy. When the government assumed full control of the Albuquerque school in 1886, Presbyterians established nearby a separate school for Pueblo children. The new school, however, did not attract sufficient students and was closed after the 1889–90 school year. This experience led mission officials to rely less on federal monies and policies at the school that they opened in Tucson in 1888.[10]

The early boarding schools in New Mexico suffered from poor leadership, inadequate facilities, and Jesuit opposition. In 1890 mission officials merged the Mora and Las Vegas schools. This arrangement, however, did not prove satisfactory. After much debate, mission officials in 1895 relocated the boys enrolled at the Las Vegas school to the site of the former Albuquerque Indian School; two years later that school took the name Menaul School. The girls enrolled at Las Vegas were transferred to Miss Allison's flourishing boarding school in Santa Fe.[11] In the Utah field inadequate facilities posed the greatest problem. In 1890 fewer than sixty pupils boarded in the Utah schools, and boarding space was so limited that it was reserved for only those who were able to pay the full boarding charge.[12]

Despite these difficulties, by 1890 boarding schools had become essential to the Presbyterian strategy for the Southwest. Missionaries and mission officials believed that the hoped-for cultural regeneration of the pupils would flourish in the more regimented boarding environment. Attendance problems that plagued the day schools were, of course, minimized in the boarding schools. Missionaries rigidly designated times for classes, work, worship, and study. Students were usually up before 6 A.M. and in bed by 10. Teachers from all three fields believed that boarders progressed much faster academically and socially than day school students. An observer at Albuquerque's Menaul School marveled that "dirty, procrastinating, untrained, Mexican boys" were quickly transformed into "tidy, dishwashing, bedmaking, caretaking, studious, Bible-loving, hymnsinging, [and] wide-awake" young men.[13]

Another attraction of boarding schools was the opportunity they offered for teaching students manual skills and the dignity of labor. Many educational leaders of the era extolled the virtues of industrial education, particularly for minority students. Presbyterian mission leaders shared this enthusiasm. R. W. D. Bryan, the superintendent of the Albuquerque Indian School, suggested in 1884 that "the most important part of the education of these Indians is to train them to continuous labor, and to inspire them with the ambition to accumulate wealth by their own industry." Bryan's pupils and those at the Tucson Indian Training School performed the cooking and cleaning tasks necessary for the maintenance of their schools and also learned such trades as farming, carpentry, house painting, and shoemaking. Industrial training at the New Mexico and Utah schools was initially limited to the more routine tasks necessary for school maintenance, including food preparation, dishwashing, cleaning, washing, ironing, and chopping wood. However, after the New Mexico boys' boarding school moved to the larger Albuquerque campus in 1895, the boys engaged in gardening and livestock raising. All students participated in work assignments, and for many of them work duties served as a means of defraying expenses.[14]

The purpose of the work duties was to prepare students for everyday life, and missionaries stressed that they were not engaged in actual job training. From Mora, New Mexico, a teacher suggested in 1887 that work activities taught pupils that "there is a better way of living." The year before, the matron of the girls' home at the Mt. Pleasant, Utah, school observed: "We cannot hope to make teachers of everyone who may enter this home, but we ought . . . to make practical, common sense women out of them." In 1895 the carpenter at Tucson Indian school suggested that he would be satisfied if "his boys" learned to perform routine household repairs and other odd jobs necessary on a farm.[15]

The boarding environment also provided greater opportunities for missionaries to present the gospel message. Prayer was said at the beginning and closing of each day and before every meal. Specific times were set aside daily for Bible study, and some teachers used every available opportunity to tell students "the old, old story" and to talk with them about their immortal souls. Sabbath routines were particularly regimented. For example, students at the Albuquerque Indian School rose early every Sunday morning, sang a prayer before breakfast, and devoted an hour and a half to learning hymns and Bible verses before dinner. After dinner they attended Sabbath School for an hour and a half and recited scriptures until supper time; a similar routine followed supper. Such schedules were intended not only to inculcate a religious message but also to assure that mission school students did not participate in activities that the intensely sabbatarian Presbyterians considered undesirable for the holy day. Teachers in the boarding schools were obviously less hesitant than their colleagues in the day schools to promote religious aspects of their work. A teacher at the Santa Fe boarding school reported in 1896 that her school "made no avowed effort to convert children to Protestantism" but that the students' parents knew that their children would be expected to attend Presbyterian services every Sunday, read from the Bible, and learn the Presbyterian catechism. A minister assigned to the girls home at the Mt. Pleasant, Utah, school was much bolder. Conversion, he asserted, was the chief aim of the boarding program, and he considered it a failure if a girl "stayed a great length of time and did not become a Christian." Another Utah minister reported in 1891 that nearly 100 percent of the boarding school pupils "either became Christian or marvelously changed." This record, he concluded, justified expansion of boarding facilities at the Utah schools.[16]

Finally, mission officials anticipated that their nascent network of boarding schools would prepare native youths for even more advanced educations that would equip them for the ministry and other positions of church leadership. From the mid-1880s Utah missionaries spoke of making the Salt Lake Collegiate Institute a college that would be the capstone of the Presbyterian mission school network among the Mormons. In 1890 Charles Cook suggested that the greatest need in the Pima-Papago field was a Bible school to prepare native "teachers, helpers, and missionaries." Missionaries in New Mexico periodically made similar appeals.[17]

While progress was made on this front prior to 1900, it fell short of missionary expectations. In Utah financial support from Sheldon Jackson helped Presbyterians initiate a college program in conjunction with Salt Lake Collegiate Institute in 1895. The new Sheldon Jackson College, however, suffered numerous problems which continued well into the twentieth century, when the school was renamed Westminster College. In the New Mexico field several efforts were made to provide training for native evangelists and ministerial candidates. During the 1890s the ill-fated College of the Southwest in Del Norte, Colorado, maintained a "training program for Mexican evangelists," and the Synod of New Mexico conducted summer institutes in Las Vegas for the same purpose. These programs, however, proved less than satisfactory. At the century's end New Mexico Presbyterians still debated the best means of preparing native church leaders. In the Indian fields even less progress was made, and Cook's long-anticipated Bible school for Indians was not opened until 1911.[18]

The boarding school program represented the Presbyterians' most concerted effort to recreate their cultural norms in the Southwest. Yet even as missionaries engaged busily in establishing boarding schools in each of the three fields, other more subtle developments were under way that fostered very different results. Missionaries who remained in the Southwest any considerable length of time recognized that for any school program, day or boarding, to be effective, the trust and friendship of the people they came to serve had to be won. Consequently, missionaries found it necessary to go out among the people and win their confidence. This goal, of course, was not always easy. Missionaries had to counter local suspicion, hostility from native religious leaders, communication barriers, and, most seriously, their own ethnocentrism. Winning the trust of the people they came to serve required adjustments in the missionaries' outlook and expectations. Not all teachers were able to make such adjustments, and evidence suggests that those who did not were usually among the missionaries who departed the Southwest after relatively brief tenures. The missionaries who did reach out to the native peoples, however, usually found that their effort was not in vain.

Teachers from all three fields discovered that visiting in the homes of the native peoples was usually necessary to convince parents to send children to the mission schools. Such visits, however, invariably produced even more far-reaching consequences. Although the impoverished conditions that they encountered often repulsed the teachers, they usually found the native people polite and cordial. As the newcomer, however, the missionary had to take the initiative. In 1893 a teacher recently appointed to Laguna Pueblo reported that she had been received warmly. "Toward this end," she added, "I have had to eat with apparent relish most questionable viands, praise the babies, take long walks with the girls, [and] interest myself in the games of the boys." A New Mexico teacher reported in the same year that to reach her people she "learned Spanish, ate beans almost exclusively, [and] lived in a little adobe house." The year before a teacher in Richmond, Utah, observed: "Every day ... I am more convinced that it's our lives that are going to tell for Jesus among these people. They set themselves not to believe what we teach or preach. But ... *persistent kindness* — and *'practicing what you preach'* will ... do good." Ample evidence suggests that these experiences and attitudes were not unique.[19]

Dedicated missionaries discovered many areas in which to use their talents in the Southwest, and teachers invariably found that school duties formed only one part of their daily routine. For example, the absence of anything resembling modern health care provided an avenue for many teachers to reach the native southwesterners. Although few of the teachers had formal medical training, their knowledge of medical practices often exceeded those of most of the natives of the isolated regions that they served. Moreover, after they learned of the great need for health care in their fields, some teachers took nurse's training during their summer vacations. Mission teachers in New Mexico frequently reported that even "slight knowledge of simple remedies" enabled them to meet the needs and win friendship of people who otherwise resisted them. From Gunnison, Utah, Mrs. M. M. Green reported in 1888 that "the people forget [L.D.S.] proscriptions against missionaries" when illness strikes their families. A year later, she even managed to win the support of the local Mormon bishop, who allowed her to teach afternoon classes in preventive health measures in the L.D.S. meeting house. According to the bishop, Mrs. Green "was doing more good than anyone else in Gunnison."[20]

Missionaries wore an endless array of other hats in serving the peoples of their communities. From time to time they performed the duties of midwife, home economist, lawyer, lobbyist, agricultural specialist, and undertaker. Some mission teachers followed the example of early settlement house workers, such as Jane Addams and Ellen Starr of Chicago's Hull House, and attempted to introduce higher culture and forms of etiquette to their people. For example, a Taos, New Mexico, teacher offered Saturday afternoon classes in drawing and art, and in Utah a teacher offered a Saturday morning kitchen school in which she taught simple rules of housekeeping.[21]

Other missionaries concerned themselves with the more practical needs of their people. John Menaul introduced new farming methods, vegetables, and fruit trees at Laguna Pueblo. With cooperation from government officials, he even attempted to improve the native food supply by stocking nearby lakes with German trout. Charles Cook performed similar services during his forty-year career among the Pimas and Papagos. In the 1890s Cook led the Pimas in resisting white settlers who illegally cut off the Indians' traditional water supply. Cook wrote letters to federal officials, organized the Pimas, and lobbied mightily in their behalf.[22]

Missionaries like Menaul and Cook (undeniably the most effective Presbyterian workers among the southwestern Indians) understood that bridging the language barrier was also essential to their efforts. Consequently, both men devoted themselves to learning the unwritten native tongues. Menaul even went further and, using his talents as a printer, produced copies of *McGuffey's Reader,* the Presbyterian Shorter Catechism, and a number of tracts in the Laguna's Keresan language. Other missionaries similarly recognized the importance of learning the native tongues. From Zuni Pueblo in 1889 Carrie Pond boldly questioned the federal Indian Office's English only policy for contract schools; teaching the Zunis in English, she wrote, "is like throwing rubber balls against the wall—they bounce back into our faces." Teachers in the New Mexico field reached similar conclusions, and consequently most of them learned at least some Spanish.[23]

Naturally such cordial interaction tempered some of the ill will and many of the negative stereotypes held by both natives and newcomers at the time Presbyterians first arrived in the Southwest. A Mormon girl who had become friends with a Presbyterian teacher observed that she was surprised to find that the missionary was "so nice and friendly" and that the Presbyterians "did not worship idols." For her part, the teacher commented, "You don't know how glad I was to receive such well meant kindness."[24] Records from the late 1880s and 1890s reveal that this situation was not unique.

Natives in all three fields watched over trusted teachers when they fell ill, presented them with gifts when they returned from vacation, and invited them to participate in local celebrations and festivities. When teacher Sue Zuver was assaulted and robbed in her Penasco, New Mexico, home in 1895, the predominantly Catholic population of that town sent a posse of cowboys after the culprit and threatened to lynch him if he ever returned to their village. In Utah in 1888 the people in one predominantly Mormon town asked a mission teacher, who had endured much hostility, to become a justice of the peace. When she declined, one old man offered to take the position if she would advise him on particulars. The people of Trementina, New Mexico, became so attached to teacher-nurse Alice Blake that they called her "mother of us all."[25]

Clearly, mission officials had expected that missionary kindness would win the friendship of the native peoples and abate their initial suspicions and fears. They did not, however, anticipate that this interaction would have a similar effect on the missionaries. While negative stereotypes of the southwestern peoples continued to appear in missionary letters and reports, both first-hand experience and the passage of time eroded many of the harshest Presbyterian criticisms of the southwestern peoples. For example, after eight years in New Mexico one teacher reported that she found it increasingly difficult to write about her work. "The novelty has long since departed," she explained; "everything has become so familiar that it does not call for the same comment."[26]

Most missionaries only gradually relinquished the traditional stereotypes of the southwestern populations. Upon discovering that the people among whom they labored did not conform to the stereotypical images, some missionaries suggested that these peoples were exceptions to the norm. For example, soon after arriving at her northern New Mexico station, one missionary observed that the people of that community were "so different from Mexicans generally"; another teacher reported the people in his village were "more enterprising and thrifty than the average Mexican."[27]

With the passage of time, however, some missionaries recognized that what their predecessors had believed was typical was actually the exception. Several Utah missionaries, for example, reported that polygamy was not so widespread as often assumed and that many Mormons actually rejected it. Furthermore, some missionaries observed that the southwestern people were as different and varied among themselves as any other people. "Mexican girls," commented one teacher in 1896, "are like American girls, bright and dull, lovely and not so lovely." Five years later a *Home Missions Monthly* article entitled "Misjudging the Mexicans" observed that the American stereotype of the Mexican was "based on a few who are of the lowest type [and] totally inaccurate for the broader population."[28]

Dr. Taylor Ealy and mission school pupils at Zuni Pueblo, late 1870s (Courtesy of Smithsonian Institution)

Original church and schoolhouse in Mt. Pleasant, Utah, early 1870s (Courtesy of Pierce Historical Hall, Wasatch Academy, Mt. Pleasant, Utah)

Students and parents arriving at mission school in Santa Fe, New Mexico, ca. 1880 (Courtesy of Menaul Historical Library)

Campus of Albuquerque Indian School in 1887 (In 1895 this became the campus for Menaul School for New Mexican boys.) (Courtesy of Menaul Historical Library)

Matilda Allison and pupils at her Santa Fe mission school, probably in the mid-1880s (Courtesy of Menaul Historical Library)

Elementary classroom at Wasatch Academy, Mt. Pleasant, Utah, in 1899 (Courtesy of Pierce Historical Hall)

Girls at Allison School in Santa Fe, ca. 1905 (Courtesy of Menaul Historical Library)

High school classroom at Wasatch Academy, Mt. Pleasant, Utah, in 1899 (Courtesy of Pierce Historical Hall)

Teachers and pupils of Menaul School, Albuquerque, New Mexico, in 1899 (Courtesy of Menaul Historical Library)

Girls in Wasatch Academy dormitory, Mt. Pleasant, Utah, early 1900s (Courtesy of Pierce Historical Hall)

Boys in Albuquerque Indian School dormitory, 1880s (Courtesy of Museum of New Mexico)

Sheldon Jackson, early promoter of missions to exceptional populations (Courtesy of Menaul Historical Library)

Duncan McMillan, early Presbyterian missionary to Utah and founder of Wasatch Academy (Courtesy of Pierce Historical Hall)

James Menaul, New Mexico synodical missionary in the 1890s and promoter of mission schools (Courtesy of Menaul Historical Library)

John Menaul, longtime minister, physician, and teacher to the Navajos, Laguna Pueblos, and New Mexicans (Courtesy of Menaul Historical Library)

Alice Hyson, mission teacher in Taos, New Mexico (Courtesy of Menaul Historical Library)

Alice Blake, mission school teacher and nurse to Trementina, New Mexico (Courtesy of Menaul Historical Library)

Matilda Allison, early mission teacher in Santa Fe (Courtesy of Menaul Historical Library)

Charles Cook, longtime minister, teacher, and friend of the Pima and Papago Indians of southern Arizona (Courtesy of Cook School, Tempe, Arizona)

Some missionaries went even further and suggested that the peoples they had come to change compared favorably with many Americans. In 1900 a New Mexico teacher observed that the worst of the native peoples were "no worse than some of the Americans living in the territory." Five years earlier a southern Colorado teacher commented that "there are some traits about these people [New Mexicans] that we would do well to copy." In particular, missionaries praised New Mexican and Indian kindness, hospitality, patience, and perseverance. One New Mexico missionary conceded in 1893 that "she had learned many a lesson" from the people she had come to teach.[29]

Missionary reports from the Southwest in the late 1880s and 1890s sometimes contradicted many of the earlier descriptions of the exceptional populations and their cultures common in the Sheldon Jackson era. Missionaries in New Mexico, for example, defended adobe architecture, traditional New Mexican cuisine, and the efforts of native farmers (particularly their communal irrigation efforts). More significantly, the Presbytery of Santa Fe denounced a congressional report of 1888 that recommended against New Mexico statehood as "untruthful and slanderous." The Presbytery particularly objected to denigrating depictions of New Mexican social and sexual mores and concluded that the native people of their territory compared favorably with those of "other territories . . . [and] many, if not all states."[30]

Some missionaries even tempered criticisms of New Mexican Catholicism. In 1898 veteran missionary R. W. Hall reported that there were few "fanatical Romanists" in his field. Most interesting of all were changes in missionary attitudes toward penitentes. After commenting negatively on penitente practices in 1891, one longtime New Mexico teacher conceded: "They do this thinking they please God. I am sure they do it with a devout feeling." Other missionaries offered even more positive appraisals. The November 1900 issue of *Home Mission Monthly* carried several eye-witness accounts of penitente rituals that contrasted greatly with those presented twenty years before in Jackson's *Rocky Mountain Presbyterian*. Penasco mission teacher Sue Zuver suggested that the penitentes' "earnestness and zeal [were] sufficient to shame some of our modern Christians." Another missionary described a penitente procession with such adjectives as "benighted" and "depressing," but she suggested that it so vividly depicted the suffering of Jesus that she "could understand something of the hold the Catholic church keeps upon the [New Mexicans]."[31]

Mormons generally did not fare as well in missionary eyes, but over time Presbyterian attitudes toward them softened slightly. Occasionally a missionary commented on Mormon hospitality, friendliness, and hard work, and in 1901 one longtime missionary vehemently defended the Mormons. In a letter to Utah synodical missionary Samuel Wishard, Laura Work expressed "astonishment and indignation" at the "melodramatic complaint" of a northern Utah mission teacher that had recently been printed in a eastern newspaper. In response to charges of Mormon disloyalty to the United States and allegations that Mormons had been hostile toward missionaries, Miss Work (who had once taught in the town described in the article) observed that "no teacher who conducts herself with dignity and kindliness will ever suffer indignity" at the hands of Mormons. The article, she concluded, was "unjust to the Mormon people and unfortunate to all concerned." More common, however, was the observation of Miss Josie Curtis, a veteran of twenty-nine years in the Utah field. "We may well hate the degrading system and influence of Mormonism," she wrote near the end of her long career, "but never the Mormon people as we know them."[32] These observations leave no doubt that the Presbyterian crusade to transform the Southwest had also changed some of the missionaries.

Despite the popular image that missionaries were unusually rigid and uncompromising, the adjustments that Presbyterians made in the Southwest were not unique. Writing fifteen years ago, mission theologian Louis Luzbetak labeled such adjustments "incipient adaptation." While conceding that missionary accommodations were often superficial, Luzbetak observed that missionaries have often been among the first westerners to appreciate anomalous, non-Western peoples. In support of this contention he offered a number of missionaries — from the sixteenth to the twentieth centuries, Catholic and Protestant, famous and little known — who made such adjustments. In recent years a number of other scholars have offered other examples of missionaries who became champions of the peoples among whom they labored.[33]

The missionaries' sobered expectations and more tolerant views of the three southwestern peoples, however, did not immediately change Presbyterian goals for the mission schools. Many Presbyterians in the 1890s still perceived enough shortcomings in the exceptional populations to justify continued efforts for their regeneration. Furthermore, the continued absence of widespread public education in much of the Southwest convinced Presbyterians of the need to maintain the mission schools. Finally, while the missionaries' new-found appreciation of the native southwestern culture was undeniably genuine, it did not convince national mission officials and eastern supporters (much less the missionaries themselves) that the mission effort was unnecessary. Indeed, the opposite occurred.

For many Presbyterians the more positive views of the southwesterners were evidence that their efforts had not been in vain. In the absence of the victory that had once appeared imminent, missionaries invariably pointed to other signs of progress. Like most missionaries, Presbyterians in the

Southwest considered conversions to their faith an important barometer for their work. While admitting that they had little success in converting adults, missionaries often noted that youths in the mission schools did embrace Presbyterianism. For example, a report from Utah in 1888 announced that all but five of the twenty-three students who graduated from Salt Lake Collegiate Institute that spring "professed Christ before leaving school." In 1891 a Raton, New Mexico, teacher reported that twenty-nine of her former pupils were members of Raton's Second Presbyterian Church. Missionaries optimistically expected that each of these youthful converts would become an active church member who, in time, would bring many brethren into the Presbyterian fold.[34]

The missionaries' close identification with Anglo-American customs and culture led them to detect other signs that their efforts had not been in vain. Missionaries in all three fields attributed cleaner homes, more diligent work habits, and improved farming methods to their influence. In 1893 Mary DeSette at Zuni Pueblo reported that the mother of one of her best pupils had introduced many improvements in her home, including neatly made beds, tablecloths, and clean dishes. Charles Cook reported that at harvest time the Pima boys educated at the Tucson Indian Training School were "the leaders and their fathers [were] the pupils." In an article entitled "Proofs of Progress," a Taos, New Mexico, missionary noted that the natives of his community had adopted "our" agricultural equipment and machinery, improved methods of home construction, and American modes of dress and food. He attributed these changes to "the progress of our age, our American civilization, and especially the leavening influence" of the mission schools. Missionaries in Utah similarly claimed that they had influenced Mormons to improve their homes and farming methods. More significantly, they suggested that their influence had weakened the power of the L.D.S. hierarchy, pressured Mormons to improve their own schools, and influenced Mormons to resist polygamy.[35]

Non-Presbyterians occasionally echoed these comments and lauded the Presbyterian effort. For example, a Smithsonian ethnologist who visited Albuquerque in 1885 praised the Indian school in that town for "operating upon the body, mind, and heart of these Indians and preparing them to be something more than drones in this struggle for pre-eminence." Government officials in New Mexico and Utah often praised the "elevating influence" of Presbyterian schools on their territories. In 1890, for example, Utah's governor suggested that Presbyterian influence was "doing more to suppress evil than all the jails, callabooses, and policemen of the country."[36]

Because of their understanding of culture, most missionaries believed that native southwesterners who embraced aspects of Anglo-American physical culture would ultimately adopt the full package of mainstream American culture, including Protestant Christianity. A few particularly perceptive missionaries, however, recognized that this assumption was fallacious. For example, one teacher lamented in 1895 that Presbyterian mission schools in Utah produced "Mormon teachers, elders, priests, bishops, and missionaries." A decade later a missionary from Arroyo Hondo, New Mexico, observed: "The majority seem to me more anxious for the education we can give them than the pure gospel we wish to teach them." Most missionaries, however, failed to recognize what today is labeled selective acculturation.[37]

Even if the Presbyterians' optimism proved illusory, it did have one positive consequence. The missionaries' deep religious faith and their belief that progress had been achieved made them impervious to the increasingly widespread racial explanations of the innate inferiority of such exceptional peoples as the native southwesterners. While many of their fellow late-nineteenth-century Americans embraced social Darwinism's deterministic view of human history, Presbyterian missionaries remained confident that the native southwesterners were as capable as any other peoples. Moreover, they openly criticized those who thought otherwise. At the New Mexico synod's 1895 teachers' institute, the Reverend T. C. Moffett of Flagstaff, Arizona, condemned the application of the principle of survival of the fittest to the human experience. "THE DEVIL," Moffett emphasized, "DOES NOT TAKE THE HINDMOST, CHRIST TAKES THEM."[38]

While few Presbyterian missionaries recognized it at the time, their mission school effort in the Southwest reached its zenith in the early 1890s. In the decade and a half after the establishment of the Woman's Executive Committee had placed the school work on a more certain basis, several thousand young Indians, New Mexicans, and Mormons had been educated in Presbyterian schools. Simultaneously, Presbyterians had learned a great deal about the native southwesterners and the tenacity of human culture. Sobered by southwestern realities, Presbyterians made significant adjustments in their mission strategy. However, while many southwestern missionaries in the 1890s recognized flaws in their church's earlier approach to southwestern pluralism, they had not rejected the basic rationale for the missionary effort in the Southwest. Indeed, many missionaries shared the sober optimism of longtime New Mexico teacher Elizabeth Craig. "Truth forbids my seeing great results," Miss Craig observed in 1893, "but in faith I can look forward to the time when there will be wonderful changes in New Mexico."[39] For Presbyterians in the 1890s victory in the Southwest was no longer imminent, but it was still expected.

Notes

1. 19th Annual Report, Board of Home Missions, 1889, 27. As late as 1900 the Utah Presbytery suggested that the 1878 General Assembly's authorization of home board-operated mission schools had intended for that work to be under local supervision (Minutes, Presbytery of Utah, April 9, 1900, 6:62–64).

2. 23rd Annual Report, Board of Home Missions, 1893, 5; "Words from Workers," *HMM* 7 (July 1893): 209; Report of Superintendent of School Work to Board of Home Mission and Woman's Executive Committee, 1895, 4; D. S. Dodge, "The Board of Home Missions," *HMM* 13 (March 1899): 104–5.

3. "Rev. Roberts' Address on Home Missions," *PHM* 11 (July 1882): 151; 16th Annual Report, Board of Home Missions, 1886, 21; 18th Annual Report, Board of Home Missions, 1888, 22–23; Minutes, Utah Presbytery, April 5, 1888, 3:53; 20th Annual Report, Board of Home Missions, 1890, Appendix.

4. Minutes, Presbytery of Utah, March 31, 1884, 2:52; "Our Mormon Work," *HMM* 2 (May 1888): 149; "Signs of Promise in the Mexican Field," *HMM* 10 (November 1895): 18; Minutes, Synod of New Mexico, October 6–9, 1899, 31; "Course of Study of the Presbyterian Mission Schools for the Synod of New Mexico," PHS, RG 104, Box 1, F-6.

5. Minutes, Presbytery of Utah, March 31, 1884, 2:52; "Course of Study for New Mexico"; Minutes, Synod of New Mexico, October 6, 1899, 31, September 6–9, 1895, 16; *HMM* 8 (June 1894): 180. For other comments on the mission school as a crucible for patriotism, see Mary McWhirt, "A Patriotic Picnic," *HMM* 13 (November 1898): 19; George McAfee, Report of Superintendent of School Work to Board of Home Missions and Woman's Executive Committee, 1896, 2.

6. "Utah Presbytery: Convention of Presbyterian Teachers in Utah," clippings from *Salt Lake Daily Tribune,* March 30, 31, 1883, SHS 60:84–85; Program for the Presbyterian Teacher's Convention for August 1885, G. W. Martin File, Paden Collection, Westminster College; R. G. McNiece, "Utah Presbytery," *PHMy* 15 (October 1885): 232; Minutes, Presbytery of Utah, March 20, 1887, 2:139–40; Minutes, Synod of New Mexico, October 3–4, 1891, 10, September 14–17, 1893, 15, September 6–9, 1895, 15–16; Minutes, Presbytery of Santa Fe, September 14, 1893, 3:238; *Proceedings of the First Institute of the Presbyterian Mission School Teachers* (Albuquerque: Spanish Tracts Press, 1894).

7. Comments on early, non-official, boarding arrangements in Presbyterian schools are found in M. E. Griffith to S. Jackson, July 3, 1878, SJCC; J. M. Roberts, "Fernando de Taos," *PHM* 10 (June 1881): 317; "Utah — Pleasant Grove," *PHMy* 13 (March 1884): 64. Regulations regarding the matter of boarding students were given in "To Our Mission Teachers," PHS, RG 51, Box 1, F-5. Among other things, these guidelines limited the number of boarding students in any school to two per teacher and stipulated that teachers could charge boarding scholars no more than $75 per year.

8. Letter from Mrs. B. M. Armstrong, August 3, 1879, reprinted in 9th Annual Report of Ladies Union Mission School Association, 1879, SHS 53:422; J. M. Shields

to S. Jackson, April 19, 1880, SJCC; M. Allison, "Mission Work in Santa Fe," *HMM* 1 (September 1886): 251. Similar sentiments are expressed in the following letters to Jackson from the SJCC: John C. Pyle, August 17, 1878; Jose Ynes Perea, February 29, 1881; Thomas Thompson, June 14, 1882. Pratt's Carlisle Indian School is examined in Prucha, *The Great Father,* 2:694-700. Also see Pratt's memoirs, *Battlefield and Classroom: Four Decades with the American Indian, 1876-1904,* ed. Robert Utley (New Haven: Yale University Press, 1964).

9. Accounts of the early histories of these schools are found in Lillie G. McKinney, "History of Albuquerque Indian School," *New Mexico Historical Review* 20 (April 1945): 109-38; John M. Hamilton, "A History of the Presbyterian Work among the Pima and Papago Indians of Arizona" (M.A. thesis, University of Arizona, 1948), 151-75; Barber and Agnew, *Sowers Went Forth,* 51-54, 60-61, 64; Carl Wankier, "History of Presbyterian Schools in Utah" (M.A. thesis, University of Utah, 1968).

10. The superintendent of the Albuquerque school, R. W. D. Bryan, commented on some of the problems of cooperating with government officials in his letters to S. Jackson, August 22, December 22, December 29, 1882, SJCC. Presbyterian reaction to the government's assumption of full control of the Albuquerque school are found in *PHMy* 15 (August 1886): 173; 17th Annual Report, Board of Home Missions, 1887, 19. Mrs. C. E. Walker comments on the establishment of the Tucson school (to Mrs. Alexander Whillin, May 16, 1886, PHS, RG 105, Box 2, F-12).

11. Comments on the problems at Mora and Las Vegas are found in Gabino Rendon to Paul Warnsuis, November 1941, PHS Microfilm: Selected Correspondence and Reports of the Spanish Southwest, Board of Home Missions, Presbyterian Church, U.S.A.; Woman's Executive Committee to Rev. J. Burkhead, November 12, 1886, PHS, RG 105, Box 2, F-12; Anna McNair, "Words from Workers — Mexican," *HMM* 6 (March 1892): 112; "News Budget from New Mexico," *HMM* 9 (November 1894): 11; Minutes, Presbytery of Santa Fe, April 11, 1894, 3:248. The decision to close the Las Vegas school and establish a boys' school in Albuquerque is discussed in *HMM* 10 (November 1895): 2; Minutes, Synod of New Mexico, September 1896, 16, 21; and a packet of letters between School Superintendent McAfee and several New Mexico missionaries written in 1895, PHS, RG 104, Box 1, F-16. The new Albuquerque school was named for synodical missionary James Menaul, who died in 1897.

12. Report of Superintendent of School Work to Board of Home Missions and Woman's Executive Committee, 1896, 6.

13. Descriptions of daily routines at the Albuquerque Indian School and the Mora boarding schools are found in Miss Leila Butler to Mrs. Allen, February 17, 1882, SHS 55:119; "New Mexican Column," *PHM* 10 (October 1881): 381; *PHMy* 13 (August 1884): 184-85; "What the Schools Are Doing," *PHMY* 14 (April 1885): 90. Lora Shields, "Pueblo Industrial Institute," *PHM* 10 (July 1881): 334; "N.M. — Albuquerque Training School," *PHM* 11 (October 1882): 238; M. Allison, "Words from Workers — N.M.," *HMM* 3 (February 1889): 84; *Albuquerque School for Mexican Boys* (Woman's Board of Home Missions, 1904).

14. R. W. D. Bryan, "The Albuquerque Industrial School for Indians," *PHMy* 13 (November 1884): 254; "The Albuquerque School," *PHMy* 14 (February 1885): 35; *HMM* 9 (August 1890): 218; Miss M. Beekman, "Words from Workers — Mexican," *HMM* 6 (May 1892): 179. David Tyack comments on the widespread support for industrial education during this period (*The One Best System* [Cambridge: Harvard University Press, 1974], 186–89).

15. Mrs. J. A. Cook, "Words from Workers — N.M.," *HMM* 1 (May 1887): 154; Mrs. G. S. Murphy, "Words from Workers — Utah," *HMM* 1 (November 1886): 17; *HMM* 9 (May 1895): 145.

16. Leila Butler, "Albuquerque, N.M.," *SHS* 57:37; O. E. Boyd, "A Sabbath at Albuquerque," *PHMy* 13 (January 1884): 17; "News Budget—New Mexico," *HMM* 10 (January 1896): 64; "Words from Workers — Utah," *HMM* 2 (May 1888): 157; Rev. J. A. L. Smith, "Words from Workers — Mormon," *HMM* 5 (August 1891): 227.

17. "Our Mormon Work," *HMM* 2 (May 1888): 149; Charles H. Cook to Miss S. F. Lincoln, November 18, 1890, PHS, RG 51, Box 1, F-25; Minutes, Synod of New Mexico, October 8-10, 1889, 23-24.

18. Carl Wankier examines the early history of Westminster College ("History of Presbyterian Schools in Utah," 52–70). Norman J. Bender does the same for the training program for Mexican evangelists at the College of the Southwest ("A College Where One Ought to Be," *Colorado Magazine* 49 [Summer 1972]: 213–14). The Gilchrist Family Papers at the Menaul Historical Library in Albuquerque contain a number of informative records about the several efforts to prepare native New Mexican church leaders. The brothers F. M. and J. J. Gilchrist were prominently involved in the work at Del Norte and the summer institutes in Las Vegas.

19. Miss Jennie Coltman, "Words from Workers — Indian," *HMM* 7 (September 1893): 256; Miss Dox, "Words from Workers — NM," *HMM* 7 (July 1893): 209; M. E. McCartney to Mrs. Greenleaft, March 28, 1892, PHS, RG 51, Box 2, F-3. Teachers sometimes even spent summer vacations "winning" friends in their fields: M. E. McCartney, "Words from Workers — Utah," *HMM* 3 (October 1889): 278; Miss Alice Hyson, "Vacation," *HMM* 11 (November 1896). Many other records from each of the three fields describe missionaries visiting native homes to win native friendship. See, for example, Lora B. Shields to S. Jackson, February 19, 1881, SJCC; Lora Shields to F. E. H. Haines, February 11, 1881, PHS, RG 105, Box 1, F-4; "Words from Workers — N.M.," *HMM* 2 (July 1888): 210; Jennie Ordway, "Words from Workers — N.M.," *HMM* 3 (October 1889): 276; E. W. Craig, "Words from Workers — Mexican," *HMM* 6 (November 1891): 12; "Words from Workers — Utah," *HMM* 3 (April 1889): 133; "Words from Workers — Utah," *HMM* 2 (October 1888): 277; Rev. W. A. Hough, "Utah," *PHM* 11 (May 1882): 112; Mrs. Day, "Utah — American Fork," *PHMy* 13 (December 1884): 283; Miss Gertrude Whiteman, "Words from Workers — Utah," *HMM* 3 (June 1889): 181; Report of Superintendent of School Work to Board of Home Missions and Woman's Executive Committee, 1895, 7-8.

20. See the following accounts from *HMM*: Alice Hyson, "Words from Workers— N.M.," 3 (September 1889): 251; "Words from Workers — Mexicans," 5 (October

1891): 276, 6 ((November 1891): 2. No mission teacher served the health needs of her people more than Alice Blake, who worked more than forty years in the New Mexican field. Cheryl Foote insightfully examines Blake's efforts and their significance for the broader issue of Anglo–New Mexican cultural interaction ("Let Her Works Praise Her," chap. 6). See Mrs. Green's accounts in *HMM* 2 (August 1888): 230, 3 (April 1889): 132. Also see Bertha Leadingham, "The Plaza and Its Hope," *HMM* 18 (September 1904): 268.

21. *HMM* 10 (November 1895): 13; Alice Green, "Words from Workers — Utah," *HMM* 1 (May 1887): 155. There are many parallels in the work of the southwestern mission teacher and early settlement house workers such as Addams. These are abundantly apparent in Allen F. Davis, *American Heroine: The Life and Legend of Jane Addams* (New York: Oxford University Press, 1973).

22. Menaul's efforts at Laguna are examined in Banker, "Presbyterian Missionary Activity in the Southwest," *Journal of the West* 23 (January 1984): 56–59. A firsthand account of Cook's effort in defense of Pima water rights is "The Distress of the Pima Indians," *HMM* 16 (February 1902): 86. Also see Hamilton, "A History of Presbyterian Work among the Pima and Papago Indians of Arizona," 76–95; Minnie Cook, *Apostle to the Pimas* (Tiburon, Calif.: Omega Books, 1976), chap. 15.

23. John Menaul, Laguna Pueblo, 3d Annual Report, 1878–79, SHS 55:117; Miss Carrie Pond, "Words from Workers — N.M.," *HMM* 4 (December 1889): 38. Miss Celia Morgan reported that she had originally insisted on teaching her Corrales, New Mexico, pupils in English only. However, parental objections and threats to withdraw children from her school convinced her to teach in both Spanish and English ("Words from Workers — N.M.," *HMM* 1 [January 1887]: 62–63).

24. "Utah," *PHMy* 12 (September 1883): 214.

25. Accounts of native friendliness toward missionaries are found in *HMM* 10 (November 1895): 13; "Utah — Report from Mrs. M. E. Knox," *PHM* 11 (October 1882): 237; Ella M. Bloom to Mrs. Delos Finks, PHS, RG 51, Box 1, F-25; *HMM* 16 (December 1901): 26; "Words from Workers — Utah," *HMM* 2 (January 1888): 60. Miss Zuver's experiences are recounted in *HMM* 9 (February 1895): 75, and "News Budget from N.M.," *HMM* 11 (November 1896): 11. The justice of the peace story from Utah is told in *HMM* 2 (October 1888): 266. Foote, "Alice Blake of Trementina: Mission Teacher of the Southwest," 237.

26. "Signs of Promise in the Mexican Field," *HMM* 11 (November 1895): 18.

27. Mrs. A. M. Granger, "Words from Workers — N.M.," *HMM* 2 (January 1888): 58; "Schools, Teachers, and Helpers," *HMM* 7 (November 1893): 14.

28. "Mormonism," *PHM* 11 (October 1882): 238; "Gleanings," *HMM* 11 (November 1896): 7; "Mistakes in Judging Mexicans," *HMM* 16 (November 1901): 7–8. An 1896 article in the same magazine criticized the typical white stereotype "that all blacks are alike" and called on Presbyterians to recognize that among all peoples there are "grades of morality, intelligence, and refinement" (W. E. Partee, "A Sociological Question," *HMM* 10 [April 1896]: 132).

29. "La Maestra," *HMM* 10 (November 1895): 6–8; "Bright Gleams Here and

There," *HMM* 15 (November 1900): 15; Miss Dox, "Words from Workers," *HMM* 7 (July 1893): 209. Also see "Glimpses of Mexican Life," *HMM* 14 (November 1899): 10; "Instituto de los Maestros," *La Aurora* 3 (April 24, 1902); *HMM* 14 (November 1899): 1.

30. "Seen in New Mexico," *HMM* 11 (November 1896): 9; "Mexican Cookery," *HMM* 16 (November 1901): 6; "Extracts from Teachers' Letters — Mexican," *PHMy* 14 (September 1885): 211; Minutes, Presbytery of Santa Fe, April 5, 1888, 3:12–15.

31. Miss E. W. Craig, "Words from Workers — Mexican," *HMM* 6 (November 1891): 12; Sue M. Zuver, "Zeal of Mexican Romanists," *HMM* 15 (November 1900): 7; "Penitente Processions," *HMM* 15 (November 1890): 10–11. Sarah Deutsch comments in detail on the broader duties of women mission teachers in New Mexico and concludes that they were more likely than their male counterparts to drop the negative stereotypes and adopt a more positive view of New Mexican culture (*No Separate Refuge,* 71–77).

32. "News from the Western Fields — Utah," *RMP* 9 (January 1880); Laura B. Work to Rev. S. E. Wishard, June 19, 1901, PHS, RG 51, Box 2, F-15. Miss Curtis's comment is recorded in 38th Annual Report, Woman's Board of Home Missions, 1917. Comments similar to Miss Curtis's are found in *HMM* 10 (May 1896): 147; "Happenings in the Field," *HMM* 12 (June 1898): 182.

33. Louis J. Luzbetak, "Two Centuries of Cultural Adaptation in American Church Action: Praise, Censure, or Challenge?" in *American Missions in Bicentennial Perspective,* ed. R. Pierce Beaver (South Pasadena, Calif.: William Carey Library, 1977), 338–42. Missionaries cited by Luzbetak as particularly broad-minded and flexible include Catholics St. Francis Xavier (missionary to Japan), Mateo Ricci (China), Robert de Nobili (India), and friars, such as Bartolome de las Casas, in Spanish America. Among Protestants he points to the nineteenth-century administrator of the ABCFM, Rufus Anderson, and Robert Speer, who headed the Presbyterian foreign missions board during the first third of this century. Henry Warner Bowden points to similar accommodations by missionaries among American Indians and concludes that missionaries who were able to make such adjustments enjoyed more success than those who did not (*American Indians and Christian Missions* [Chicago: University of Chicago Press, 1981]). Students of the Protestant missionary experience in China have reached similar conclusions. See, for example, Irwin T. Hyatt, *Our Ordered Lives Confess: Three Nineteenth-Century American Missionaries in East Shantung* (Cambridge: Harvard University Press, 1976), and James M. McCutcheon, "The Missionary and Diplomat in China," *Journal of Presbyterian History* 41 (December 1963): 224–36. Finally, several scholars have presented persuasive evidence of this phenomena among Presbyterian home missionaries during roughly the same period being covered in this study. See, for example, Michael L. Stahler, "William Speer: Champion of California's Chinese," *Journal of Presbyterian History* 48 (Summer 1970): 113–29, and Paula K. Benkhart, "Changing Attitudes of Presbyterians toward Southern and Eastern European Immigrants, 1880–1914," *Journal of Presbyterian History* 49 (Fall 1971): 222–45. Perhaps most germane to the present study is Ted C. Hinckley's carefully argued

"Sheldon Jackson as Preserver of Alaska's Native Culture," *Pacific Historical Review* 33 (November 1964): 411–24. In recent years William G. McLouglin has written extensively about missionaries among the Cherokees; his most recent work, *Champions of the Cherokees: Evan and John B. Jones* (Princeton: Princeton University Press, 1990), examines a remarkable father-son Baptist missionary team who engaged in many activities similar to those described in this chapter.

34. "Words from Workers — Utah," *HMM* 2 (May 1888): 157; "Words from Workers — Mexican," *HMM* 5 (February 1891): 5. It is impossible to determine how many native southwesterners converted to Presbyterianism. The home board's church membership statistics did not distinguish ethnic or religious backgrounds of communicants; consequently, they include missionaries, their families, and other Anglo Protestants along with native converts. In 1900 the home board reported to the General Assembly that about 900 New Mexicans and approximately the same number of southwestern Indians had joined Presbyterian churches. The majority of Indian converts were Pimas won to Presbyterianism by the persistent efforts of Charles Cook. Cook reported in 1898 that over 400 Pimas, one-fifth of the tribe, had joined the Presbyterian church. ("Changing Conditions in Arizona," *HMM* 12 [February 1898]: 81). Statistics on Mormon converts to Presbyterianism are even more uncertain. T. Edgar Lyon cites a study in 1885 that indicated Presbyterian church membership in Utah at that time was 387; this figure, of course, was for all Presbyterians, not just converts from Mormonism. Lyon suggests that the total evangelical population in Mormon-dominated areas in 1900 was less than 5,000. As Lyon suggests for the Utah field, the fact that Presbyterians before 1900 rarely cited statistics of native conversions indicates that missionaries did not consider such a useful gauge of the success of their labors, and, indeed, that their effort had fallen short of their expectations ("Evangelical Protestant Missionary Activities in Mormon-dominated Areas, 1865–1900," 246–47).

35. "Our Missionaries," *HMM* 7 (June 1893): 176; C. H. Cook, "Changing Conditions in Arizona," *HMM* 12 (February 1898): 81–82; Mrs. Howard Billman, "Words from Workers — Indians," *HMM* 6 (August 1892): 230–31; Rev. S. W. Curtis, "Proofs of Progress," *HMM* 7 (November 1892): 13; "A Transforming Power," *HMM* 6 (November 1891): 10–11; J. McLain, "Mormonism As It Is Today in Utah," *HMM* 3 (May 1889): 148–50; 16th Annual Report, Board of Home Missions, 1886, 20; Rev. Clemenson, "Words from Workers — Utah," *HMM* 6 (July 1892): 211.

36. "The Albuquerque School," *PHMy* 14 (February 1885): 35; *HMM* 4 (May 1880): 146. Also see the report of Indian reform leader Herbert Welsh, "The Indians of Santa Fe," *Independent*, June 1884, clipping, SHS 56:67–68; and the comments on the impact of the New Mexico schools from the *Las Vegas Stockgrower and Farmer*, reprinted in *HMM* 8 (November 1893): 2.

37. *HMM* 9 (September 1895): 247; "Three Points of View," *HMM* 20 (November 1905): 16. Alice Blake made a similar observation in "Encouragements and Outlook among the Mexicans in the U.S.," *HMM* 22 (November 1907): 4.

38. *Proceedings of the First Institute of the Presbyterian Mission School Teachers . . . September 10–12, 1894* (Albuquerque, N.M.: Spanish Tract Work, 1894).

Michael C. Coleman presents evidence that while missionaries often viewed Native Americans with a "near absolute ethnocentrism" they did not succumb to harsh racist explanations of Indian inferiority ("Not Race, But Grace: Presbyterian Missionaries and American Indians," *Journal of American History* 67 [June 1980]: 41–60). Coleman develops this theme further in *Presbyterian Missionary Attitudes toward American Indians, 1837–1893* (Jackson: University Press of Mississippi, 1985).

39. "Topic for the Month — The Mexicans," *HMM* 7 (November 1893): 8.

7

Hard Times and
Changing Conditions

By the final decade of the nineteenth century the Presbyterian mission school cause in the Southwest had achieved a degree of prominence. In the twenty-five years since Presbyterian missionaries first encountered the exceptional populations, the promotional efforts of Sheldon Jackson and the Woman's Executive Committee had made the Presbyterian Church, U.S.A., aware of the unique challenges of southwestern pluralism. Local women's auxiliary groups met regularly to discuss articles from *Home Mission Monthly*, prepare missionary boxes, and to present their mites to the cause of home missions. Southwestern missionaries spoke annually before general assemblies and frequently visited local churches to persuade churchmen of the importance of their work. And Presbyterians in general responded warmly to these efforts. Yet even as these successes were being achieved, deep-seated economic, social, and cultural changes were transforming the missionaries' own society and church. These developments, along with significant changes within the Southwest, posed new and formidable challenges for the mission schools.

The most immediate problems for the Presbyterian missionary cause in the Southwest during the 1890s were financial ones. Even with the impressive efforts of the Woman's Executive Committee, funding for mission schools had never been adequate to keep up with the rapid expansion of that work. By 1890 Presbyterians conducted seventy-six schools with nearly 4,500 pupils in the Southwest. In addition, the home board conducted twenty-seven schools among nonsouthwestern Indians and sixteen schools among the mountaineers of southern Appalachia; these schools enrolled nearly 3,000 students. Furthermore, the Woman's Executive Committee also cooperated with the Board of Missions for Freedmen in conducting more than eighty schools for blacks in the South. These ever-increasing responsibilities led the home board to comment in its 1890 annual report that "the main drawback has been that the [school] work has outrun the means."[1]

The onset of unprecedented, nationwide financial woes in 1893 severely strained the board's already inadequate funds. In 1894 the home board reported a deficit in excess of $66,400. This deficit was the board's largest ever; more significantly, it represented the fifth consecutive year that board receipts fell short of expenditures, leaving an accumulated indebtedness of nearly $260,000. Of this amount, $101,000 belonged to the education department, which oversaw the mission school work in the Southwest.[2]

These financial exigencies created numerous problems for missionaries in the field. Between 1893 and 1898 the number of teachers commissioned in all Presbyterian home mission fields dropped from 325 to 277, a decrease of 15 percent; during the same years the number of teachers commissioned for the Southwest dropped from 164 to 122, a 25 percent decline. Furthermore, the average annual salary for mission teachers decreased from $443 to $411. Payment of salaries was irregular, and the board found itself unable to make anticipated repairs and improvements in mission facilities. Teachers in all three fields echoed the lament of Matilda Allison from the Santa Fe boarding school for girls. "Never in the history of the school," she despaired in 1895, "have we needed courage, faith, and patience more than now."[3]

The home board initially resisted closing the schools, but as the nationwide panic and the board's deficits deepened, it had no other alternative. In the spring of 1894 the board announced that no new work would be initiated. In the face of continued shortfalls, the Woman's Executive Committee recommended that the relatively expensive boarding school programs be curtailed. Accordingly the home board directed superintendents of the boarding schools to send home all students who did not have scholarship support or who could not pay their own tuition.

These policies proved particularly painful in areas where the Presbyterian effort appeared to be making headway. For example, home board officials reported in 1895 that the Tucson Indian school had "been too successful for our debt ridden economy" and consequently "must have its wings clipped." A year later the superintendent of the Tucson school reported that he had complied with board policy and that enrollment had dropped from 150 to 125. "This would seem to be a time for enlarging rather than limiting the work at Tucson," he lamented. Meanwhile, the board also closed a number of its less promising day schools. Sixteen southwestern mission schools closed their doors during the trying years between 1892 and 1900, and Presbyterians opened no new schools in the Southwest during the half decade after 1895.[4]

These financial woes were only the most apparent problem besetting the Presbyterian cause in the Southwest during the final decade of the nineteenth century. Since the Civil War deep-seated economic, social, and cultural changes had gradually altered the United States. By the watershed years of the 1890s profound changes in the American outlook and orientation were becoming apparent. These developments distracted Presbyterian attention away from the Southwest and toward what appeared to be more pressing concerns.

Since the colonial period Americans had faced westward, and the winning of the frontier had occupied much of the nation's energy and attention. However, as historian Frederick Jackson Turner observed in 1893, America's frontier era had passed. Economic, political, and altruistic energy that had long been directed toward the West suddenly became refocused on new frontiers—overseas and in the increasingly urban eastern United States.[5]

The very factors that distracted American (and Presbyterian) attention away from the West also led to a significant change in the public's perception of that region. Traditionally, Anglo Americans had viewed the West as a place to be conquered and exploited. Furthermore, most nineteenth-century Americans shared the Presbyterians' belief that the West's "benighted" native peoples should be incorporated into the "superior" American mainstream. By the 1890s, however, a few American observers began to question these assumptions. The end of the frontier, the final defeat of the Indians, and the advent of serious and seemingly more mundane concerns in the East combined to lead Americans to develop a romantic fascination with the "Old West" and the Southwest in particular. Journalist Charles F. Lummis led the way in this development with his popular magazine *Out West* and a number of anecdotal works, including *The Land of Poco Tiempo*. More serious writers, including archaeologist-historian Adolph A. F. Bandelier and Hubert Howe Bancroft, followed Lummis's lead and made the Southwest more respectable in eastern eyes. Bandelier's widely read *The Land of the Delight Makers* (a fictional account of life among the ancient Pueblos) reflected the romanticism that was the most distinguishing characteristic of this new literature of the Southwest.[6]

Like the earlier, generally negative, view of native southwesterners, this romantic outlook revealed as much or more about the Anglo Americans who held it as about the people they described. Historian John Higham has suggested that the 1890s was "an iconoclastic era" in which some intellectuals strove "to break out of the frustrations, the routine, [and] the sheer dullness of an urban industrial culture." Disillusioned with their own society, these individuals celebrated simple peasant cultures (like those in the Southwest), and they challenged the long-unquestioned assumption that cultural homogeneity was essential for the nation's welfare. These "debunkers" found fuel for their cause in Franz Boaz's early attacks on the evolutionary school of anthropology.[7]

What effect did this shift in outlook have on Presbyterian attitudes toward their missions in the Southwest? There is no tangible evidence that writers such as Lummis influenced those missionaries who began to have more positive views of the native southwesterners late in the nineteenth century. Nevertheless, there can be little doubt that the less hostile literary images of southwestern natives and the questioning of the superiority of American culture helped erode the mind set that had made Presbyterians so determined to bring the exceptional populations into the American cultural and religious mainstream.

Perplexing changes within the nation's Anglo-Protestant majority that were mirrored within the Presbyterian church itself posed greater (although usually indirect) problems for the southwestern missions. As important representative institutions of the broader American society, the nation's mainline Protestant churches could not escape the profound changes of the late nineteenth century. Since the American Revolution, Protestant churches had played an important role in defining the nation's purpose and values. By the final decade of the nineteenth century, however, an increasingly heterogeneous society threatened the Protestant hegemony. Furthermore, the rise of science and the advent of secular pragmatism challenged much traditional wisdom of the age. In response to Darwin's theory of evolution, the study of comparative religion, and higher criticism of the scriptures, Protestant theologians and church officials divided into conservative and liberal camps.[8] Yet another issue fostered contention over the missionary work of the churches in particular. In the optimistic, humanitarian atmosphere of the late nineteenth century, some leading churchmen challenged the traditional idea that missions should exist primarily "to save the heathen from damnation." By the turn of the century mission officials and missionaries in the home and foreign fields increasingly emphasized that missions should address the physical needs of the target populations. This spirit flourished in the social gospel movement that called the Protestant churches to concern themselves with the social problems that rapid industrialization and unregulated immigration had created in the eastern cities. In practically every denomination, this issue also split churchmen along conservative and modernist lines.[9]

While these matters preoccupied theologians and church officials during the 1890s and early 1900s, the average Protestant in the pew remained largely oblivious to them. Like most other mainline Protestants, Presbyterians avoided serious conflict over the new issues until well into the twentieth century.[10] The experiences of missionaries in the Southwest lend credence to this conclusion. One searches missionary letters and reports in mission periodicals in vain for comments on theological questions. Preoccupied with their concrete effort to reach native southwesterners, the missionaries had little time for such matters. Most southwestern missionaries undoubtedly shared the outlook of Sheldon Jackson, who chaired the influential Committee on Bills and Overtures at the 1898 General Assembly. Jackson reportedly made light of charges before his committee that the writings and teachings of the Union Seminary professor Arthur C. McGiffert exhibited irreverence toward the scriptures. Jackson was more concerned, some theological purists complained, with reports that nearly three hundred reindeer that he had recently introduced into Alaska had died.[11]

Even though the new issues of the 1890s appear not to have had any direct affect on the Presbyterian cause in the Southwest, they affected it indirectly. Historian Robert Handy has suggested that the rise of a "crusade mentality" temporarily healed divisions within the mainline Protestant churches and prevented serious schisms until the trying post–World War I era. During the decades flanking 1900, conservatives and liberals within the Protestant denominations, including the Presbyterian Church, U.S.A., generally cooperated in such old crusades as sabbatarianism and prohibition and in new thrusts in foreign missions and missions to the cities.[12] By the final years of the nineteenth century, when economic woes were already straining church budgets, these seemingly more urgent matters distracted Presbyterian energy and funds away from the Southwest and the mission schools among the exceptional populations.

A comparison of the receipts of the home and foreign mission boards during the final two decades of the nineteenth century illustrates this pattern. In 1880 the foreign board's receipts of $585,845 exceeded those of the home board by more than $290,000. Thanks to Jackson's lobbying and the efforts of the Woman's Executive Committee, this difference steadily diminished over the next fifteen years, and by 1895 the home board's fund-raising effort surpassed that of the foreign board by more than $40,000. During the financially troubled final five years of the century, however, the earlier financial supremacy of foreign missions returned. Between 1895 and 1900 receipts for home missions declined 22 percent ($201,136). In contrast, the foreign board during the same period increased its revenue by 7 percent ($60,692). In 1900 foreign mission receipts exceeded those of the home board by nearly $220,000. Thus, in this period when the nation as a whole exhibited increased interest in matters overseas, financially pressed Presbyterians clearly decided that foreign missions were more worthy of their support than missions at home (see table 7).[13]

Even within the educational department of the Board of Home Missions, the school work in the Southwest became relatively less important during the final years of the 1800s. In the school year 1879–80 (the year the Woman's

Executive Committee was established), all but two of the home board's twenty-eight schools for exceptional populations were in the Southwest (the other two were in Alaska). During the 1880s, however, the Woman's Executive Committee assumed responsibility for schools among the mountain people of the southern Appalachians and also agreed to contribute to the school work of the Board of Missions for Freedmen. During the 1890s the committee's school responsibilities increased further. In 1894 they agreed to establish a limited number of schools among "foreign populations in the great cities" of the East, and after the Spanish-American War the women established schools in newly acquired Puerto Rico and the nation's quasi-colony of Cuba. This broadening of responsibilities resulted in a gradual decline in the relative importance of the school work in the Southwest (see table 8). In 1890 the top three areas for Presbyterian mission schools were the Utah, Indian, and New Mexican fields. Ten years later Presbyterians conducted more schools among the mountaineers of southern Appalachia than in any of the three southwestern fields. Indeed, enrollment in the Appalachian schools for 1900 exceeded the combined enrollments of the schools in the next two fields, Utah and New Mexico (see table 9).

The home board's budget troubles in the mid-1890s worked against the interests of the school work in yet another way. In 1892 members of the home board conferred with leaders of the Woman's Executive Committee

Table 7. Comparative Receipts of the Board of Home Missions and the Board of Foreign Missions, 1880–1900

Year	Home Missions	Foreign Missions
1880	$295,615	$585,845
1885	$513,875	$699,984
1890	$831,170	$852,815
1895	$934,260	$892,392
1900	$733,124	$953,084

Sources: Records and Minutes of General Assembly: 1895 and 1900.

Table 8. Comparative Statistics for Presbyterian Mission Schools, 1890, 1895, 1900

	Total		Southwestern			
Year	Number	Enrollment	Number	% of Total	Enrollment	% of Total
1890	118	7478	76	64	4393	59
1895	114	9466	59	52	4722	50
1900	126	8466	56	44	3171	38

Source: Annual Reports of Board of Home Missions, 1890, 1895, 1900.

Table 9. Mission Fields with Largest Numbers of Presbyterian Schools, 1890, 1895, and 1900

Year	Fields	Number of Schools	School Enrollment
1890	Mormon	37	2374
	Indian*	33	2264
	New Mexican	32	1627
1895	Mormon	30	2665
	Southern Appalachian Mountains	26	2537
	New Mexican	26	1774
1900	Southern Appalachian Mountains	37	2986
	Mormon	29	1478
	New Mexican	24	1405

* These figures include all Presbyterian mission schools for Indians, *not* just those in the Southwest.

Source: Annual Reports, Board of Home Missions: 1890, 1895, 1900.

"to ascertain whether or not they [might] be using too large a proportion of the money derived from friends of missions" in their school work. Some board officials were concerned that the home board had barely $500,000 "for the general work of evangelization," while the women spent more than $300,000 for the conduct of schools among peoples who made up less than one-sixth of the nation's population. In light of the great fund-raising success of the women, church officials had rejected the earlier notion that women should support only the work of other women and that the nurturing work of education was the only suitable field for women's support. Consequently, with their own general budgets inadequate for the many demands placed upon them, home missions officials in the mid-1890s turned to the women to contribute directly to the broader work of home missions. The women responded ambivalently. On the one hand, they protested that their budgets were still inadequate to conduct the mission schools fully and efficiently. Nevertheless, they gradually agreed to broaden their responsibilities.[14]

Finally, in the early years of the twentieth century the mission school effort in the Southwest fell further behind in the contest for home mission attention and dollars, as innovative and charismatic leaders directed Presbyterian attention to other concerns. In New York City the Reverend Charles Stelzle pioneered in missions to working men and immigrants as he introduced normally conservative Presbyterians to the social gospel. Simultaneously, Dr. Warren H. Wilson, a minister trained in rural sociology, initiated bold reforms in rural church work, particularly in the southern Appalachians. As secretary of the home board's Department of Town and Country Life, Wilson suggested in 1911 that the new home missions should be directed at a "frontier no longer geographical, but sociological." Unfortunately, the school work in the Southwest had no new Sheldon Jackson to present its case in comparably stirring fashion.[15]

With more and more demands placed on smaller and smaller budgets, mission officials by the mid-1890s carefully scrutinized existing mission causes. Not surprisingly, some church leaders pointed to changes in the Southwest as justification for reduction of the work there. The geographical isolation that had long been the region's most distinctive characteristic had diminished significantly in the final quarter of the nineteenth century. Railroads had brought Anglo-American immigrants, culture, and technology to the region. The Southwest's major cities—Salt Lake City, Albuquerque, and Phoenix—offered evidence that the Southwest was becoming less exceptional. More seriously for the Presbyterian mission school cause, widespread public-supported schools began to appear in the region during the final years of the nineteenth century.[16]

The greatest changes occurred in Utah. During the 1880s territorial and federal officials (and, of course, Protestant missionaries) strove to undermine the most distinctive aspects of the Mormon religion (i.e., polygamy) and L.D.S. dominance of the territory's economy and political system. Mormons resisted these efforts, but by the 1890s L.D.S. officials reversed their strategy. Rather than continued resistance to Gentile pressure, Mormon leaders made limited concessions to it. The most notable development was L.D.S. President Wilford Woodruff's manifesto in 1890 that instructed Mormons to comply with federal laws that prohibited polygamy. Shortly thereafter Woodruff affirmed Mormon support for the American principle of separation of church and state.[17]

The territorial legislature's approval of a public school law in 1890 proved even more directly significant for the Presbyterian cause in Utah. This measure ended years of Mormon-Gentile conflict over the school question and removed yet another major impediment to Utah statehood. In 1892, 62 percent of Utah's children enrolled in public schools, which were largely staffed by non-Mormon teachers. The following year educators at the Chicago World's Fair praised Utah's public school system and urged other western states and territories to emulate it.[18] Finally, in 1896 Congress approved a bill recognizing Utah statehood. All these developments raised serious questions about the need to continue Presbyterian missions in Utah and particularly cast a pall over the network of mission schools. Six schools were closed between 1889 and 1893, and with the advent of nationwide financial woes, appeals to reopen these schools fell on deaf ears at home missions headquarters.

Presbyterian enthusiasm for mission schools for Indians similarly waned in the 1890s. The passage of the Dawes Act in 1887 represented the zenith of the Protestant-dominated Indian reform movement. The failure of this and other reforms to fulfill the lofty expectations of their sponsors discouraged the self-proclaimed friends of the Indian. Moreover, increased Catholic participation in Indian education dampened Protestant support for the contract system's arrangement for church-government cooperation in Indian education. Following the leadership of Benjamin Harrison's commissioner of Indian affairs, Thomas Jefferson Morgan, major Protestant denominations charged that the contract system violated the principle of separation of church and state and called for its abrogation. Presbyterians belatedly joined this cause. In 1893 and 1894 the home board assumed full financial responsibility for its Indian day schools, and the following year they declined all federal support for Indian education. The Presbyterians did not attempt to disguise their motives. An article in *Home Mission Monthly* in 1893 called for a "vigorous effort" to arouse public opinion against the "evils of sectarian appropriations." The concurrence of this action and nationwide financial woes severely set back Presbyterian efforts in Indian education.[19]

The federal government's decision to expand its involvement in Indian education eased Presbyterian disengagement from Indian mission schools. The record of Richard Henry Pratt's Carlisle Indian School convinced many Americans in the 1880s that a network of government-operated, off-reservation boarding schools offered the best means to resolve the Indian problem. This attitude contributed to the government's decision in 1886 to assume full responsibility for the Presbyterian-operated school in Albuquerque. Four years later the government established large boarding schools in Santa Fe and Phoenix. These schools, of course, served the Pueblos, Navajos, Pimas, and Papagos, who had long been the object of Presbyterian attention, and consequently made it easier for the financially strapped home board to reduce its efforts in Indian education. Citing inadequate finances, increased government involvement in Indian education, and "small returns," mission officials closed the Presbyterian day schools at Jemez Pueblo (1894), Zuni Pueblo (1896), and Laguna Pueblo (1901). During this same period mission officials responded coolly to appeals to expand the relatively successful boarding school at Tucson and to reinitiate mission school work among the Navajos.[20]

Developments were not quite so ominous for the Presbyterian mission school cause in New Mexico as in the Utah and Indian fields. During the final quarter of the nineteenth century, the schooling question continued to divide New Mexico's citizens. The native, Spanish-speaking, Catholic majority called for a parallel system that would provide public funding for both sectarian and nonsectarian schools. The Anglo-Protestant newcomers wanted a public school system comparable to what they had known in the eastern states. Several times between 1875 and 1890, reformers introduced bills for public, nonsectarian schools in the territorial legislature; each time, however, strong Catholic opposition defeated the measure. Meanwhile, Catholics continued to operate a number of schools, and many counties simply contracted with the Catholic church to conduct their public schools. Disgruntled Anglos objected that this violated the principle of separation of church and state. They also charged that the system was inadequate. In 1887, for example, only 37 percent of New Mexico's children attended schools, and critics observed that most teachers were poorly trained, that the school year was too short, and that school facilities were inadequate.[21]

New Mexico's territorial legislature finally approved a public school law in 1891, when the political bosses of the Santa Fe Ring recognized that such a provision was necessary to gain statehood. For long thereafter, however, New Mexico's public schools proved less than adequate. During the 1890s school enrollment in New Mexico hovered between 50 to 60 percent, the school year averaged ninety days, and funding remained inadequate. In 1891, for example, New Mexico's average per pupil expenditure of $12.27 per year fell nearly six dollars below the national average. Furthermore, local school boards continued to operate independently, and the tradition of contracting nuns and priests with public school funds persisted in many areas. Finally, public schools remained particularly scarce and inadequate in the territory's isolated northern mountains until well into the twentieth century. All of these considerations, along with the relative success of the missionary work among the New Mexicans, convinced eastern Presbyterians and mission officials of the need to continue the mission school effort in New Mexico. Even under these circumstances, however, thirteen New Mexico mission schools closed during the period from 1892 to 1900, and in 1899 New Mexico synodical missionary Robert Craig suggested that Presbyterians should encourage use of the public schools "as far as possible in after days."[22]

The southwestern missionaries and home missions officials and Presbyterians in the East who were sympathetic with the cause in the Southwest did not passively accept the retrenchment that accompanied the economic crisis and unprecedented changes of the 1890s. Missionaries invariably protested when schools were closed or when anticipated expansion of their work was delayed. In particular, they objected that the new public-supported schools were inadequate. For example, while missionaries in the Indian fields conceded that the new government-operated schools had larger budgets, superior facilities, and many excellent teachers, they suggested that many government teachers were un-Christian and that the curriculum in the government schools was too secular. Most seriously, missionaries suggested that the failure of government schools to provide religious instruction would harm Indian youth. "Christian schools must be maintained," wrote the home board's superintendent of school work in 1896, "or the Indian is doomed to worse than extermination." Missionaries in the field frequently echoed this sentiment.[23]

Missionaries in Utah and New Mexico were similarly critical of the new public schools in their territories. They repeatedly charged that Mormons and Catholics dominated the local schools and used them to inculcate their peculiar doctrines. Missionaries at isolated rural stations in each of the two territories frequently observed that public schools had not yet penetrated their areas and thus called for continued support for their work. Finally, Presbyterians frequently criticized the teachers employed in the new public schools of Utah and New Mexico. In the latter territory Presbyterians reported that politics influenced the appointment of teachers and that the majority of teachers could not speak English and had less than a fourth-grade education. An article in *Home Mission Monthly* in 1895 recounted a story of a young teacher in Utah to illustrate the poor quality of that territory's public schools. The teacher ("a son of an LDS bishop") wrote "a tripp to the moon" on the blackboard of his classroom. When a pupil corrected his spelling, the teacher reportedly explained that had the trip been on earth it would have been spelled with one *P*, but that "since it referred to celestial bodies, two *P*'s were required."[24]

Reports from Utah in the 1890s also commented on other, more serious, matters. Missionaries correctly recognized that the transformation of Mormonism in the 1890s posed a serious threat to the continuation of their work. Since their arrival in Utah, Presbyterians had pointed to polygamy and L.D.S. domination of local territorial governments to justify their missions. Because of their understanding of culture, they expected that the eradication of these peculiarly Mormon traits would require nothing short of the destruction of Mormonism. When this expectation proved fallacious, missionaries charged that Mormon officials had "hoodwinked the nation." Following Woodruff's manifestos of 1890, Utah missionaries observed that "polygamy still flourishes in Utah" and that L.D.S. officials had "in no way modified [their] determination to control secular government in Utah." Utah statehood, many missionaries later observed, only emboldened Mormon officials to rid themselves of the Presbyterians and their mission schools. Finally, by the late 1890s some missionaries began to recognize that the greatest problem with Utah's public schools was not their poor quality. A committee of Utah Presbytery warned in 1899 that the state's public schools had vastly improved and that the Presbyterian mission schools would be left behind if they did not make comparable improvements. Clearly, the Presbyterian cause in Utah was in a state of crisis as the nineteenth century ended. Nevertheless some Presbyterians remained optimistic. "Our final victory is sure," proclaimed a committee of Utah Presbytery in 1897, "for God is on our side."[25] Above all else belief that God was indeed on their side sustained the Presbyterian cause in the Southwest through the trying years of the 1890s and carried it into a new and uncertain century.

Notes

1. 20th Annual Report, Board of Home Missions, 1890, 24, 27; Inez More Parker, *The Rise and Decline of the Program of Education for Black Presbyterians of the United Presbyterian Church, U.S.A., 1856–1970* (San Antonio: Trinity University Press, 1977), 36.

2. 24th Annual Report, Board of Home Missions, 1894, 3; *HMM* 8 (February 1894): 73, 9 (January 1895): 50; "An Outlook Sketch from Headquarters," *HMM* 9 (September 1895): 250.

3. Report of Superintendent of School Work to Board of Home Missions and Woman's Executive Committee, 1896, 6, 10; George McAfee, "Our Schools," *HMM* 12 (January 1898): 62–63; Mrs. Frederick H. Pierson, "The Outlook — From the Office at '53,' " *HMM* 9 (September 1895): 251–53; Emmeline G. Pierson, "Report of the Corresponding Secretary," *HMM* 11 (July 1897): 197; Matilda Allison, "The Situation at Santa Fe," *HMM* 10 (November 1895): 9; E. M. Fenton, "Voices from the Field — N.M.," *HMM* 11 (July 1897): 205–6; "Words from Workers — Utah," *HMM* 10 (February 1896): 73–74.

4. 24th Annual Report, Board of Home Missions, 1894, 3; *HMM* 9 (January 1895): 50; "Outlook from the Office at '53,' " 252; "Three Points of View," *HMM* 10 (February 1896): 89; McAfee, "Our Schools."

5. Broad overviews of the Gilded Age are found in John A. Garraty, *The New Commonwealth* (New York: Harper and Row, 1968), and Carl Degler, *The Age of the Economic Revolution* (Glenview, Ill.: Scott, Foresman, 1977).

6. General accounts of the romanticization of the West are found in Paul A. Carter, "Out West," in *Writers of the Purple Sage: Origins of a National Myth* (Tucson Public Library and Arizona Historical Society, 1983), and Earl Pomeroy, *In Search of the Golden West* (New York: Alfred A. Knopf, 1957), 35–46, 158–164. Burl Noggle comments on the more romantic views of the Southwest that appeared in the 1880s and 1890s ("Anglo Observers of the Southwest Borderlands, 1825–1890: The Rise of a Concept," *Arizona and the West* 1 [Summer 1959]: 129–31). For a thorough account of Lummis's career and writing see Edwin R. Bingham, *Charles F. Lummis: Career in the Southwest* (San Marino, Calif.: Huntington

Library, 1955). Bandelier's career is examined in Bernard L. Fontana, "A Dedication to the Memory of Adolf A. F. Bandelier, 1840–1914," *Arizona and the West* 2 (1960).

7. John Higham, "The Reorientation of American Culture in the 1890s," in *The Origins of Modern Consciousness*, ed. John Weiss (Detroit: Wayne State University Press, 1965), reprinted in Higham, *Writing American History: Essays on Modern Scholarship* (Bloomington: Indiana University Press, 1970), 73–102; F. H. Matthews, "The Revolt against Americanism: Cultural Pluralism and Cultural Relativism as an Ideology of Liberation," *Canadian Review of American Studies* 1 (Spring 1970): 4–31.

8. Arthur M. Schlesinger in "A Critical Period in American Religion, 1875–1900," originally published in *Massachusetts Historical Society Proceedings* 64 (October 1930–June 1932): 523–46, was one of the first historians to suggest that the 1890s represented a watershed in American religious history. In subsequent years a number of scholars have examined and modified Schlesinger's thesis. Two particularly useful recent studies are George M. Marsden, *Fundamentalism and American Culture: The Shaping of Twentieth-Century Evangelicalism, 1870–1925* (New York: Oxford University Press, 1980), and Ferenc M. Szasz, *The Divided Mind of Protestant America, 1880–1930* (Tuscaloosa: University of Alabama Press, 1982). Robert T. Handy offers a concise analysis of these same developments (*A Christian America: Protestant Hopes and Historical Realities*, 2d ed., rev. [New York: Oxford University Press, 1984], chap. 3).

9. A number of scholars have examined the debate over conduct of missions. See, for example, Paul A. Varg, "Motives in Protestant Missions, 1890–1917," *Church History* 23 (March 1954): 68–82; R. Pierce Beaver, "Missionary Motivation through Three Centuries," in *Reinterpretation of American Church History*, ed. Jerald C. Brauer (Chicago: University of Chicago Press, 1968), 129–32; Charles W. Forman, "A History of Foreign Mission Theory in America," in *American Missions in Bicentennial Perspective*, ed. R. Pierce Beaver (South Pasadena, Calif.: William Carey Library, 1977), 69–95; Sidney E. Mead, "Denominationalism: The Shape of Protestant America," *Church History* 23 (December 1954): 304–5. There are a number of informative studies of the social gospel movement, including Charles H. Hopkins, *The Rise of the Social Gospel in American Protestantism, 1865–1915* (New Haven: Yale University Press, 1940); Robert T. Handy, ed., *The Social Gospel in America* (New York: Oxford University Press, 1966); Henry F. May, *Protestant Churches and Industrial America* (New York: Harper and Brothers, 1949).

10. Lefferts Loetscher, *The Broadening Church: A Study of Theological Issues in the Presbyterian Church since 1869* (Philadelphia: University of Pennsylvania Press, 1957), chaps. 6, 7, and 8; May, *Protestant Churches and Industrial America*, 192–93; Dieter T. Hessell, "The Social Gospel in the Presbyterian Church," 1969, unpublished essay in the Presbyterian Historical Society, Philadelphia.

11. Loetscher, *The Broadening Church*, 71.

12. Handy, *A Christian America*, chaps. 5, 6.

13. This pattern was not unique to Presbyterians. See Handy, *A Christian America*, 111.

14. Report of Standing Committee on Home Missions to General Assembly, 1892, 22d Annual Report, Board of Home Missions, 1892, 153; Mrs. E. G. Pierson, Report of Corresponding Secretary of Woman's Executive Committee, 23d Annual Report, Board of Home Missions, 1893, 164–67; Mrs. Pierson, "19th Annual Report of Woman's Board," *HMM* 12 (July 1898): 197–98.

15. Stelzle's efforts have not received the attention from historians that they deserve. Dieter Hessell comments on the work of Stelzle's Department of Church and Labor and draws primarily from Stelzle's voluminous writings ("The Social Gospel in the Presbyterian Church," 7–9). These include *Messages to Workingmen* (Revell, 1906); *The Church and Labor* (Houghton Mifflin, 1910); and his autobiography, *A Son of the Bowery* (Doran, 1926). Wilson's efforts have received more (but not adequate) attention. A good recent overview is James H. Madison, "Reformers and the Rural Church," *Journal of American History* 73 (December 1986): 645–68. Madison calls Wilson "the most important figure in early twentieth-century rural church reform." Also see Seth William Hester, "The Life and Works of Warren H. Wilson and Their Significance in the Beginnings of the Rural Church Movement in America" (M.A. thesis, Drew Theological Seminary, 1946). Wilson also wrote extensively. For a listing of his most important works, see the Madison article.

16. Howard Lamar, *The Far Southwest, 1846–1912: A Territorial History* (New York: W. W. Norton, 1970), provides a detailed overview of the transformation of the Southwest during this era.

17. Historians have devoted considerable attention to these developments. See Lamar, *The Far Southwest,* 378–411; Robert J. Dwyer, *The Gentile Comes to Utah: A Study in Religious and Social Conflict,* rev. 2d ed. (Salt Lake City: Western Epics, 1971), 190–249; Arrington and Bitton, *The Mormon Experience,* 176–84; Larson, *The "Americanization" of Utah for Statehood,* 94–264. Grant Underwood's essay "Revisioning Mormon History" suggests that historians have exaggerated the transformation of Mormonism during this period (*Pacific Historical Review* 55 [August 1986]: 403–26).

18. Frederick S. Buchanan, "Religion and Secular Change in Utah Schools, 1870–1890" (paper presented at Western History Association annual conference, October 9–12, 1985; copy provided courtesy of Dr. Buchanan). Also see S. S. Ivins, "Free Schools Come to Utah," *Utah Historical Quarterly* 22 (June 1954): 321–42; Lamar, *The Far Southwest,* 405.

19. In 1889 Catholics received $347,672 out of the $530,905 that the government awarded for contract schools. In contrast, the Presbyterians, with $41,825, were the most active Protestant participants in this arrangement. Francis Paul Prucha has contributed much to the understanding of the debate that these figures fostered. Chap. 27 of *The Great Father: The United States Government and the American Indians,* vol. 2 (Lincoln: University of Nebraska Press, 1984), provides an overview of these matters that draws heavily from two other of his works: *American Indian Policy in Crisis: Christian Reformers and the Indian, 1865–1900* (Norman: University of Oklahoma Press, 1976) and *The Churches and the Indian Schools, 1888–1912* (Lincoln: University of Nebraska Press, 1979). Com-

ments on the Presbyterian decision to withdraw from the contract system are found in the 23d and 24th annual reports, Board of Home Missions, 1893, 164–65; 1894, 38. Also see "The Annual Meeting," *HMM* 7 (July 1893): 196.

20. Prucha, *The Great Father,* 2:815–22; Margaret Connell Szasz, *Education and the American Indian: The Road to Self-Determination since 1928* (Albuquerque: University of New Mexico Press, 1977), 9–10. Historians have examined the programs of several of the government boarding schools. See, for example, Robert A. Trennert, "Peacefully If They Will, Forcibly If They Must: The Phoenix Indian School, 1890–1901," *Journal of Arizona History* 20 (Autumn 1979): 297–322; Lillie McKinney, "A History of Albuquerque Indian School" (M.A. thesis, University of New Mexico, 1943). Official explanations for the closing of the Pueblo day schools are found in Minutes, Synod of New Mexico, September 7–10, 1894, 15 (re the Jemez school); *HMM* 11 (January 1897): 50 (re the Zuni school); and Minutes, Synod of New Mexico, October 4–9, 1901, 31–32 (re the Laguna school). "Field Items," *HMM* 13 (February 1899): 90, carries an appeal to expand the work at Tucson. New Mexico synodical missionary Robert Craig complained about foot dragging in reinitiating work among the Navajos in 98th Annual Report, Board of Home Missions, 1900, 34–35.

21. Jane Atkins, "Who Will Educate? The Schooling Question in Territorial New Mexico, 1846–1911" (Ph.D. diss., University of New Mexico, 1982), 362–96, provides an in-depth overview of these developments. Also see Dianna Everett, "The Public School Debate in New Mexico, 1850–1891," *Arizona and the West* 26 (Summer 1984): 107–34; Robert W. Larson, *New Mexico's Quest for Statehood, 1846–1912* (Albuquerque: University of New Mexico Press, 1968), 124–28, 159–61; Lamar, *The Far Southwest,* 167–68, 178–201.

22. Atkins, "Who Will Educate?" 397–407; Craig, Synodical Missionary's Report, Minutes, Synod of New Mexico, October 6–9, 1899, 31. That more schools were closed in New Mexico during the 1890s than in the other two fields is somewhat misleading. Eight of the thirteen schools that were closed had been opened between 1888 and 1891, a period of rapid and haphazard expansion in the New Mexican field. Most of these schools never became firmly established, and consequently they were the first to be closed when hard times arrived.

23. Report of Superintendent of School Work to Board of Home Missions and Woman's Executive Committee, 1896; 95th Annual Report, Board of Home Missions, 1897, 42; Frazier S. Herndon, "The Government–The Church," *HMM* 15 (February 1901): 88; *HMM* 16 (November 1901):1–2; M. E. Dissette to Mrs. Pierson, May 13, 1901, PHS, RG 51, Box 2, F-11.

24. Presbyterian comments on New Mexico's public schools are found in Minutes, Synod of New Mexico, October 3–4, 1891, 13; E. G. Pierson, "Presbyterian Home Missions among Spanish-speaking Peoples, *HMM* 12 (November 1897): 8; "From Our N.M. Stations," *HMM* 15 (November 1900): 14; "Bright Gleams Here and There," *HMM* 15 (November 1900): 16; Harriet R. Benham, "Impressions of a New Worker," *HMM* 15 (November 1900): 5; Robert M. Craig, "Conditions among the Mexicans" (New York City: Board of Home Missions, no date, reprinted on PHS microfilm, Presbyterian Church, U.S.A., Board of Home Missions, Spanish

Missions in Southwest, Selected Works: Item 4). For Presbyterian comments on Utah's public schools, see Minutes, Utah Presbytery, August 27, 1891, 3:264; Miss Anna Noble, "Words from Workers—Utah," *HMM* 5 (November 1890): 12; "Words from Workers — Mormon," *HMM* 5 (January 1891): 178–79; "Do Not Close the Schools," *HMM* 9 (May 1895): 149–50; Minutes, Presbytery of Utah, August 24, 1895, 4:204; Samuel Wishard, "The Woman's Board and Mission Schools," *HMM* 13 (May 1899): 152–53. The story about "the tripp" to the moon is recounted in "Lights and Shades of the Mormon Field," *HMM* 9 (June 1895): 157.

25. Missionaries in Utah wrote frequently and extensively about the problems that beset their cause in the 1890s. For general comments on the Mormon transformation, see *HMM* 5 (January 1890): 50; Minutes, Presbytery of Utah, August 24, 1893, 4:15–17; "Protest, Protest," *HMM* 7 (September 1893): 253–54; Alice M. Peck, "Words from Workers — Mormon," *HMM* 9 (January 1895): 63; "An Outlook Sketch from Headquarters," *HMM* 9 (September 1895): 251; "The Present Situation in Utah," Minutes, Presbytery of Utah, 5:183. Comments on increased L.D.S. hostility against Presbyterian missionaries after Utah statehood are found in 95th Annual Report, Board of Home Missions, 1897, 42; "Since Statehood," *HMM* 14 (October 1900): 271; "The Real Governing Power in Utah," *HMM* 10 (May 1896): 150; Report of Superintendent of School Work to Board of Home Missions and Woman's Executive Committee, 1896, 9.

8

Missions in Transition

For many friends of Presbyterian missions the optimistic expectations for the mission schools in the Southwest seemed closer to fulfillment as the twentieth century dawned than ever before. After the retrenchment of the 1890s eleven new schools opened between 1900 and 1905, and enrollment in the schools increased by more than 8 percent during this period.

Reports from the field seemed to portend even greater efforts and results in the years ahead. In 1902 the home board's superintendent of school work commented that the school in Tucson was "known far and wide in the far West as the most successful Indian school in that great country." A year later he announced the opening of a new day school in northern New Mexico and concluded, "No church ever had such an opportunity as the Presbyterian church now has in New Mexico to preach the gospel with immediate and splendid success." "Our schools," he concluded, "have opened the whole country to us." From the Utah field in 1906 came news of increased enrollments, "fewer discouragements," and "many encouragements."[1]

From the vantage point of ninety years later, it is apparent that the burst of expansion in mission schools and resulting optimism was short lived. To be sure, Presbyterians opened three more schools in the New Mexico field and six more Indian schools after 1905, but most of these were very small and remained open only briefly (see table 10 and map 5). Rather than initiating a new era of advance for Presbyterian mission schools in the Southwest, the first two decades of the twentieth century were the last gasp of the aggressive mission school policy that Sheldon Jackson had initiated forty years before. Presbyterians did not abandon their commitments in the Southwest in this period, but they did make major adjustments in hopes of fulfilling those commitments. The mission school that had long been

Table 10. Presbyterian Mission Schools Established in the Southwest, 1900–1923

New Mexican Field

Location	Opened	Closed
Chimayo	1901	*
Trementina	1901	1919
Truchas	1903	1959
Jarales	1903	1906
Ranchitos de Taos	1903	1910
Tierra Amarilla	1906	1911
Santa Fe**	1908	1913
Chamisal	1909	1919

Mormon Field

Location	Opened	Closed
Franklin	1900	1908
Preston	1903	1909
Rigby	1904	1907
Panguitch	1903	1913

Indian Field

Location/Tribe	Opened	Closed
Jewett (Navajo)	1903	1913
Ganado (Navajo)***	1901	1986
Jemez (Pueblo)	1910	1914
Phoenix (Pima-Papago)***	1911	****
Sells (Papago)	1912	1914
San Miguel (Papago)	1914	1949
Topawa (Pagago)	1921	1926
Stotonic (Pima)	1919	1932

* Present-day John Hyson School.

** Mary James School. In 1913 the Allison School for Girls expanded and took over the campus of the James School and became known at Allison-James. At that time the boys of the James School transferred to Menaul School in Albuquerque.

*** The school opened at Ganado in 1901 was in the home of the Reverend and Mrs. C. H. Bierkemper. This school gradually expanded until 1914, when the Jewett School was transferred to Ganado. At that time the school at Ganado became known as Kirkwood Memorial School.

**** Cook Bible School, now the Cook Christian Training School.

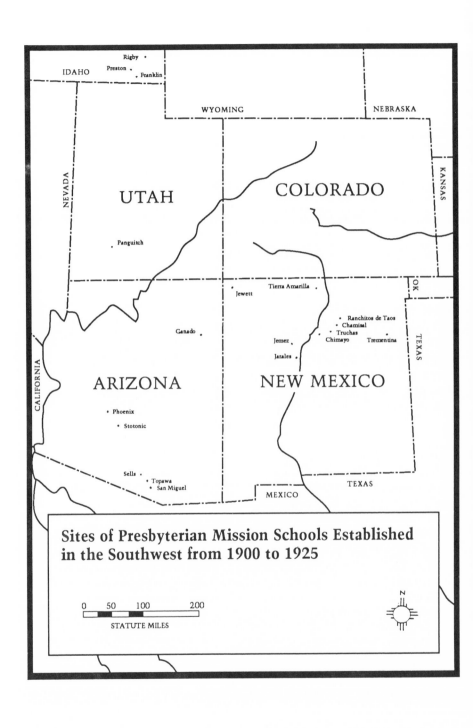

IDAHO
Rigby
Preston
Franklin

WYOMING

NEBRASKA

NEVADA

UTAH

COLORADO

KANSAS

Panguitch

Jewett

Tierra Amarilla

OK

CALIFORNIA

Ganado

Ranchitos de Taos
Chamisal
Truchas
Jemez
Chimayo
Trementina

TEXAS

Jarales

ARIZONA

NEW MEXICO

Phoenix

Stotonic

Sells
Topawa
San Miguel

TEXAS

MEXICO

Sites of Presbyterian Mission Schools Established in the Southwest from 1900 to 1925

```
0    50   100       200
|====|====|=========|
     STATUTE MILES
```

the key to the Presbyterian cause in the Southwest would play a less prominent role in their new southwestern strategy.

Many factors combined to make this a transitional era in the history of Presbyterian missions in the Southwest. Most significantly, the changes within the region that had raised doubts about the need to continue Presbyterian missions there in the 1890s accelerated in the years after the turn of the century. Improved transportation and communication systems effectively ended the Southwest's long-standing isolation from the rest of the nation and brought increased numbers of Anglo-Protestant immigrants into the region. Moreover, statehood for Utah in 1896 and for New Mexico and Arizona in 1912 belatedly incorporated these areas into the national political system and made them appear less exceptional to many Americans.[2]

The expansion of public-supported primary education in the new southwestern states presented the greatest challenge to the continuation of Presbyterian mission schools. When public schools first appeared in the region, Presbyterians had protested that their inadequacy justified the continuation of the mission schools. By the early twentieth century, however, Presbyterian missionaries praised Utah's public schools as "superior" and "splendid" and warned that their own schools must improve if they were to compete effectively.[3] In New Mexico missionaries continued to comment on unsatisfactory facilities, poorly qualified teachers, and Catholic domination of the public schools in the state's more isolated regions. Nevertheless, progress had been made in less remote population centers, such as Las Vegas and Raton (where Presbyterians had long conducted schools). The enabling act for New Mexico statehood in 1912 strengthened the state's commitment to provide free, nonsectarian public schools.[4] In the Indian fields the government continued to expand its educational work during the early 1900s.[5]

Few Presbyterians at the time argued that public education in the Southwest had improved to the point that the mission schools should be abandoned completely. But the traditional Presbyterian commitment to public education led some observers to question the wisdom of continued expansion of the mission school effort. These persons noted that the General Assembly action in 1878 that had authorized the home board to initiate schools for exceptional populations had clearly stated that mission schools not be established in states or territories "which [had] or [were] likely soon to have school laws." The General Assembly had allowed for "temporary exception to this rule," but by the early years of the twentieth century some Presbyterians suggested that the time for such exceptions had passed.

The reappearance of nationwide financial difficulties from 1907 to 1909 made the debate over the future of the mission schools more acute. Actually, the board's budget shortfalls during this period were minor compared to those of the 1890s. However, the aforementioned expansion of public education in the Southwest and an ever-growing number of new demands on the home board made the southwestern mission school work appear more expendable in the first decade of the twentieth century than in the last decade of the nineteenth. Consequently, the board consolidated the work at a number of its struggling one-teacher schools in New Mexico and closed day schools in several Utah communities where adequate public schools had been established. Between 1905 and 1910 the number of Presbyterian schools in the Southwest decreased 43 percent, from fifty-eight to thirty-three, and the number of pupils decreased 27 percent, from 3,386 to 2,488 (see table 11).[6] That these cuts and the return to economic prosperity by 1910 did not end the debate about the future of the mission schools, however, indicated that more than financial considerations were at issue.

Significant changes in home missions leadership during this period greatly influenced Presbyterian responses to the changing conditions in the Southwest. Death and retirement removed from the church and home board many of the individuals who had played instrumental roles in the initiation and enlargement of the school work in the Southwest. Sheldon Jackson died in 1909. Although he had not been directly involved in southwestern missions since the early 1880s, Jackson had always maintained interest in that work. More significantly, he symbolized the old home missions that had been concerned primarily with winning souls in the western territories. In the same year that Jackson died, Mary E. James resigned as president of the Woman's Board of Home Missions. She had headed the woman's mission agency since 1886, when school work in the Southwest represented the

Table 11. School Statistics, 1900–1920

	1900	1905	1910	1915	1920
New Mexican					
Schools	24	27	19	13	10
Pupils	1405	1478	1290	1070	768
Mormon					
Schools	29	29	11	7	3
Pupils	1478	1732	1027	598	439
Indian					
Schools	2	2	3	2	4
Pupils	247	176	171	169	270
Total					
Schools	55	58	33	22	17
Pupils	3130	3386	2488	1837	1477

major object of women's concern. Another longtime friend of southwestern missions, the home board's superintendent of schools, Robert Craig, also resigned from his duties in 1909. As New Mexico's synodical missionary for a decade prior to his appointment to the schools superintendency in 1906, Craig had been a strong promoter of schools for Indians and New Mexicans. He continued this support during his tenure as the board's superintendent of school work.[7]

It would be misleading to suggest that the home mission leaders who replaced these individuals were not supportive of mission efforts in the Southwest. They did not, however, have the personal attachment that their predecessors had shown for that work. Their vision for home missions was broader in scope and reflected many of the changes that had taken place in the United States and the Presbyterian Church, U.S.A., since the pivotal years of the 1890s. The Reverend Charles L. Thompson, who served as secretary of the home board from 1898 to 1914, typified in many ways the new home missions. As head of the home board, he was a strong promoter of the social gospel, Protestant cooperation in home missions, and specialization in the conduct of missions. He championed, in particular, Charles Stelzle's work among immigrants and laborers in eastern cities and Warren H. Wilson's innovative efforts to revitalize rural churches. In a history of Presbyterian home missions written after his retirement, Thompson observed that during his years as board secretary missionary thought turned away from its traditional preoccupation with the West and "toward congestions of population far this side of the frontier."[8] The mission administrators who surrounded Thompson, including M. Katherine Bennett, who replaced James as president of the woman's board, and David R. Boyd and Marshall C. Allaben, who served in the superintendent of schools position during the second decade of the twentieth century, also strongly identified with the new home missions.[9]

While new missions concerns distracted the attention of home mission officials from the Southwest, the new mission outlook also influenced the development of official board policy toward the region. The spirit of Progressivism that so thoroughly pervaded every facet of American society during this period left its imprint on Presbyterian mission leaders. Like many other social and political planners of the Progressive era, Presbyterian mission officials were concerned with efficiency. This commitment convinced home board officials to emphasize what Secretary Thompson called "intensive" mission activities, as opposed to the "extensive" approach that typified the old, frontier-oriented home missions. While traditional religious motives were still apparent, the new home missions embraced the social gospel. And, as one historian of Protestant uplift has noted, in this new approach to missions "the Kingdom here and now tended to displace the

Kingdom coming at the end from the center of concern."[10] As good Progressives, the new home missions leaders also emphasized that their church must keep abreast of the rapid and unprecedented changes that their society was undergoing. In 1914 Superintendent of Schools Allaben observed: "There is always a danger of getting into ruts in all lines of educational and evangelistic work." "It behooves us," he concluded, "to be watchful lest golden opportunities slip from our grasp through our failure to keep pace with the changes of our day and generation."[11]

These considerations had important implications for Presbyterian missions in the rapidly changing Southwest. At the annual meeting of the Woman's Board of Home Missions in 1911, home board secretary Thompson reported on improved public education in Utah and suggested that "gradually it will become the duty of all Gentile people . . . to stand by the public school system." A year later Bennett spoke before the same audience about the growth of public education in the isolated areas of the country that Presbyterian mission schools served. While observing that "the time when mission schools [would] be unnecessary was still far away," Bennett reminded her audience that "it never has been, and never can be, the desire of the Woman's Board to compete with the public schools."[12]

Neither Thompson nor Bennett believed Presbyterians should abandon their southwestern missions, but they made clear that the time for major adjustments in that work was at hand. Consequently, they called for the gradual discontinuation of primary-level day schools as public schools effectively entered areas of Presbyterian work. Secondly, both Thompson and Bennett pointed to other areas of work worthy of Presbyterian support. Citing the continued absence of adequate public-supported secondary schools in the Southwest, they called on Presbyterian women to emphasize advanced levels of academic work at their boarding schools. Furthermore, they suggested that greater attention be devoted to the training of native church leaders and to non-educational mission activities directed toward improving the quality of life in the isolated areas that Presbyterian missions long had served. Ending the paternalism that had long characterized the Presbyterian effort was an underlying goal of this blueprint for the new Presbyterian missions in the Southwest.[13]

Despite protests from missionaries and other Presbyterians in the mission fields, the recommended de-emphasis on primary-level day schools was carried out. In 1905 Presbyterians in the Southwest conducted fifty day schools with 2,362 pupils. Fifteen years later they operated only ten, with fewer than six hundred pupils (see table 12).

The decline was most severe in the Utah field, where all of the twenty-five day schools that had served more than 1,100 pupils in 1905 were closed

Table 12. Statistics for Day Schools, 1900–1920

	1900	1905	1910	1915	1920
New Mexican					
Schools	22	25	16	11	8
Pupils	1279	1254	930	808	509
Mormon					
Schools	25	25	7	4	0
Pupils	986	1108	392	240	0
Indian					
Schools	1	0	0	0	2
Pupils	50	0	0	0	51
Total					
Schools	48	50	23	15	10
Pupils	2315	2362	1322	1048	566

by 1920. A gradual softening of Presbyterian attitudes toward Mormonism facilitated the new policy. In 1907 the home board observed "whatever justification there was in the past for an aggressive antagonism toward Mormonism . . . it would be better to confine the work in Utah to simple teaching and preaching of the gospel." Despite occasional outbursts of anti-Mormon sentiment, this more cordial attitude prevailed in the second decade of the twentieth century; Mormon-Gentile cooperation during World War I further reduced tensions between the two groups.[14] Less hostile attitudes toward Mormonism made it easier for Presbyterian missionaries in Utah to accept the discontinuation of their day schools. After several years of resistance to the new policy, a committee of Utah Synod reported in 1915 that "a careful study of the present methods of work will reveal that the results attained have not been commensurate with the labors of the missionaries and the expenditures of home mission funds." Consequently, the committee recommended that the Utah work be concentrated "in a few strategic centers." Over the next five years Presbyterians closed their four remaining day schools in Utah.[15]

The number of mission day schools in the New Mexico field also declined during the first two decades of the twentieth century, but not as drastically as in Utah. This was largely due to the continued absence or inadequacy of public schools in many of the areas served by Presbyterian schools.[16]

Shortly after his 1913 appointment to the schools superintendency, Marshall Allaben toured the New Mexico field and attended an interdenominational conference of southwestern missionaries in Albuquerque. At the conference Allaben led a discussion about the future of the mission day schools. The participants concurred that Protestants should "support in every way" New Mexico's public school effort but concluded that the existing situation required the continuation and strengthening of the mission day schools. The New Mexico missionaries, however, agreed that their mission boards should expand their support for boarding schools offering advanced work. More specifically, they suggested that the mission schools should do more to prepare teachers for the public schools. Six months later Allaben commented in his annual report that "pronounced changes are occurring throughout New Mexico" and that Presbyterians should be "alive to the necessity of readjusting [their] work." In 1919 M. Katherine Bennett participated in a similar discussion at another interdenominational conference of southwestern missionaries. By that time opinion about the future of the day schools was divided. Some missionaries and mission officials called for their discontinuation, while others protested that conditions in the plazas demanded that the day schools be continued. All participants, however, agreed that the various churches should continue to support large, well-equipped boarding schools.[17]

When public schools effectively entered communities with mission schools, Presbyterians usually withdrew. For example, Alice Blake in 1920 announced the closing of her relatively successful mission school in Trementina. She observed that the new public school teacher (a native Presbyterian) was not allowed to read from the Bible or teach religion. Otherwise, she concluded, "his work does not differ from the mission school itself." On the other hand, Presbyterians kept open their schools in communities where public schools did not exist or where they were inadequate. Nevertheless, by 1920 only eight Presbyterian day schools with slightly more than five hundred pupils remained in operation (see table 12 and map 5). Seven of these schools were located in still isolated areas of the Sangre de Cristo mountains north of Santa Fe; the other was in the equally remote San Juan mountains of southern Colorado.[18]

The Indian fields in some respects proved the exception to the pattern of declining emphasis on day schools. This, however, was partly because Presbyterians conducted so few day schools among Indians at the turn of the century. Indeed, they had closed their one remaining Pueblo day school, at Laguna Pueblo, in 1901. From 1910 to 1914 a mission teacher attempted with meager success to reinstitute a day school at Jemez Pueblo. Similarly, the effort to reinitiate a mission day school among the Navajos, begun at Ganado in 1901, convinced mission and government officials that only boarding schools could be effective among those Indians. Although initiated tardily, Presbyterian day schools proved more effective among the tribes of southern Arizona. Between 1912 and 1921 missionaries opened day schools for Papago children at Sells, San Miguel, and Topawa and for Pima children at Stotonic that served as feeders to the Tucson boarding school. Although the schools at San Miguel and Stotonic remained open for a number of years, their enrollments were never large, and when the federal government established schools nearby, Presbyterians withdrew from these stations (see table 10 and map 5).[19]

Mission officials were quick to point out that the gradual withdrawal from the southwestern day schools was not retrenchment. And, indeed, the closing of the day schools represented only one-half of the equation in the new Presbyterian educational strategy for the Southwest. According to this new plan, the mission dollars saved from the closing of the day schools were redirected to a variety of other mission activities, most notably the boarding schools.

Presbyterians had, of course, conducted boarding schools among the three southwestern populations since the 1880s. The boarding schools that the new generation of mission officials envisioned, however, differed significantly from the earlier ones. First, because of the continued absence of adequate public high schools in much of the Southwest, mission officials emphasized that the boarding schools should concentrate on secondary-level academic work. Second, they called for many of the elements of the new progressive education, such as industrial education, child-centered schooling, and character building to be incorporated into the boarding school curricula. Finally, mission officials called for improved quality in the boarding schools programs and facilities. Speaking of the academies in Utah in 1913, superintendent of schools Marshall Allaben observed that "if we are to bring in large numbers of pupils . . . we must have the variety of work and fullness of equipment which will suit the demands of students possessing different gifts and having different ideals." In short, the new emphasis on boarding schools called not for more schools but for better ones. And, indeed, during the period from 1910 to 1920 the number of Presbyterian boarding schools in the Southwest actually decreased from ten to seven, and the number of boarding pupils declined from 1,166 to 911 (see table 13). At the end of this period, however, most observers agreed about the excellence of the remaining Presbyterian boarding schools.[20]

The shift to the new boarding schools came most quickly in the Utah field. The home board's superintendent of schools, Dr. David Boyd, observed in 1909 that although public-supported primary schools had become widespread in Utah, few public high schools existed in the state's rural areas. Young people from those regions who wished to continue their educations beyond the primary level had to leave their homes. After observing that only one of the state's Mormon-operated private academies had boarding facilities, Boyd exclaimed: "Here is our great opportunity!"[21]

Table 13. Statistics for Schools that Offered Advanced Work and Had Boarding
Departments,* 1900–1920

	1900	1905	1910	1915	1920
New Mexican					
Schools	2	2	3	2	2
Pupils	126	224	360	262	259
Mormon					
Schools	4	4	4	3	3
Pupils	492	624	635	358	439
Indian					
Schools	1	2	3	2	2
Pupils	197	176	171	169	213
Total					
Schools	7	8	10	7	7
Pupils	815	1024	1166	789	911

* These statistics reflect total enrollments at those schools that offered advanced work and
had boarding departments. Included in the enrollments were day students and some
students engaged in primary-level work. Figures for post-secondary educational work (e.g.,
Westminister College, Albuquerque Training Schools, and Cook Bible School) are not
included in these statistics.

By 1910 four Utah schools—Wasatch Academy in Mt. Pleasant, New
Jersey Academy in Logan, Hungerford Academy in Springville, and the Salt
Lake Collegiate Institute—had boarding departments and offered secondary-
level work.[22] Since the turn of the century each of these schools had awarded
a few high school diplomas, but the graduating classes were usually small
and in some years there were no graduates at all. Moreover, the programs
of these schools fell short of the new Presbyterian ideal for boarding-school
education in several other ways. In each of them primary- and preparatory-
level students (grades one through nine) outnumbered those enrolled at the
academy (high school) level. Furthermore, in 1910 fewer than 25 percent
of the pupils in the so-called boarding schools in Utah were actually boarders.

These conditions convinced mission officials in the East and mission
educators in Utah that significant changes had to be made if the Utah
academies were to fulfill their newly envisioned role. This conclusion
hastened the decision to withdraw from the day schools and to concentrate
attention and funding on the boarding schools. It also led to other significant
developments. In 1910 the home board turned over its property in Salt Lake
City to the trustees of struggling Westminster College on the provision that
the Salt Lake Collegiate Institute be continued as the college's preparatory

division with a sizable boarding enrollment. Two years later, "in the interests of efficiency and economy," the board merged the work of Hungerford and Wasatch academies at the campus of the latter. While the newly consolidated Wasatch Academy and Salt Lake Collegiate Institute continued along co-educational lines, the board determined that the New Jersey Academy in Logan could operate most effectively as a boarding school for girls exclusively.[23]

Presbyterians strove to strengthen the new consolidated schools. Over the course of the decade between 1910 and 1920, new dormitories were constructed and boarding enrollments increased. By the 1919–20 school year, for example, all but three of Wasatch Academy's 230 students were boarders. Simultaneously, each of the academies phased out its primary divisions and increased enrollment in its high school departments. In turn, the number of graduating seniors increased steadily, and many of the graduates continued their educations beyond the high school level. Wasatch Academy, for example, reported that nine of ten members of its graduating class of 1916 attended college or other post-secondary educational institutions.[24]

Simultaneously, the Presbyterian vision for its Utah academies also broadened. In an article entitled "The Challenge of Utah," published in 1918, superintendent of schools Allaben mentioned "the conditions of ranch life in the West" rather than Mormonism as the major reason for Presbyterian boarding schools in Utah. Indeed, Allaben refrained from commenting on the L.D.S. church at all and concluded with the query: "Must we be fed tales of attrocities [sic] in order to support our work in Utah?"[25]

Developments in the New Mexico field roughly paralleled those in Utah. Although day schools remained open in a number of isolated villages, New Mexico Presbyterians gave increased attention to their boarding schools. Construction of a large new building enabled Menaul School to more than double its enrollment in 1904, and by 1910 it had 185 students. Advanced course work was gradually added to the curriculum, and in 1906 Menaul graduated its first high school class. The high school division grew slowly, however, and in 1916 only twenty-seven of the school's 154 students (18 percent) were in the high school. Following the arrival of Harper C. Donaldson as superintendent in 1916, the school added several new buildings and entered a period of sustained growth and vitality that won it the praise of church officials and many New Mexico educational and political leaders. In 1914 a county school superintendent (a native New Mexican and Roman Catholic) wrote that he wished Menaul "had room for 500 of our boys." Another state educational leader (an Anglo Protestant) commented that "the great majority of Mexican youths who are pushing to the front and making something of themselves" were Menaul graduates.[26]

Meanwhile, similar developments were under way in Santa Fe. In 1907 the woman's board had opened the Mary James boarding school for boys, adjacent to the campus of the Allison School for girls "with hope that coeducation might solve the problem of establishing future Christian Protestant homes among the Mexicans." Six years later, however, home mission officials decided to close the James School and consequently transferred the boys enrolled at Santa Fe to Menaul School. Thereafter, the Allison School for girls assumed control of the campus of the former boys' school. The new, enlarged Santa Fe school took the name Allison-James and offered course work from the first through the tenth grades. When nearly all of the sixteen eighth-grade graduates of the class of 1919 expressed interest in continuing their educations, the board approved a plan to initiate a four-year high school program. By 1921 nearly one-fourth (twenty-three) of the school's ninety-seven pupils enrolled in the high school division, and at the end of the decade the enrollment of high school students at Allison-James had climbed to 46 percent (51 of 113). Like Menaul School, Allison-James benefited during these important transitional years from strong leadership. Miss Ruth K. Barber, who arrived at Allison-James in 1916 and became superintendent in 1920, played an important role for many years in the history of the school and the broader Presbyterian mission cause in New Mexico.[27]

The emphasis on boarding schools offering more advanced academic work also characterized Presbyterian educational missions among southwestern Indians during the first two decades of the twentieth century. Progress toward this end, however, was slower than in the other two fields. At the beginning of this period the Tucson Indian Training School was the only successful Presbyterian educational venture among southwestern Indians. In 1900 enrollment neared 200, and the school implemented a graded system through the eighth grade; two years later, four Pima youths became the school's first eighth-grade graduates. The move to a new campus of 150 acres in 1908 allowed the school to expand its educational offerings, particularly in the field of vocational education. Four years later board officials praised the Tucson school as the "largest and best equipped" of the Presbyterian Indian schools.[28]

The arrival of new superintendent Martin L. Girton in 1915 provided further cause for optimism. Under his leadership the faculty strengthened the school's eight-year course of study and the campus added a number of new buildings. In 1925 Girton reported an enrollment of 183 and a waiting list of over 100. Furthermore, the school gradually placed increased emphasis on more advanced work; by 1924 fewer than one-fifth of the pupils were in the lower three grades. In 1921 the school purchased a small cottage in downtown Tucson and designated it the Graduate Home. This facility provided an opportunity for girls who completed the eighth grade at the training school to continue their educations at the Tucson public high school while continuing to live under Presbyterian guidance. Several years later the school provided a similar facility for boys. All but two of the school's fifteen eighth-grade graduates in 1932 continued their educations at the local high school. Finally, in the mid-1930s the school gradually phased out the lower grades and simultaneously added high-school-level work.[29]

In the early twentieth century Presbyterians also reinitiated missionary work among the Navajos and opened mission schools and medical stations at Ganado, Arizona, and Jewett, New Mexico. In 1914 the board consolidated the two programs and announced plans for a large boarding school at Ganado to be named Kirkwood Memorial School. Although enrollment for the first full year at Ganado was only twenty-five, mission officials remained optimistic. In 1918 the home board announced a five-year plan that called for expenditures of $125,000 toward the construction of a plant at Ganado that would have boarding capacity for 200 students. In 1926 enrollment reached 155, and the pupils ranged from six-year-olds to adults in the evangelical training program. In that same year Kirkwood school added the first year of high school work to its curriculum. Four years later it graduated a high school class of four; by 1934 the lower grades were dropped, and the school was conducted as a junior-senior high school.[30]

The vision for the new mission boarding school called for not only the addition of advanced levels of work but also upgraded academic standards. Toward this end the home board raised its qualifications for mission school personnel. In 1913 schools superintendent Allaben announced that in addition to the general requirements for missionary service, those seeking teaching positions should have "the equivalent of a normal school or college education." When Ruth Barber arrived at Allison-James School in 1916, she reported that most of the teachers were college graduates. Six of the seven teachers at New Jersey Academy for the academic year 1919–20 had college diplomas and two had completed master's degrees. In 1920 the woman's board implemented a leave-of-absence policy to enable teachers to further their educations. The following school year six Presbyterian mission teachers took advantage of this policy, including three who attended Columbia University's Teachers College.[31]

With guidance from the professional educators who served as the home board's superintendents of schools during this period, the boarding school faculties sought to improve the quality of their offerings. Each school, for example, devised a course of study that followed general board guidelines while allowing for its own circumstances. In 1916 a candidate for the position of superintendent of schools for the state of New Mexico expressed hope that "the state course of study would soon be as thorough" as that of the Presbyterian schools.[32]

Academic work, however, was never an end in itself in the mission schools. By involving students in literary societies, dramatic productions, and the publication of school newspapers, for example, teachers stressed the practical applications of the academic skills that they taught. More significantly, however, Presbyterian educators emphasized that traditional literary education represented only one facet of the many-sided programs of their boarding schools. In accord with the prevailing ideals of progressive education, the Presbyterian schools sought to offer an education that was "vitally related to real life."[33]

While the new boarding schools retained many distinctive characteristics of the earlier schools, missionaries adjusted these to meet new needs and to fit the progressive ideals. Religious instruction, for example, remained an important element in boarding school life. Students enrolled in Bible courses, memorized verses of scripture, attended regular Sabbath services, and participated in Gospel Teams and Christian Endeavor societies. Each school designated a time every year for special evangelistic services. But while school officials usually reported on the number of conversions from these activities, they were quick to add that "there was no compulsion at all." Moreover, mission teachers in the early twentieth century showed greater sensitivity to the religious orientations that so many of their pupils had inherited. For example, following two weeks of evangelical services at Menaul School in 1909, the school's superintendent reported that the evangelist (a native New Mexican) had "preached the truth in a very convincing and forcible way" but had said nothing "that would cause the young men of the Romanist faith to be offended." Teachers in the Utah schools similarly recognized that the surest way to lose influence on Mormon students was to directly attack their religion.[34]

Like many mainstream Protestants of the era, Presbyterian mission school teachers emphasized the practical application of the religion that they offered to their pupils. Upon the encouragement of their teachers, boarding school students participated in such activities as the temperance crusade and extension work in communities surrounding their schools. These activities, along with the more formal religious experiences of teaching Sunday schools in the community and leading religious services on campus, were intended "to give [the students] a definite idea of Christian service . . . so that when they go out [from the school] they may be better fitted to help their people."[35]

The applied Christianity taught in the mission boarding schools and character building that progressive educators of the era so strongly promoted were virtually indistinguishable. Indeed, a New Mexico teacher commented that one of the most important functions of the mission schools was "to develop and train character." Mission teachers also identified character closely with responsible citizenship in the American democratic system. Toward this end the schools promoted patriotism and encouraged participation in student governments that taught responsibilities of voting and office holding. Furthermore, the New Mexico and Indian schools required students to speak English and used a variety of incentives, including both punishment and rewards, to assure compliance with this policy.[36]

The traditional Presbyterian emphasis on the importance of work and the dignity of labor found its counterpart in the early twentieth century in the industrial education then being promoted by progressive educators. Since the establishment of the earliest Presbyterian schools in the Southwest, mission pupils had worked as a means to keep down costs and learn new skills and work habits. In the second decade of the twentieth century, however, mission officials called for more systematic vocational training that would enable students "to earn a living in their own communities." The boarding schools with their larger enrollments, better facilities, and twenty-four-hour-a-day programs proved well suited for such pursuits. Large farms at Tucson Indian Training School and Menaul School provided opportunities to teach boys about modern farm machinery and improved seeds, produce, and strains of livestock. All of the schools added new academic offerings in domestic science, agriculture, carpentry, and commercial arts to complement and reinforce what students learned in their work assignments. Presbyterians, however, did not embrace vocational training as an end in itself, and mission officials were adamant that it not supplant the cultural and spiritual emphases that were the other two essential elements in their "important three-sided work." Above all else, requiring students to perform regular work duties enhanced community spirit and taught students responsibility, self-reliance, and leadership skills, as it reduced the costs of their educations.[37]

Another significant innovation of the new boarding schools was increased emphasis on athletics and physical culture. This, of course, followed developments in the broader American society. All of the schools fielded athletic teams that competed with a variety of opponents in the major sports. Mission teachers, however, were careful to keep sports in a proper perspective. Along with team sports, they encouraged individual forms of recreation, including tennis, swimming, and hiking. Moreover, they related these activities to broader educational objectives. The principal of Logan Academy commented in 1919: "Self-activity in entertainment and outdoor jaunts is encouraged with the definite purpose of so filling the girls lives with wholesome interest that they shall not have time for folly." Three years later, the superintendent at Menaul School suggested that athletics and recreation helped teach "proper physical care" and "such moral lessons as fair play and self-control."[38]

Presbyterian mission schools in the Southwest had always sought to teach cleanliness and personal hygiene. In the late teens, however, the woman's board went a step further. Citing "the decay of the American family," it directed the principals of its schools to devise separate courses for boys and girls to teach them "worthy ideals of personal and family life." Without mentioning the word *sex,* a veteran mission teacher who oversaw the development of these programs commented: "Whether or not we approve of it, we must recognize that the silence is broken and children and young people must now be given wise scientific instruction if they are to be saved from forces militating against their welfare for time and eternity." By 1921 she reported that nearly all of the schools had introduced programs for female students for this purpose. At Tucson Indian Training School, for example, teachers and girls found time to discuss "the mysteries of life and duties of motherhood" during sewing class. At New Jersey Academy all freshmen girls enrolled in a year-long biology course that took them from a general study of living things to laboratory examination of "the manner of birth" of a variety of plants and animals. The course culminated with discussion of "the mysteries of [the girls'] own lives" that showed them "the necessity for moral purity."[39]

Even as the Woman's Board of Home Missions sought to strengthen the programs in each of its boarding schools, it recognized that physical improvements at the schools were also needed. Some facilities were renovated, and a few new buildings were raised during the second decade of the twentieth century. American involvement in World War I, however, interrupted these developments. In the immediate postwar euphoria, the women announced that a $250,000 New Era Fund had been established for purposes of improving the physical plants at its scattered network of schools. A significant part of this money was spent at the southwestern boarding schools to renovate old structures and erect new administration-classroom buildings, dormitories, gymnasiums, and homes for teachers.[40]

While the boarding high school was the centerpiece of the new Presbyterian strategy in the Southwest, the second decade of the twentieth century saw Presbyterians pursue several other new mission endeavors in the region. One of these, a more concerted effort to prepare native church leaders, resulted from both the successes and shortcomings of the boarding school programs. On the one hand, the growing number of graduates from the boarding schools convinced mission officials of the need to offer even more advanced work. On the other hand, they worried that many boarding school graduates were not "fully useful for Christian ministry." Consequently, many Presbyterians in the Southwest believed their church should do something to prepare these young people for Christian service "before the church [lost] its grasp on them."[41] Although the financially pressed home board was reluctant to endorse such programs, local Presbyterians in each of the three fields made halting progress toward establishing several post-secondary programs.

Presbyterians in Utah had talked of the need for a college as a capstone to their educational work since the 1880s. However, Sheldon Jackson College, established in 1895, was beset by serious financial problems, competition with other Protestant denominations, and confusion about the college's relationship with the mission boards. During the five years that the college conducted classes (1897–1902), enrollments were small, and only three students completed the college course of study. The change in name to Westminster College in 1902 did little to alter the situation. For another decade presidents of the school came and went with regularity, and the college existed in name only.[42]

The arrival of Hebert W. Reherd as president in 1913 finally brought stability to Westminster. Less than a month after assuming his position, Reherd issued a bold plan of action. Among other things, it called for the enrollment of a college freshmen class in the fall of 1914, improvement of the physical plant, and accelerated fund-raising efforts. Enrollment increased immediately in both the preparatory (the Collegiate Institute) and junior college divisions. Of the ninety-nine students enrolled at the end of Reherd's first year, twenty were in the junior college. By 1922 the Collegiate Institute had 131 students, and Westminster College had thirty-five.[43]

The most acclaimed development at Westminster, however, came in another area. Since 1911 the college's persistent financial difficulties and the growing spirit of "cooperative Christianity" had convinced Westminster trustees of the desirability of placing their school on an interdenominational basis. Reherd agreed wholeheartedly, and in the early 1920s he proclaimed his school "the most striking example in America of Protestant Christian cooperation in college education." Reherd's efforts to secure significant financial contributions from other major Protestant denominations lagged, but by 1921 eleven of the college's eighteen trustees were members of non-Presbyterian denominations. While the faculty remained predominantly Presbyterian, the student body was diverse. For the school year 1921–22, 25 percent of the 166 pupils were Presbyterian and another 20 percent were affiliated with other Protestant churches. Most notably, only four students were identified as Mormon. However, the remainder of the student body (eighty-seven or 52 percent of the total enrollment) had no church affiliation, which (in most cases) meant they were from apostate Mormon families.[44] Like the academies in Mt. Pleasant and Logan, Westminster College increasingly assumed the role of a Gentile island in a Mormon sea. As heirs to an effort that had originally sought to win converts from Mormon heresy, many Presbyterian educators in Utah learned by the 1920s to accept their minority status within the state's predominantly Mormon society.

Initial efforts to establish a training school for native evangelists in the New Mexico field suffered many of the same difficulties as the early efforts to establish a college in Utah. After several efforts toward this end proved less than satisfactory in the 1890s, Presbyterians in 1901 opened the Albuquerque Training School in conjunction with Menaul School. Under the direction of the Reverend Henry C. Thompson, a veteran missionary of twenty years in Mexico, the school was intended "not [as] a theological seminary [but as] a training school for native evangelists." Thompson stressed theory and practice, and his students conducted Sunday schools and preaching services at surrounding churches. Nine students (seven New Mexicans and two Indians) enrolled during the first year. But in spite of Thompson's grand vision for his work, subsequent enrollments never equalled that of the first year. In 1907 the financially strained home board discontinued the program.[45]

New Mexico Presbyterians protested the closing of the Albuquerque Training School, and in 1911 the home board tentatively approved reinitiating that program. After two years' delay, the Reverend Lansing Bloom opened classes at Albuquerque's Spanish Presbyterian Church in October 1913. Only three students enrolled. More seriously, a "lack of harmony" plagued the school. The school's synod-appointed directors disagreed among themselves and did not meet regularly. The synod, in turn, charged the home board with "lack of moral support." Finally, the school's non-seminary status disqualified its students from receiving financial support from established Presbyterian funds for ministerial candidates. Perhaps most disappointing of all was the failure of Menaul School graduates to show interest in the program. At that time Menaul had only a few high school graduates each year, and those students who wanted to continue their educations apparently preferred to pursue regular college-level work at the state university or at Presbyterian-related colleges in the East. The problem-plagued training school did not reopen for a second year, and subsequent pleas to reinstitute a school for native church leaders fell on deaf ears. Several Menaul School graduates, however, enrolled in Presbyterian seminaries after completing regular college programs. By the early 1920s a number of these young native ministers had returned to New Mexico to serve their own people.[46]

Friends of Indian missions also stressed the importance of preparing native church leaders. In 1912 the home board assumed responsibility for an interdenominational Bible Training School at Tochalco, Arizona, on the Navajo reservation. When fire destroyed the facilities of that school in 1920, the board transferred its program and director, the Reverend Fred Mitchell, to Ganado, where so much of the Presbyterian work among the Navajos had been consolidated. Thereafter, Mitchell's Bible school became an important part of the Ganado program, and its students and graduates performed evangelistic work throughout the reservation. Eventually, when the Kirkwood Memorial School offered more advanced levels of work, it absorbed the former training school.[47]

In 1911 Presbyterians established a similar school in conjunction with the Tucson Indian Training School. The new school took the name Charles H. Cook Bible School in honor of the missionary who spent forty-three years among the Pimas and Papagos. After two years in Tucson, Cook School moved to Phoenix to be nearer the center of southern Arizona's Indian population. During the first year in Phoenix, the school enrolled thirteen men and seven women (all of whom were wives of male students). The school operated on a self-support plan. In the mornings male students pursued courses in English, Bible, church history and government, and elementary theology; afternoons and Saturdays they worked at odd jobs in the community to help cover their personal expenses. Wives of Cook students received instruction several afternoons each week. On Sundays students taught church school classes and worked with Y.M.C.A. groups at the nearby government Indian school and preached and visited at Indian churches on the Pima reservation. Each school year concluded with a three-week field course during which students applied what they learned in the school room at isolated locations on the Pima and Papago reservations. In 1919 the school broadened its curriculum to include instruction in more practical areas, including music, hygiene, sanitation, and domestic science. By the completion of the ninth year, forty-six students (mostly Pimas but also Papagos, Mohaves, Apaches, Navajos, and Maricopas) had enrolled at Cook Bible School. Eighteen pupils had completed the three-year training program, and all of them (plus several who did not graduate) were commissioned as salaried workers of the Presbyterian church.[48]

Medical missions and community work were other essential elements in the new Presbyterian strategy for the Southwest. Since the 1870s missionaries had provided health care and a variety of social services to the native peoples of the Southwest. These efforts, however, were largely spontaneous. Furthermore, although home mission officials approved and, indeed, urged missionaries to engage in this work, it was not a central part of the official mission policy. The success of these endeavors (or lack thereof) depended largely on the personality and perseverance of the individual missionary. By the progressive years of the early twentieth century, however, such piecemeal efforts were deemed inadequate. The prevailing emphasis on the social gospel in the mainline Protestant churches (and in Charles Thompson's Presbyterian Board of Home Missions in particular) called for a more thorough and systematic Presbyterian response to the physical and social needs of the native southwesterners.

The Presbyterians who reinitiated missions among the Navajos in the first decade of the twentieth century considered medical work essential to the success of that venture. Several medical doctors served at the Jewett, New Mexico, station before its consolidation with the work at Ganado in 1912, and from the time the Reverend Charles Bierkemper opened the latter station in 1901, he pleaded with board officials to assign a doctor to join him. In 1906 the board finally complied, but the doctor who was appointed remained only briefly. Two years later Dr. James Kennedy arrived at Ganado. The Navajos called Kennedy "the walking doctor" because of his willingness to make house calls to isolated hogans throughout the vast Navajo country. Under Kennedy's direction the home board constructed a twelve-bed hospital at Ganado in 1912. In the 1920s, in accord with the board's decision to concentrate its Navajo work at Ganado, the medical work increased greatly, and in 1930 Presbyterians, with support from the Russell Sage Foundation, constructed a seventy-five-bed hospital there. Even the commissioner of Indian affairs, John Collier, who rarely had kind words for missionaries, reported that it was "the best hospital in the Indian Southwest."[49]

During this same period Presbyterians also attempted to systematize their medical work in northern New Mexico. Several tours of the region convinced mission officials that such was sorely needed and that it would provide another avenue, in addition to the schools, for reaching native New Mexicans. In 1915 the home board constructed a two-bed hospital in Embudo, where a nurse had already been employed for several years. Later the same year Dr. Horace Taylor, a veteran medical missionary who had served many years in Puerto Rico, opened the Rincones Medical Center, out of which he served a vast area on the western slope of the Sangre de Cristos from Espanola to Taos. After several setbacks the medical missions in northern New Mexico expanded in the 1920s, as Presbyterian doctors and nurses provided health care to many of the isolated plazas that mission schools had served for many years.[50]

Like the medical missions, the community work that mission officials called for in the years after 1910 was not really so new. But it did place work that missionaries had performed spontaneously for many years on a more systematic basis. A variety of activities were initiated under this rubric, including mother's clubs, literary societies, Bible study groups, 4-H clubs, child care, and recreation for children. A wide array of classes for adults were also offered, including first aid, cooking, sewing, housekeeping, hygiene, gardening, and animal husbandry. While community work was initiated in all three of the southwestern fields, it was most strongly emphasized in areas where Presbyterian day schools were being closed. Mission officials stressed that this new type of mission was proof that their church was not abandoning fields that had long been the objects of its concern.[51]

No less than the kind acts of earlier generations of missionaries, the medical missions and community work won many friends for the Presbyterian cause, if not so often for Presbyterianism. This work helped build bridges between natives and newcomers that more purely evangelical activities and, indeed, even the school work could not have created. Presbyterian medical missions proved particularly effective in winning native trust and friendship. Several years after medical work was formally initiated in northern New Mexico, the annual report of the woman's board reported that many Catholic families that did not patronize mission schools would not hesitate to call on a Presbyterian nurse or doctor. A report from Ganado in 1921 told of an old Navajo man who had long resisted the white man's medicine and religion. After the recovery of his ill child following surgery at the Ganado hospital, however, the man "at least converted to the medical work."[52]

The community work was equally effective in fostering more cordial relations between missionaries and the native southwesterners and eroding negative stereotypes. In 1924 missionaries at Chimayo, New Mexico, reported that the people of nearby Cordova invited them to extend their work to that community. Consequently, the missionaries and members of their Chimayo Christian Endeavor Society helped organize a Sunday School that met in a private residence in Cordova. Although the village had only five Protestant residents, average attendance in the Sunday School was forty-seven, and the superintendent for the Presbyterian-sponsored endeavor was Roman Catholic! Similarly, community work in Utah fostered more cordial relationships with Mormons. In 1921 the woman's board reported that in Utah "the spirit of meeting community needs has broken down great walls of prejudice which kept scores of people from our hall in the past." Later in the same year a veteran Utah missionary of thirty-seven years (the last eleven as a community worker) suggested that community work was simply "neighborliness." "And," she concluded, "there are many who need it."[53]

The cordial interaction and extended contact with native southwesterners that resulted from these new areas of mission endeavor left its mark on Presbyterian missionaries. To be sure, negative stereotypes persisted in the mission literature, and hostility between missionary and native southwesterner did not disappear completely. But even the most negative Presbyterian descriptions of Indians, New Mexicans, and Mormons in the early twentieth century were mild compared to the images of those peoples that the Presbyterians who pioneered in the Southwest a half century earlier had presented. In the first two decades of the 1900s missionaries from all three southwestern fields increasingly commented on positive traits of the peoples among whom they labored: Mormon loyalty to home, family, and church; Indian honesty and simplicity; and the pride, independence, courtesy, and "splendid character" of the New Mexican. Again a few missionaries even suggested that their own people would do well to emulate many of the traits of the southwestern peoples.[54]

Like the small mission day schools that they were intended to replace, Presbyterian boarding and training schools and medical and community missions in the Southwest filled significant voids and helped bring the distinctive peoples of that long-isolated region into contact with the broader American society. As such, these new mission endeavors were very much in accord with the goals that had led the Presbyterian Church, U.S.A., to initiate missions in the Southwest. As arenas for relatively cordial ethnocultural interaction, however, the new mission endeavors—much like the earlier mission schools—unconsciously fostered results that would have surprised the generation that planted Presbyterian seeds in the Southwest a half century earlier.

Notes

1. Comments on expanded Presbyterian efforts are abundant. See, for example, George McAfee, "A Forward Movement in the Mission Fields," *HMM* 17 (January 1903): 62; "The Navajo Field," *La Aurora* 6 (April 15, 1905): 8; Warner, "Protestant Missionary Activity among the Navajo, 1852–1912" (Ph.D. diss., University of New Mexico, 1978), 339–45, 369–77; Report of Superintendent of School Work to Board of Home Missions, 1902, 6; 104th Annual Report, Board of Home Missions, 1906, 72.

2. Howard R. Lamar, *The Far Southwest, 1846–1912: A Territorial History* (New York: W. W. Norton, 1970), provides an informative overview of developments in the Southwest during this period. Also see Gerald D. Nash, *The American West in the Twentieth Century: A Short History of an Urban Oasis* (Albuquerque: University of New Mexico Press, 1977), 11–16.

3. Presbyterian comments on improvements in Utah public education are abundant. See, for example, "Freshly Gathered Items — Mormon Field," *HMM* 20 (October 1906): 307; "Introducing Our Missionaries," *HMM* 22 (August 1908): 240; 107th Annual Report, Board of Home Missions, 1909, 63; Report of Superintendent of School Work to Board of Home Missions, 1909, 13.

4. The November 1909 issue of *HMM* (vol. 24) carried a number of articles that commented on the poor state of public education in New Mexico. See, for example, L. C. Galbraith, "Opportunities for Mexicans," 5; Dora M. Fish, "Embudo Plaza," 13; "The Why of Mission Schools in New Mexico," 15. Also see Tom

Wiley, *Politics and Purse Strings in New Mexico's Public Schools* (Albuquerque: University of New Mexico Press, 1965), 35–36.

5. Margaret Connell Szasz, *Education and the American Indian: The Road to Self-Determination since 1928* (Albuquerque: University of New Mexico Press, 1977), 11–12. Even though the federal effort in Indian education was expanding, it was still inadequate in the Southwest; hence it posed little immediate threat to Presbyterian schools for Indians.

6. Comments on the consolidation of several of the smaller New Mexico schools are found in Dr. David R. Boyd to Mr. M. D. J. Sanchez, August 18, 1910, PHS, Missions in the Southwest: Selected Correspondence and Reports. Also see George McAfee, *Home Missions among the Mexicans* (New York: Woman's Board of Home Missions, 1912), 8. The closing of schools in Utah is reported in 107th Annual Report, Board of Home Missions. 1909, 63.

7. Boyd and Brackenridge, *Presbyterian Women in America*, 49. James's personal commitment to the southwestern schools is evident in "Forecast and Rally," *HMM* 18 (September 1904): 265. Announcement of Craig's resignation is made in "Administrative Changes," *HMM* 23 (October 1909): 278–79.

8. Charles L. Thompson, *The Soul of America: The Contribution of Presbyterian Home Missions* (New York: Flemming H. Revell Co., 1919), 150, quoted in Robert Handy, "Charles L. Thompson: Presbyterian Architect of Cooperative Protestantism," *Journal of Presbyterian Historical Society* 33 (December 1955): 219. Handy uses the terms *new* and *old* home missions to make the distinctions presented here. Other historians have commented on this change in missions strategy. See, for example, Paul A. Varg, "Motives in Protestant Missions, 1890–1917," *Church History* 23 (March 1954): 68–82; Henry Warner Bowden, "An Overview of Cultural Factors in the American Protestant Enterprise," in Beaver, *American Missions in Bicentennial Perspective*, 41–62; Charles W. Forman, "A History of Foreign Mission Theory in America," in ibid., 69–95.

9. Bennett played a crucial role in the developments that led to the incorporation of the Woman's Board of Home Missions as an independent agency. Boyd and Brackenridge, *Presbyterian Women in America*, and Hayes, *Daughters of Dorcas*, devote attention to her work in the broader context of the history of Presbyterian women. Also see "M. Katherine Bennett," *Notable American Women*, 3 vols. (Cambridge: Harvard University Press, 1971), 1:134. Boyd and Allaben were both professional educators who had served as college presidents. As superintendents of schools for the home board, they strove to put the school work on a more efficient and systematic basis. See "Administrative Changes," *HMM* 23 (October 1909): 278–79; *HMM* 26 (August 1912): 246.

10. R. Pierce Beaver, "Missionary Motivation through Three Centuries," in *Reinterpretation of American Church History*, ed. Jerald C. Brauer (Chicago: University of Chicago Press, 1968), 131. This new departure, however, was not so radical as it might first appear. Presbyterian missionaries had always been concerned about the physical needs of the native southwesterners. Similarly, even though the new missionaries spoke less frequently about the eternal fate of Indians, New Mexicans, and Mormons, they were nonetheless concerned about the spiritual lives of these peoples.

11. Report of Superintendent of School Work to Board of Home Missions, 1914, 10. Similar thoughts are expressed in *HMM* 25 (November 1910): 1, and Edward P. Childs, "A Business Proposition," *HMM* 25 (March 1911): 103.

12. Address of Dr. Charles L. Thompson to Woman's Board of Home Missions, May 18, 1911, PHS, RG 105, Box 5, F-6; M. Katherine Bennett, "Annual Address of the President," *HMM* 26 (July 1912): 221-22.

13. Address by Dr. Charles L. Thompson to Annual Meeting of Woman's Board of Home Missions, May 18, 1911, PHS, RG 105, Box 5, F-6; M. Katherine Bennett, "Annual Address of the President," *HMM* 26 (July 1912): 221-22.

14. 105th Annual Report, Board of Home Missions, 1907, 33; *HMM* 21 (June 1907): 170. Mary H. Martin of New Jersey Academy in Logan, Utah, commented on improved Mormon-Gentile relations during World War I in "From the Mormon Front," *HMM* 32 (July 1918): 200-201. Cooperation in support of the war led Mormon and Gentile, she wrote, "to recognize each other's worth."

15. Minutes of Church Extension Committee, Synod of Utah, June 28, 1915, PHS, RG 195, Box 1, F-5. For a brief time in the early 1920s Presbyterian missionaries helped conduct a school in the former mission school building at Ferron, Utah, with approval of the Woman's Board of Home Missions. Financial support, however, came from the community rather than from Presbyterian mission funds. See "A Unique Work," *HMM* 37 (December 1922): 42.

16. David Boyd, School Department Report, 1909, PHS, RG 104, Box 1, F-12, comments on the inadequacy of New Mexico's public schools. See also Galbraith, "Opportunities for Mexicans," 5; Fish, "Embudo Plaza," 13; "The 'Why' of Mission Schools in New Mexico," 15; Report of Superintendent of School Work to Board of Home Missions, 1913, 41-42.

17. Report of Superintendent of School Work to Board of Home Missions, 1914, 10. Comments on the two interdenominational conferences are found in Marshall C. Allaben, "Conference of Workers among Spanish-Americans," *HMM* 28 (November 1913): 14; M. Katherine Bennett, "The Interdenominational Spanish Council," *HMM* 33 (May 1919).

18. Alice Blake, "New Outlook from an Old Field," *HMM* 34 (May 1920): 165; Harriet Elliot, "Truchas in the Mountains," *HMM* 33 (May 1918): 162.

19. Comments on the difficulties at the Ganado day school are found in Charles H. Bierkemper to Miss Ella A. Boole, July 16, 1906, PHS, RG 51, Box 3, F-1, and August 1, 1906, F-3. Navajo agent Peter Paquette commented on the same problems in a letter to the commissioner of Indian affairs, March 22, 1910, NA, RG 75, Central Classified Files: 11792-1910 (Navajo), File 806. Information sheets on the southern Arizona day schools are included in the Dick Smith Collection, Arizona Room, Arizona State University Library. Also see John M. Hamilton, "History of Presbyterian Work among the Pimas and Papagos of Arizona" (M.A. thesis, University of Arizona, 1948), 73-75, 141-43.

20. For descriptions of the new progressive education, see Timothy L. Smith, "Progressivism and Education, 1880-1900," *Harvard Educational Review* 31 (Summer 1961): 168-93; Lawrence A. Cremin, *The Transformation of the School: Progressivism in American Education, 1876-1957* (New York: Alfred A. Knopf,

1961). The Allaben quote is from the Report of Superintendent of School Work to Board of Home Missions, 1913, 54–55.

21. Report of Superintendent of School Work to Board of Home Missions, 1909, 13.

22. The Logan school assumed this name in 1890, when the women of the Synodical of New Jersey made a substantial contribution toward the establishment of a new campus. In 1925 it changed names again and became simply Logan Academy (Harold S. Loo, "History of New Jersey–Logan Academy," 20, 60).

23. 11th Annual Report, Board of Home Missions, 1913, 72–73; David R. Boyd, "Our Work in Utah," *HMM* 25 (October 1911): 287–88; M. Katherine Bennett, "Solving Problems in Utah," *HMM* 26 (October 1912): 299–301; Wankier, "History of Presbyterian Schools in Utah," 27–28, 71, 73–74, 102–4; Loo, "History of New Jersey–Logan Academy," 39–41.

24. Reports of the Superintendent of Schools to the Board of Home Missions, 1913, 54–55, 1914, 32, 44; 38th and 41st Annual Reports, Woman's Board of Home Missions, 1917, 1920, 41; Herbert W. Reherd, "The Future of Church Educational Work in Utah," *HMM* 28 (October 1914): 282–83; Wankier, "History of Presbyterian Schools in Utah," 27, 100–105; Loo, "History of New Jersey–Logan Academy," 39–41.

25. Marshall Allaben, "The Challenge in Utah," *HMM* 33 (December 1918): 26–29.

26. Barber and Agnew, *Sowers Went Forth,* 84–85; Buck, "An Inquiry into the History of Presbyterian Educational Missions in New Mexico," 43–44; J. C. Ross, "Menaul School," *La Aurora* 13 (June 15, 1914). Donaldson remained as superintendent at Menaul until 1954.

27. 112th Annual Report, Board of Home Missions, 1914, 79; Olinda A. Meeker, "The Evolution of Allison-James School," *HMM* 31 (November 1916): 5–6; Barber and Agnew, *Sowers Went Forth,* 85–86, 93. Also see the following annual reports of the Woman's Board of Home Missions: 40th, 1919, 35–36; 41st, 1920, 39; 42d, 1921, 40. "History of Allison-James School," 1935, PHS, RG 101, Box 9, F-2. Miss Barber served at Allison-James until 1934, when she became principal at Menaul School, a position she held until 1959.

28. Hamilton, "A History of Presbyterian Work among the Pima and Papago Indians of Arizona," 167–79; "Outline of Tucson Indian Training School Development," PHS, RG 103, Box 1, F-2; 111th Annual Report, Board of Home Missions, 1912, 71.

29. Hamilton, "A History of Presbyterian Work among the Pima and Papago Indians of Arizona," 181–89; M. L. Girton to Marshall Allaben, January 28, 1916, Records of Tucson Indian Training School, Arizona Historical Society; 43d Annual Report, Woman's Board of Home Missions, 1921, 22. M. L. Girton remained as superintendent of the Tucson school until 1941.

30. For a general overview of these developments, see Warner, "Protestant Missionary Work with Navajo Indians, 1846–1912" (Ph.D. diss., University of New Mexico, 1977), 339–45, 369–77; Edgar W. Moore, "The Bierkempers, Navajos, and the Ganado Presbyterian Mission," *American Presbyterians* 64 (Summer 1986):

125-36; "Fifty Years of Serving the Master at Ganado," *Ganado News Bulletin* 2 (June 1951): 1-5. Firsthand accounts of the difficulties that plagued the early work at Ganado and Jewett are found in Charles H. Bierkemper to Miss Ella A. Boole, July 16, 1906, PHS, RG 51, Box 3, F-1; *HMM* 26 (February 1912): 81. The Report of the Superintendent of School Work to the Board of Home Missions, 1914, 6, and *HMM* 28 (May 1914): 169, comment on the consolidation of the work at Ganado in 1914. Comments on the work after that time are found in 113th Annual Report, Board of Home Missions, 1915, 118; 41st Annual Report, Woman's Board of Home Missions, 1920, 31; *HMM* 35 (February 1921): 86; Report of Ganado Mission School by E. H. Howard, Supervisor of Indian Schools, April 29, 1924, NA, RG 75, Central Classified Files, 42513-1924 Navajo, File 806.

31. Reports of Superintendent of School Work, 1913, 65, 1914, 26; Ruth Barber to Lois Huebert, July 22, 1961, quoted in Huebert, "A History of Presbyterian Church Schools in New Mexico" (M.A. thesis, University of New Mexico, 1962), 62; Woo, "A History of New Jersey-Logan Academy," 49; Annual Reports, Woman's Board of Home Missions (1921), 31, (1922), 2.

32. Ralph McConnell, "Latest News from Our Boarding School for Mexican Boys," *HMM* 31 (November 1916): 24. Comments on planning and upgrading the academic programs in the mission schools are found in 112th Annual Report, Board of Home Missions, 1914, 22-23; M. L. Girton to Marshall Allaben, January 28, 1916, Records of Tucson Indian Training School; 45th Annual Report, Woman's Board of Home Missions, 1924, 23.

33. Rachel L. Wood, "Varied Activities at Menaul: Literary Life," *HMM* 35 (May 1921): 158; Charles L. Johns, "The Growth of Wasatch Academy," *HMM* 37 (December 1923): 34-36; "Progress at New Jersey Academy," *HMM* 28 (October 1914): 291.

34. Ruth K. Barber, "The Girlhood of New Mexico," *HMM* 35 (May 1921): 156; "Good News from Allison School," *La Aurora* 6 (April 1, 1905); M. L. Girton, "An Indian Christian Endeavor Society and Its Influence," *HMM* 31 (August 1917): 242; W. W. McKirahan, "The Place of Wasatch Academy as a Christian Agency," *HMM* 30 (October 1916): 294-97. Ross's comments about the 1909 services at Menaul are found in "Glad Words from Menaul School," *La Aurora* (March 1, 1909). Calls for more subtle approaches in dealing with Mormonism are found in Report of Superintendent of School Work to Board of Home Missions, 1913, 43; 118th Annual Report, Board of Home Missions, 1920, 38.

35. A. V. Lucero, "A Former State Senator Measures Results," *HMM* 34 (May 1920): 149; "Making Missionaries in Mission Schools," *HMM* 36 (August 1922): 230; Harper C. Donaldson, "The Life Service Band," *HMM* 37 (May 1923): 149-50.

36. L. C. Galbraith, "Opportunities for Mexicans," *HMM* 24 (November 1909): 6; Harper Donaldson, "Varied Activities at Menaul: Development of Leadership," *HMM* 35 (May 1921): 157; 42d Annual Report, Woman's Board of Home Missions, 1921, 27-33. The euphoria of the World War I years proved particularly conducive to the promotion of patriotism in the boarding schools. See the annual reports of the woman's board, 1918, 25; 1919, 27. Comments on the English-only policy in

the New Mexican and Indian schools are found in *Glimpses of Allison-James School for Mexican Girls at Santa Fe, New Mexico,* 1915, PHS, RG 101, Box 9, F-2; Esther Buxton, "Our Southwestern Mountaineers," *HMM* 32 (November 1917): 8; M. L. Girton, "Scholarship News," January 14, 1919, Records of Tucson Indian Training School.

37. Accounts of student work and industrial training at the boarding schools abound in *HMM* and other missionary literature of the era. See, for example, Report of Superintendent of Schools to Board of Home Missions, 1913, 38; Edna A. Bright, "The School a Factor in Home-Making," and Charles Johns, "A Sturdy Presbyterian Institution: Wasatch Academy," *HMM* 27 (October 1913): 282–83, 284–86; "Progress at New Jersey Academy," *HMM* 28 (October 1914): 291; M. L. Girton, "Glimpses of Our Work among Pimas and Papagos," *HMM* 33 (February 1919): 82; M. Frances Robe, "Varied Activities at Menaul: Dormitory Life," *HMM* 35 (May 1921): 157–58; 42d Annual Report, Woman's Board of Home Missions (1921); M. L. Girton, "Tucson Progress All Along the Line," 38 (February 1924): 80–81.

38. *Glimpses of Allison-James School for Mexican Girls at Santa Fe, New Mexico*; M. L. Girton, "Scholarship Letter," February 21, 1918, Records of Tucson Indian Training School; Mary H. Martin, "A Chat about Logan Academy," *HMM* 33 (December 1918): 44; Harper C. Donaldson, "Varied Activities at Menaul," 35 (May 1921): 158.

39. Florence Stephenson, "Social Hygiene in Our Schools," *HMM* 35 (October 1921): 247–48; article from Tucson Indian Training School for *Wireless Message* (January 14, 1918), Records of Tucson Indian Training School; Bessie L. Coat, "Glimpse of New Jersey Academy," *HMM* 31 (November 1917): 290. Missionary reports offer little indication that similar programs were devised for male students.

40. 41st Annual Report, Woman's Board of Home Missions, 1921, 38–39; "Building Progress," *HMM* 36 (July 1922): 204–5; 45th Annual Report, Woman's Board of Home Missions, 1924, 18.

41. The home board expressed these concerns in its 118th Annual Report, 1920, 6. At that time it was specifically concerned about the need for such a program in New Mexico.

42. Wankier, "A History of Presbyterian Schools in Utah," 52–65; Emil Nyman, "A History of Westminster College: The McNiece Period, 1875–1913," Westminster College Archives. Nyman reports that the college had three graduates; Wankier suggests, however, that there was only one.

43. Wankier, "A History of Presbyterian Schools in Utah," 78–81. Reherd remained as president of Westminster College until 1939. In 1944 the college discontinued its preparatory department and added a full four-year college program.

44. Firsthand accounts of the interdenominationalizing of Westminster College are found in Rodney W. Roundy, "Cooperation in Educational Work in Utah," *HMM* 36 (December 1922): 40; Dr. Robert Kelly, *Cooperation in Education in Utah: Report on Westminster College of Salt lake City* (New York: Home Missions Council, 1922). The statistics cited in this paragraph are from Kelly, 14–15.

45. A brief overview of earlier leadership training programs in the New Mex-

ican field is in chap. 6 of this study. Minutes, Synod of New Mexico, October 4–9, 1901, 41, October 6-9, 1902, 43; 100th Annual Report, Board of Home Missions, 1902, 40, 240. Thompson frequently reported on the work of his school. See, for example, "The Training Class for Preachers," *HMM* 17 (November 1902): 13–14; "The Albuquerque Training Class," *HMM* 19 (November 1904): 7–9. The decision to close the school is explained in "Report of the Synodical Missionary," *La Aurora* 8 (November 15, 1907); "Dr. Thompson Goes to New York," *La Aurora* 9 (November 15, 1908). Also see Barber and Agnew, *Sowers Went Forth,* 82–84.

46. For accounts of the effort to reopen the training program and of the problems that beset the school that opened in 1913, see the following minutes of the Synod of New Mexico, September 24–28, 1908, 39; October 19–23, 1911, 38; September 25–28, 1913, 29–31; September 24–28, 1914, 33. Olinda Meeker reported that Menaul graduates had enrolled in Princeton, the University of Chicago, Maryville and Tusculum Colleges (Tennessee), Hanover College (Indiana), Emporia College (Kansas), and Park College (Missouri) ("Some of the Fruits," *HMM* 28 [January 1914]: 62). Appeals for reopening another school for native leaders were made in 118th Annual Report, Board of Home Missions, 1920, 46; Rodney Roundy, "Getting Together in the Southwest," *HMM* 35 (May 1921): 150. Roundy called Presbyterians to support an interdenominational training school.

47. The transfer of Mitchell and his training school to Ganado is recounted in *HMM* 35 (February 1921): 86. Two informative firsthand accounts of the work of the Ganado Bible School are E. A. Trevor, "Girl of Grey Mesa Country," and Mitchell, "Training Indians for the Leadership of Their Own People," *HMM* 37 (February 1923): 80–81, 88–89. Also see Historical Data Sheet on Ganado Mission, Richard K. Smith Collection, Arizona Room, Arizona State University Library.

48. The development of Cook Bible School is recounted in the minutes of the Synod of Arizona. See, in particular, the minutes for the following meetings: September 1912, 31–32; October 16–20, 1913, 24–26; August 22–25, 1914, 18; June 17–19, 1919, 10–11; July 30–August 4, 1920, 10. For a general account of the school's history, see Hamilton, "A History of Presbyterian Work among the Pima and Papago Indians of Arizona," 95–99.

49. Joseph Poncel, "Presbyterian Educational and Medical Work in Arizona," 1952, PHS, RG 103, Box 1, F-2; Judith R. Johnson, "A Mission to the Navajos," *Menaul Historical Review* 10 (October 1983): 2–3. Collier's comment is recorded in a letter in PHS, RG 101, Box 1, F-9.

50. For an overview of the history of Presbyterian medical missions in northern New Mexico, see chap. 18 of Barber and Agnew, *Sowers Went Forth.* Also see Judith R. Johnson, "A History of Embudo Hospital," *Menaul Historical Review* 10 (June 1983): 2–3; Jake W. Spidle, Jr., *Doctors of Medicine in New Mexico* (Albuquerque: University of New Mexico Press, 1986), 185–200.

51. Sources on community work are abundant. See, for example, the following Annual Reports of the Woman's Board of Home Missions: 41st, 1920, 40; 42d, 1921, 38–40; 45th, 1925, 27. Also see the following articles from *HMM:* "Touching the Problem at Several Points," 35 (May 1921): 160–64; "Our Community Programs in Utah," 38 (December 1923): 42–43. The following articles from *HMM* comment

on extension work: Charles L. Johns, "It Began at Home," 36 (December 1921): 36–37; Edna R. Voss, "Extension Work Tried Out," 35 (October 1921): 252–55.

52. 37th and 42d annual reports, Woman's Board of Home Missions, 1916, 43; 1921, 33.

53. See the following annual reports of the Woman's Board of Home Missions: 45th, 1924, 27–28; 38th, 1917; 42d, 1921, 40. Also see Josie Curtis, "As I Look Back," *HMM* 36 (December 1921): 41.

54. Typical comments on positive Indian traits are found in *HMM* 24 (February 1910): 4; "Latest Indian Books," *HMM* 23 (March 1909): 102. Positive observations about New Mexicans and their culture are found in Prudence M. Clark, "The Fair Land," *HMM* 23 (November 1908); Alice Hyson, "Experiences with Little Mexicans," *HMM* 28 (November 1913): 16–17. Similar views of Mormons are found in "Vesper Services," *HMM* 24 (August 1910): 238; Rev. Josiah McClain, "Three Lessons from Mormonism," *HMM* 24 (October 1910): 283–84; Report of Superintendent of School Work to Board of Home Missions, 1913, 43.

Epilogue

The End of an Era

From the time Presbyterian missionaries first arrived in the Southwest, changing conditions in the region and within the missionaries's own society and church forced them to repeatedly adjust and redesign their mission strategy. The era after the First World War, however, brought changes of unprecedented significance. The 1923 annual report of the woman's board commented that the once-isolated areas that had long been a target of Presbyterian home missions were beset with "restlessness and a spirit of questioning." A host of contributing causes—the recent war, the automobile and other technological advancements, and assumption by state and local governments of responsibility for much of the work that mission agencies had formerly performed—had all created a situation that the secretary of field work, Edna R. Voss, described as "at once a problem and a challenge": "a problem," she suggested, "in that old policies and programs fail to meet the new needs"; "a challenge," she continued, in that where once there was "lethargy if not definite opposition," Presbyterians found an eagerness for "betterment" and change.[1]

Voss followed these general observations with specific proposals for the future conduct of home missions. Regarding the school work, she called for the board to continue to support the remaining day schools and community work, but with the aim of turning responsibility for these efforts over to the local communities as soon as possible. The boarding schools, she advised, should be continued, but with greater emphasis on meeting community needs and nurturing in students a spirit of Christian service toward their own people. This effort, Voss concluded, would require more and better-trained workers, increased financial support, and closer cooperation within the Presbyterian church and with the other churches and public agencies engaged in similar efforts. True to the tradition of earlier mission leaders, Miss Voss was confident that Presbyterians would be equal to the new challenge.

Although the remaining southwestern mission schools in many ways followed Miss Voss's proposed course, over the next several decades even more rapid and dramatic changes in the Southwest and broader American society rendered results that she did not foresee. While Presbyterians had little control over these changes, they were unable to escape them. Like other mainline churchmen, Presbyterians had identified closely with the idealistic and humanitarian goals of progressivism and the World War I crusade to make the world safe for democracy. When these efforts failed to attain their lofty goals, disillusionment ushered in what historian Robert Handy calls the "religious depression of the 1920s."[2] This and the economic depression that followed had ominous consequences for all of the nation's mainline Protestant churches and their mission programs in particular. The Presbyterian Board of National Missions, for example, ran a deficit for nine straight years, from 1924 to 1933. Throughout the remainder of the 1930s and the early 1940s, board revenues remained substantially below what they had been in the early twenties.[3]

While the Great Depression was the major cause for these budget woes, other factors were also at play. Presbyterian women, whose contributions had been so vital to the mission schools, lost much of their earlier enthusiasm for this work. They were particularly disappointed in 1923, when their woman's board was merged with the old home missions board to form the Board of National Missions. Despite the intent of the men who designed the new mission structure "to be generous to the ladies" and attempts by women's leaders to convince their Presbyterian sisters that they should continue to support their old areas of work, enthusiasm for the mission cause diminished. This development, of course, also reflected the general mood change of the era as well as new developments in women's roles that made many younger women less eager than their mothers and grandmothers to support mission work.[4]

These developments had varied impacts on the seventeen Presbyterian schools that remained in operation in the Southwest in 1925 (see table 14 and map 6). On the one hand, loss of enthusiasm and reduced budgets meant hardships that led to the closing of Indian day schools at Topawa (1926) and Stotonic (1932), Arizona. Economic considerations also influenced the board's decision to consolidate several of its boarding schools. In 1934 Logan and Wasatch academies were merged at the Mt. Pleasant, Utah, campus of the latter. In the same year the board also made major changes in the New Mexico field. The programs at Allison-James and Menaul were made coeducational, and the former became a junior high school and the

The End of an Era

Table 14. Presbyterian Schools in the Southwest, 1925

Boarding Schools		
School	Program	Closed
Allison-James (Santa Fe)	Junior-Senior High for girls	1958
Menaul School (Albuquerque)	Junior-Senior High for boys	—
Wasatch Academy (Mt. Pleasant)	Junior-Senior High, coed	—
New Jersey–Logan Academy (Logan)	Junior-Senior High for girls	1934
Tucson Indian Training School (Tucson)	Elementary–Junior High, coed	1959
Kirkwood Memorial School (Ganado)	Elementary–Junior High, coed	1986

Day Schools	
Location	Closed
Chacon	1958
Holman	1958
Ranchos de Taos	1958
Dixon	1958
Chimayo (John Hyson School)	—
Truchas	1959
San Miguel (Papago)	1949
Topawa (Papago)	1926
Stotonic (Pima)	1932

Colleges/Training Schools		
School	Program	Closed
Westmister College	High School, Junior College	—
Cook Bible School	Postsecondary training program for Native American ministers	—

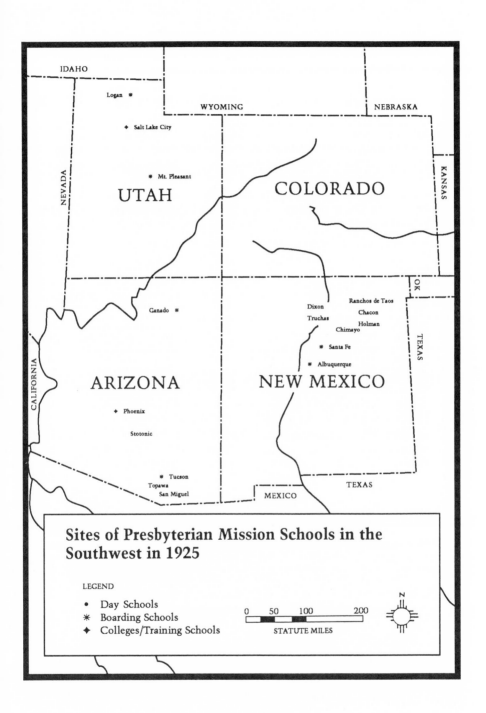

IDAHO

Logan ✳

WYOMING   NEBRASKA

✦ Salt Lake City

NEVADA

✳ Mt. Pleasant

UTAH   COLORADO

KANSAS

Ganado ✳

Dixon   Ranchos de Taos
Truchas   Chacon
         Holman
Chimayo

✳ Santa Fe

✦ Albuquerque

CALIFORNIA

ARIZONA   NEW MEXICO

TEXAS

OK

✦ Phoenix

Stotonic

✳ Tucson
Topawa   TEXAS
San Miguel   MEXICO

Sites of Presbyterian Mission Schools in the Southwest in 1925

LEGEND

• Day Schools
✳ Boarding Schools
✦ Colleges/Training Schools

0   50   100   200

STATUTE MILES

N

latter a three-year high school (tenth through twelfth grades). Menaul graduates also had the opportunity to continue living on campus when they enrolled at the nearby University of New Mexico.[5]

On the other hand, the hard times of the 1930s actually benefited the remaining Presbyterian mission programs in the Southwest in several ways. With financially hard-pressed state and local governments unable to meet the many demands for services, the Presbyterian boarding high schools, day schools and community stations in isolated areas, and hospitals and medical clinics continued to fill a significant void. Secondly, lack of opportunities elsewhere brought to the mission schools a number of talented faculty members who might otherwise never have come to the Southwest (or at least not have remained there). Strong leadership from M. L. Girton at Tucson Indian Training School, Keith Throndson and Ralph Gunn at Wasatch Academy, Harper Donaldson and Ruth Barber at Menaul, and Dr. Clarence Salsbury at Ganado's Kirkwood School and Sage Memorial Hospital enhanced Presbyterian successes during the depression decade. By the mid-1930s all of these schools had accredited high school programs that graduated increasingly larger classes. Similarly, the six day schools that remained in northern New Mexico flourished during these years, in the absence of government-sponsored efforts to improve the quality of life in their isolated communities.[6]

The two Presbyterian-related post-secondary schools in the Southwest, Cook Bible School and Westminster College, experienced greater difficulties during this period. Unlike the other schools, they were no longer directly related to the Board of National Missions. The Synod of Arizona operated Cook School on a shoestring budget until 1939, when the national missions board temporarily assumed responsibility for it. A year later the school changed its name to Cook Christian Training School and came under the auspices of the interdenominational Home Missions Council. Westminster College at this time was theoretically an interdenominational college, but the Presbyterian Board of Christian Education remained the college's single greatest source of support. Although the college experienced hardships during the Great Depression, a sharp enrollment decline during World War II created even more serious problems. Under these circumstances, the college's board of trustees decided to discontinue the high school department (the former Collegiate Institute) and expanded the college work to four years. By 1950 Westminster had become the only Presbyterian school in the Southwest with roots in the later nineteenth-century mission school effort to make the transition to a four-year college.[7]

By the mid-twentieth century Presbyterian officials contemplated even more altered conditions. World War II accelerated the already rapid pace of change in the Southwest. Increased federal spending in the region, the arrival of larger numbers of Anglo Protestants, improved transportation systems, and the contributions of many native southwesterners to the war effort brought the Southwest more into the American mainstream. Postwar economic prosperity furthered this phenomenon, and by the early 1950s public elementary schools and other modern services were within reach of even the most isolated communities of rural Utah, northern New Mexico, and the Pima, Papago, and Navajo reservations. These developments raised doubts about the need to continue the remaining Presbyterian day schools and the community and medical stations. Furthermore, as new public high schools appeared and buses on new highways carried students to them, applications to the long-popular boarding high schools diminished.[8]

Significant changes also occurred within the schools during this period. By the early 1950s the generation of effective and durable mission leaders had largely passed from the scene.[9] Furthermore, the physical plants at most of the schools were old and needed serious attention. A less tangible, but more serious, problem became increasingly apparent as the midpoint of the twentieth century neared. The vitality that had long been the hallmark of the Presbyterian schools had diminished significantly. Joseph Poncel, who was appointed superintendent of Tucson Indian Training School in 1945, made this problem painfully apparent in several letters to mission headquarters that reported declining enrollments and morale. Board-sanctioned studies of the New Mexico field in the 1950s reported similar problems. These investigations recognized that developments in the area since World War II had altered the conditions that had long made Presbyterian missions needed in the region. More specifically, the reports questioned the quality of academic work in several of the day schools and concluded that that work often competed directly with the public schools. Similarly, the advent of widespread public high schools in rural New Mexico and Utah began to deprive Menaul School and Wasatch Academy of the very students who a generation before had needed their programs the most.[10]

Finally, important philosophical considerations created another unprecedented predicament for the remaining schools. From the time Presbyterians first initiated schools for exceptional populations, few people within the church questioned that these schools should serve exclusively the young peoples of the target populations. The one exception to this was the Utah schools that, from the beginning, served Mormon, gentile, and apostate Mormon children. In the New Mexico and Indian fields, however, mission officials had always called for restrictive admission policies, and on several occasions they denied school personnel permission to admit children from "American" homes.[11] In the 1940s Presbyterian mission officials began to question this policy. Anticipating the civil rights reforms of the late 1950s and 1960s, the Board of National Missions urged school personnel and pupils to participate in interracial conferences. In 1950, four years before the celebrated Supreme Court decision *Brown* vs. *Board of Education of Topeka,* the board began to abandon its own traditional policy of operating segregated schools. In 1950 and 1951 Katharine Gladfelter, secretary of the national missions board's Department of Educational and Medical Work, made clear the board's new policy in a series of letters to the heads of the remaining schools. The board desired, Gladfelter wrote to the superintendent of Tucson Indian School, "to broaden the base of admission for students, so that the school might move in the direction of becoming an area school [and serve] all children, Anglo, Indian, Mexican, and Negro, who meet its requirements and need what it has to offer." Despite Indian and New Mexican resentment and resistance to the proposed changes, board officials moved ahead with their new policy. In a dramatic reversal of its longstanding support for schools for exceptional populations, the full membership of the Board of National Missions in 1953 ruled that its schools would no longer serve particular racial, cultural, or regional groups to the exclusion of others. An era was indeed coming to an end.[12]

In the aftermath of this decision, the national missions board conducted several conferences to discuss the future of the remaining schools. That future, however, was little in doubt. In 1955 Dr. Herman Morse, general secretary of the Board of National Missions, stated bluntly that a "primary objective of the board [was] to work itself out of [the] job" of elementary and secondary education. Two years later the annual General Assembly adopted a major policy statement that affirmed Presbyterian support for public education and declared that the church would not sponsor parochial schools. Following several thorough investigations of the mission fields, the board announced in February 1958 that Allison-James boarding school and day schools in Chacon, Holman, Ranchos de Taos, and Dixon, New Mexico, would be closed. (The day schools in Chimayo and Truchas were to remain open temporarily until local public schools could absorb their students.) Two years later, the board announced that Tucson Indian Training School would likewise be closed.[13] Soon thereafter the board provided for the gradual transfer of the properties of Menaul School, Wasatch Academy, and Ganado Mission High School to local boards of trustees. This process was completed in the early 1970s, and the Presbyterian church for the first time in more than a century was officially out of the education business in the Southwest. At the present time (1990) alumni, individual Presbyterians, and numerous Presbyterian congregations provide essential support to the work of Menaul School, the John Hyson Day School (Chimayo, New Mexico), Wasatch Academy, Cook Theological School, and Westminster College. These schools form the most obvious legacy of the once widespread Presbyterian mission school effort among the exceptional populations of the Southwest.

What then does one make of the Presbyterian mission school experience and the broader missionary effort in the Southwest? Historians have long recognized difficulties in assessing the results of missionary work. In 1939 Colin B. Goodykoontz observed in his thorough study of home missions on the American frontier that the most quantifiable results of mission work (e.g., financial costs, numbers of churches established, and numbers of converts) were "superficial tests of achievement." "The more important results," he concluded, "[are] intangible, and a statement of their significance is necessarily an excursion into the realm of opinion." Nearly half a century after Goodykoontz wrote these words, ethnohistorian James Axtell lamented that historians of religion still had not devised objective "criteria for judging the success or failure of a missionary program." He suggested, in particular, that defenders and critics of missionaries fail to consider the native perspective in assessing the results of mission work.[14] One should keep these perceptive observations in mind when assessing the impact and significance of the Presbyterian work in the Southwest that has been the focus of this study.

While heeding Goodykoontz's warning, one can best begin the process of assessing the work of Presbyterians in the Southwest with a consideration of the standard barometer for missionary success or failure — numbers of converts. In doing so, however, it is important to clarify several points.

First, Presbyterian missionaries in the Southwest emphasized repeatedly throughout the period examined in this study that winning new members for their church was not their major motive for conducting missions in the Southwest. The Presbyterians' close identification with the broader Anglo-Protestant culture led them to make native embracement of that culture their principal goal. Furthermore, Presbyterian commitment to religious freedom (which, as Sidney Mead and other historians have emphasized, meant freedom to choose one's denominational affiliation within a sphere of Protestant choices) made them ambivalent about demanding that native peoples come exclusively into their church.

Second, statistics reporting native conversions and church membership are often unreliable. Records of Presbyterian church membership from New Mexico and Utah, for example, usually did not distinguish between Anglo immigrants into the region and natives who converted. Moreover, statistics that are available often present conflicting information. For example, one source suggests that there were 2,850 Spanish-speaking members of the Presbyterian Church, U.S.A., in the entire Southwest in 1920. Another source places the figure at below 2,100 (and neither source indicates how many of these were native New Mexicans, as opposed to *Tejanos, Californios,* and recent immigrants from Mexico).[15]

While keeping these shortcomings in mind, one may use the statistics to shed light on the results of the Presbyterian effort in the Southwest. First, if number of converts is made the determining factor of success or failure, then one must conclude that Presbyterian efforts among the southwestern peoples largely failed. For example, half a century after they initiated missions to the Navajos, Presbyterians in 1919 counted fewer than 150 church members from that tribe. Five years earlier only 180 Papagos had affiliated with the Presbyterian church. Similarly there were only 1,808 Presbyterian communicants in Utah in 1910, and presumably the vast majority of these were gentile immigrants rather than converts from Mormonism. Presbyterians, of course, expended many mission dollars for these meager results. In 1885 a Baptist-sponsored study reported that Presbyterians had spent $1,162 for every church member in Utah; this figure would undoubtedly have been greater had it been "cost per convert." While it is impossible to calculate such costs for either the New Mexican or Indian field, there can be little doubt that the figure would be similarly high.

The same statistics, however, also reveal several notable exceptions to this pattern. Clearly, the most successful Presbyterian missionary venture in the Southwest was among the Pima Indians of southern Arizona. In 1919, 1,644 out of 2,000 adults of that tribe were reportedly members of the Presbyterian church.[16] While no other field came close to this record, Presbyterian missionaries also enjoyed considerable success at Laguna Pueblo and in a number of the isolated plaza communities of northern New Mexico.

Two factors were present in each of these locations. First, the missionaries who initiated Presbyterian work in these fields were practical, flexible, and unusually durable. Charles Cook served forty-three years among the Pimas and Papagos; John and Charity Menaul remained at Laguna Pueblo for fourteen years; and the most effective missionaries among the New Mexicans, such as Alice Hyson and Alice Blake, each spent long careers in the Southwest. These individuals took genuine interest in the physical, as well as spiritual, welfare of the people they served. Moreover, they all came to recognize that these native peoples had virtues of their own.

Second, in every location that Presbyterian mission efforts enjoyed some success, unique circumstances were at play that opened the door (or at least left it ajar) for missionary inroads. Ethnohistorians James Axtell and Anthony F. C. Wallace have ably demonstrated that native populations usually embrace outside religions in order to meet their own needs and, indeed, that the blending of new and old ways often revitalizes the native culture and helps it deal with the trauma of change and cultural fragmentation. These considerations make more understandable the successes that Presbyterians did enjoy in the Southwest. The Pimas, for example, were in a state of disarray due to increasing pressure from white immigrants and culture when Charles Cook arrived with the Protestant message in 1870. Laguna Pueblo, on the other hand, had always had a reputation of being more willing to experiment with new ideas than the other pueblos and had a long history of cordial relations with Europeans. In both cases these circumstances facilitated the Presbyterian cause.[17]

Similarly, the peculiar history of Roman Catholicism in northern New Mexico and the turmoil created when Archbishop Lamy in the mid-nineteenth century attempted to reform the New Mexico church enhanced Presbyterian efforts there. Soon after initiating work in Las Vegas, for example, the Reverend John Annin reported that "there is an element of this population disaffected . . . to the Romish church and ready to adopt something better." Annin's wife found it noteworthy that "more good is being done in the country where the people are less under priestly influence" than in Las Vegas, which had long been a center of Jesuit activity. And, indeed, Presbyterians enjoyed particular successes in isolated areas where Padre Martinez (the native priest whom Lamy had excommunicated) had considerable influence and where Catholic priests visited only irregularly. Finally, several *penitentes* became Presbyterians after Archbishop Lamy condemned their brotherhoods and banished them from the Catholic church. Many other members of this Catholic lay group infuriated church officials when they refused to withdraw their children from Presbyterian schools. In 1911 the *penitentes* of the village of Embudo split over this very issue, with the rebel faction becoming known as *Penitentes Presbyterianos* because they sent their children to the local Presbyterian school.[18] Similar circumstances help explain the very limited gains Presbyterians made among apostate Mormons in Utah.

Existing statistics cannot fully answer the question of the effectiveness of the mission schools in winning converts. Although the board did not keep systematic records of student conversions until 1898, narrative reports suggest that many of the early native converts came out of the mission schools. Table 15 presents statistics of conversions for the New Mexico and Utah fields for random years from 1900 to 1915 (records from all Presbyterian Indian schools were lumped together, making it impossible to present statistics for the southwestern Indian schools during that period) and from all three fields for the period from 1916 to 1923. Evaluation of these statistics depends, of course, on one's criteria for success. There can be little doubt, however, that Presbyterians expected greater results. Only on one occasion (the Indian field in 1923) did the number of converts exceed 15 percent. Moreover, for most of the period the number of converts in the Utah field remained under 3 percent and in New Mexico under 10 percent. Never-

Table 15. Conversions to Presbyterianism of Mission School Pupils, 1900–1923

		Number of Conversions	Percent of Enrollment
1900	New Mexican	48	3.3
	Mormon	62	4.2
1905	New Mexican	162	11
	Mormon	47	2.7
1910	New Mexican	199	15
	Mormon	27	2.6
1915	New Mexican	49	4.4
	Mormon	12	2
1916	New Mexican	41	4.3
	Mormon	5	1
	Indian	11	9
1920	New Mexican	53	7
	Mormon	18	5.5
	Indian	7	2.5
1923	New Mexican	70	8.3
	Mormon	6	2
	Indian	59	17

Source: Annual Reports, Board of Home Missions.

theless, one suspects that the mission school represented the Presbyterians most effective means of reaching the southwestern populations. This was particularly true in areas like northern New Mexico, where public schools arrived only in the twentieth century and where many native families recognized education as the best means of assuring better futures for their children.

Statistics also reveal that the Presbyterian hold on the peoples they did reach has diminished over time, particularly since the closing of the majority of the mission schools. For example, in 1930, 1,839 Pimas were members of the Presbyterian church; by 1966 the figure had fallen to 874. A similar pattern has occurred in northern New Mexico. Depending on what figure one chooses to accept, there were approximately two thousand New Mexican Presbyterians in 1920; in 1969 the eighteen Presbyterian churches in the predominantly Hispanic villages of northern New Mexico had about 1,300 members. Church officials report that in both of these areas and at Laguna Pueblo, Presbyterianism has held its own with the older generations but has not succeeded in reaching or retaining young people. Secondly, Presbyterian churches in rural areas of these fields have lost many members who have moved to such urban centers as Phoenix, Albuquerque, and Denver. The early twentieth-century attempt to train a corps of native Presbyterian leaders who would shepherd flocks of their own people clearly fell short of expected goals.[19]

Missionaries who remained in the Southwest any considerable time were aware of their failure to win large numbers of converts. In the early years many missionaries soothed their disappointment by observing, as did one Utah teacher, that "to be instrumental in saving even *one* soul we would spend and be spent." Gradually some veteran missionaries accepted that many of the native southwesterners were content with their religion and were unlikely prospects for conversion. Commenting on the tenacity of New Mexican Catholicism in 1900, Alice Hyson suggested (using the words of Henry Ward Beecher) that the church in which one is raised is "not simply a presentation of a creed; it [is] his home."[20]

Similarly, by the early 1900s some missionaries began to suggest that church membership was a poor barometer for measuring the results of their efforts. Like historian Goodykoontz, these missionaries believed that the most important consequences of their work were intangible. Leva Granger, who assisted in her mother's New Mexico school room as a youth and who as an adult taught in the New Mexico and Utah fields, suggested in 1901 that Presbyterians should bring to older New Mexicans "a measure of truth within their own church, rather than bringing them out of it into the Presbyterian church." "Is it not worthwhile to teach people about Jesus," she asked, "even if they continue to call themselves Catholic?" Missionaries in Utah similarly spoke of the positive effects of their work on many individuals who chose to remain in the Mormon church or who simply gave up all formal religion but lived virtuous lives. "These are results," concluded one Utah teacher, "that the church roll does not give."[21]

Missionaries from all three fields found alternative barometers to indicate that their work had not been totally in vain. First, they pointed with pride to their former pupils who had become ministers, teachers, businessmen, and "honest, hardworking farmers." Not all mission school graduates became Presbyterians, but this did not make their former teachers any less proud of their accomplishments. Second, missionaries invariably pointed to physical, material, and social changes that they attributed to their work. Presbyterians in Utah claimed that their mission schools had spurred the establishment of that state's excellent public school system and made Mormons more liberal and broad-minded. Similarly, missionaries in New Mexico and among southwestern Indians claimed cleaner and more comfortable homes, improved farming methods, and higher moral standards as important indicators of the success of their efforts.[22]

These observations reveal that the missionaries retained their close identification with Anglo-American cultural norms well into the twentieth
century. These influences, of course, limited the missionaries' perspective
in a number of ways. For example, they prevented all but a few missionaries
from recognizing that the southwestern peoples adopted aspects of Anglo-
American culture selectively and rejected those that they did not care to
embrace (which often included the missionaries' Presbyterianism). Secondly,
the missionaries' outlook prevented them from realizing that what successes
they did achieve (e.g., among the Pimas and in some areas of northern New
Mexico) resulted from unique historical and cultural circumstances rather
than the irresistible appeal of the Anglo-Protestant way. Finally, when missionaries claimed credit for many of the social and cultural changes that
occurred in the Southwest during the years flanking 1900, they failed to
see the influence of the wider world on their region. They were reluctant
to acknowledge that theirs was only one of many influences that brought
the southwestern peoples closer to the American mainstream.

It is hardly surprising that missionaries also generally failed to see another,
and less comforting, consequence of their efforts. As one of many forces
that modernized the Southwest during the one hundred years covered in
this study, Presbyterian missions contributed to cultural disintegration and
fragmentation in the region's three traditional societies. This is manifested
in tensions and internal conflicts within each of the three groups. While
not a primary concern of this study, these tensions and conflicts are apparent
throughout its pages: when outraged Laguna leaders whipped Pueblo youths
who embraced the "white man's ways" at Albuquerque Indian School;
when Mormon leaders angrily cut off vital irrigation waters to the few
among their followers who dared embrace Presbyterianism; and when New
Mexico villagers, like Embudo's *penitentes,* divided over the proper response
to the Presbyterian schools. Countless other similarly unfortunate incidents
could be cited. Moreover, conversations with New Mexican, Pima, Laguna,
and Utah Presbyterians reveal that such internecine tensions remain to this
day. To be sure, they have diminished in recent years, but that they still
linger at all is proof that the missionaries unwittingly helped foster considerable rancor and ill will.[23]

To place full blame for these difficulties on the missionaries, however,
would be both unfair to them and historically misleading. If the missionaries
cannot be given full credit for the benefits that change brought to the
southwesterners, they surely should not be saddled with full blame for the
problems that came in the wake of that process. Surely Presbyterianism is
only one factor among many that produced internal unrest as these traditional societies underwent the traumas and mixed blessings of moderni-
zation.

Preoccupation with the negative side of the missionary effort is most misleading because it leads one to overlook the positive results of that effort. Perusal of lists of the careers and contributions of mission school graduates and random conversations with many of these individuals and residents of communities served by Presbyterian missions leaves no doubt that the Presbyterian missionaries in the Southwest accomplished considerable good. Even more significantly, interaction between native and newcomer that occurred in Presbyterian schools, medical stations, and community centers fostered a spirit of cross-cultural friendship and cooperation which the first Anglo-American newcomers to the Southwest (including Sheldon Jackson's Presbyterian pioneers) had not anticipated. While not every Presbyterian missionary was changed by the experience in the Southwest, many of those who remained in the region for considerable periods of time learned that the hold of native culture is tenacious. Moreover, they learned that the cultures that they had come to change had many virtues that deserved to be preserved and that the southwesterners themselves were capable of making enlightened decisions about their own best interests.

Indeed these very emphases and attitudes are evident in the curricula, programs, and leadership of the existing southwestern schools that are the legacies of the Presbyterian mission school effort. Where Presbyterians once attempted to erase southwestern pluralism, they now celebrate it. However, one should not naively assume that Presbyterians in the Southwest have found in pluralism a new panacea. Recent developments in the remaining schools and within the church throughout the Southwest have not always been tranquil. Balancing the demands of diverse groups within a pluralistic setting is a difficult act.[24]

By the later twentieth century Presbyterians embraced a perspective on missions and religious and cultural diversity that differed in many respects from that of their predecessors of a century before. The Confession of 1967, a historical restatement of Presbyterian convictions, affirmed that "the Christian finds parallels between other religions and his own and must approach all religions with openness and respect." A decade later the 189th General Assembly called Presbyterians to support bilingual and bicultural education. In 1985 the Presbyterian Church (U.S.A.) (the result of the 1983 reunion of former Northern and Southern churches) affirmed that "diversity and pluralism [are] integral to inclusiveness and the body of Christ." More recently the church in 1990 issued the amicable report on Mormonism with which this book began.[25]

The missionary experience in the Southwest, of course, did not cause this change in Presbyterian outlook. Developments of this magnitude result from many and varied influences, of which the persons affected are often only dimly aware. Social and intellectual changes in the broader American society—particularly the new perspective on human culture offered by cultural anthropology and mainstream Protestantism's gradual relinquishment of its close identification with Anglo-American culture—obviously undergirded the new Presbyterian outlook. Nonetheless, experiences like those of Presbyterian missionaries in the Southwest confirmed in many ways this new perspective on cultural and ethnic diversity and helped nurture reconsideration of the church's role in the pluralistic American society. Indeed, the education that took place in the Presbyterian mission schools was not the simple one-way process that Sheldon Jackson and others had envisioned. The Southwest changed American Presbyterians, even as they helped change it.

Notes

1. 44th Annual Report, Woman's Board of Home Missions, 1923, 23–24. Miss Voss herself represented many of the changes that had occurred in Presbyterian home missions during the post–World War I years. Her appointment to succeed superintendent of schools Marshall C. Allaben in 1921 made her the first woman to hold that position. Secondly, the change in her title to secretary of field work suggested the diminished role mission schools played in the new Presbyterian home missions outlook. Her 1923 annual report was also the final annual report of the woman's board.

2. Robert Handy, "The American Religious Depression, 1925–1935," *Church History* 29 (1960): 3–16. In a more recent book Handy refers to this as the period of the "second disestablishment" (*A Christian America*, 2d ed. [New York: Oxford University Press, 1984]).

3. Handy, "American Religious Depression," 4–6. Statistics for the receipts of the Board of National Missions are found in Clifford Drury, *Presbyterian Panorama* (New York: Board of National Missions, 1952), Appendix C, 410. Also see John Lankford, "The Impact of the Religious Depression upon Protestant Benevolence," *Journal of Presbyterian History* 42 (June 1964): 104–23.

4. Boyd and Brackenridge comment on the controversies that followed reorganization of the Presbyterian mission boards in 1923 (*Presbyterian Women in America*, chap 4). M. Katherine Bennett, "The Past a Promise for the Future," *HMM* 38 (March 1924): 106–7, and Lucy H. Dawson, "Reorganization," *HMM* 37 (April 1923): 132, appeal for Presbyterian women to continue their support for missions. Herman N. Morse, a leading official of the new Board of National Missions, made a similar appeal in *One Hundred and Twenty-Five Years of National Missions* (New York: Board of National Missions, 1927), 25–26.

5. Miss Voss announced plans to close the school at Stotonic in a memo to M. L. Girton, June 14, 1932, PHS, RG 101, Box 1, F-9. Consolidation of Logan and Wasatch academies was recommended in a memo from Miss Voss, April 6, 1934, PHS, RG 101, Box 16, F-9; also see Woo, "A History of New Jersey–Logan Academy,"

74–75. Barber and Agnew, *Sowers Went Forth,* 111–13, discuss the merger of Menaul and Allison-James. The action in 1934 also placed the remaining community work in Utah under the direction of Wasatch Academy. Similarly, the board in that year made Menaul School superintendent Harper Donaldson superintendent of all remaining mission work in New Mexico.

6. Hamilton, "A History of Presbyterian Work among the Pima and Papago Indians of Arizona," 182–95. Wankier, "A History of Presbyterian Schools in Utah," 105–7, discusses developments at Wasatch during this period. Barber and Agnew, *Sowers Went Forth,* 11–14, do the same for Menaul School. Brief comments on Salsbury's work at Ganado are found in Judith R. Johnson, "A Mission to the Navajos," *Menaul Historical Review* 10 (October 1983): 2–3. Also see Florence C. Means, *Sagebrush Surgeon* (New York: Friendship Press, 1956). Brackenridge and Garcia-Treto, *Iglesia Presbyteriana,* 180–84, and Barber and Agnew, *Sowers Went Forth,* 105–8, 114–16, discuss the work of the day school–community centers in northern New Mexico.

7. *A Brief History of Cook Christian Training School* (pamphlet issued on the Golden Anniversary of the Founding of the School, Phoenix, 1961). Also see Smith and Nelson, *Datelines and Bylines,* 74–75; Wankier, "A History of Presbyterian Mission Schools in Utah," 85–92. George A. Works and H. M. Gage, "Statement on Westminster College," January 20, 1944, Westminster College Archives, laid the groundwork for Westminster's transition to a four-year college.

8. Gerald D. Nash, *The American West in the Twentieth Century,* chaps. 4 and 5, comments on the West during World War II and the postwar years.

9. Reherd of Westminster College stepped down in 1939; Girton retired at Tucson two years later. In 1950 Salsbury relinquished his duties at Ganado, and in 1954 Donaldson did the same at Menaul.

10. Joseph A. Poncel to Edna Voss, September 12, 1945, February 13, 1946, Records of Tucson Indian Training School, Arizona Historical Society. Poncel reported declining enrollments and that his "spoiled" and "pampered" students performed poorly in the classroom. More seriously, he suggested that after an extended period of time at the school, many pupils suffered a "definite decline in morale, spirit, and enthusiasm." Among the several board-sponsored studies of the New Mexican field, the most critical of the mission schools was Milton W. Brown, *Presbyterian Church, U.S.A.: Educational Work in New Mexico,* December 1957, PHS, Presbyterian Spanish-speaking Work in the Southwest: Selected Correspondence and Reports.

11. See, for example, Alice Blake to Mrs. Ella A. Boole of the Woman's Board of Home Missions regarding "special application for admission of an American boy" to Menaul School, April 22, June 25, 1907, PHS, RG 51, Box 3, F-10. In response to this request Menaul superintendent J. C. Ross advised Mrs. Boole against admitting the boy, June 12, 1907, PHS, RG 51, Box 3, F-18. "We will certainly have to take one less Mexican for each American pupil we receive," he wrote. Boole followed Ross's advice and informed Blake that her request had been denied. For a similar set of circumstances and results at a later time, see "Allison-James and Menaul to Become Co-educational," undated, unidentified newspaper clipping, Menaul Historical Library, Menaul School Collection, 84-2-f.

12. The board's objectives and local responses to them are clearly revealed in the following exchange of letters from the Records of the Tucson Indian Training School: Gladfelter to William Hennessey, September 1, 1950, May 2, 1951, December 19, 1951, and Hennessey to Gladfelter, March 14, December 7, 1951, Arizona Historical Society.

13. Herman N. Morse, "Guiding Principles for Educational and Medical Work" (address delivered in Santa Fe, March 12, 1955), quoted in Barber and Agnew, *Sowers Went Forth,* 130. Announcement of the closings in the New Mexico field was made in Katherine Gladfelter's memo to All Executives, February 7, 1958, PHS, RG 101, Box 9, F-1. The recommendation to close Tucson Indian Training School was made in the Report of the Study Committee on Educational and Medical Institutions, PHS, RG 101, Box 2, F-3. William Hennessey, superintendent of the Tucson school, announced the decision about its closing in letters to Friends and to Parents and Guardians, February 20, 1960, PHS, RG 101, Box 1, F-15.

14. Colin B. Goodykoontz, *Home Missions on the American Frontier* (Caldwell, Idaho: Caxton Printers, 1939), 406; James Axtell, "Some Thoughts on the Ethnohistory of Missions," *Ethnohistory* 29 (1982): 35. Historian Henry W. Bowden shares Axtell's concern. See, for example, "An Overview of Cultural Factors in the American Protestant Missionary Enterprise," in *American Missions in Bicentennial Perspective,* ed. R. Pierce Beaver (South Pasadena, Calif.: William Carey Library, 1977), 42.

15. Lela Weatherby offers the 2,850 figure without giving a source in "A Study of the Early Years of Presbyterian Work with the Spanish-speaking People of New Mexico and Colorado and Its Development from 1850 to 1920" (M.A. thesis, Presbyterian College of Christian Education, 1942), 73. Brackenridge and Garcia-Treto, *Iglesia Presbyteriana,* 161, offer the figure of 2,099 in a table indicating church membership taken from records of the Presbyterian church's Spanish-speaking department.

16. The statistics for Navajo, Papago, and Pima church membership are taken from Smith and Nelson, *Datelines and Bylines,* 65–67, 68–69. Statistics for Utah are found in Milford R. Rathjen, "The Distribution of Major Non-Mormon Denominations in Utah" (M.S. thesis, University of Utah, 1966), 42. Figures on cost per church member in Utah are presented in Rev. H. D. DeWitt, "Baptist Work in Utah" (Salt Lake City, 1885), cited in Lyon, "Evangelical Protestant Missionary Activities in Mormon-dominated Areas, 1865–1900," 131.

17. See A. F. C. Wallace, *Religion: An Anthropological View* (New York: Random House, 1966), 30; idem, *Death and Rebirth of the Seneca* (New York: Vintage Books, 1970); Axtell, "Some Thoughts on the Ethnohistory of Missions," 35–41; Florence H. Ellis, "An Outline of Laguna Pueblo History and Social Organization," *Southwestern Journal of Anthropology* 15 (1959): 327–28.

18. John Annin, "From New Mexico," clipping, 1871, SJS 53:81; Mrs. E. D. Annin to S. Jackson, January 23, 1878, SJCC. Presbyterian comments about *penitente* interest in their work are found in Alice Hyson, "Words from Workers — N.M.," *HMM* 1 (December 1886): 14–15; Report of Superintendent of School Work to Board of Home Missions, 1901, 9; 109th Annual Report, Board of Home Missions,

1911, 71. Also see Marta Weigle, *Brothers of Light, Brothers of Blood* (Albuquerque: University of New Mexico Press, 1976), 104.

19. Smith and Nelson, *Datelines and Bylines,* 65; Barber and Agnew, "The Unique Presbyterian School System of New Mexico," *Journal of Presbyterian History* 49 (Fall 1971): 221; Rev. Roe B. Lewis (retired executive for Indian ministries, Synod of Southwest), interview with author, May 27, 1985; Rev. Jaime O. Quninones (executive for Spanish ministries, Presbytery of Santa Fe), interview with author, June 22, 1987. Michael Coleman offers one of the first systematic attempts to understand Indian responses to the "white man's education" from the Indian perspective. Several Indian students that he focuses on attended Presbyterian schools. Coleman's approach offers a model that might be effectively utilized in examining how students from each of the three southwestern groups responded to the Presbyterian schools ("Motivations of Indian Children at Missionary and U.S. Government Schools, 1860–1918," *Journal of the West* 40 [Winter 1990]: 30–45).

20. Miss Lockwood, "Words from Workers — Utah," *HMM* 1 (October 1887): 272; Alice Hyson, "Hindrances to Overcome," *HMM* 15 (November 1890): 13.

21. Leva Granger, "Mistakes in Judging Mexicans," *HMM* 8 (November 1901): 8. Miss Granger made similar observations in "Mexican Work," *HMM* 17 (July 1903): 213–14; *HMM* 19 (November 1904): 2.

22. Comments on mission school graduates and changes in the three southwestern populations are abundant in the missionary literature. The following are typical samples of these comments from 1900 to 1920. Comments from the Utah field are found in *HMM* 21 (November 1906): 2; 108th Annual Report, Board of Home Missions, 1910, 18–19; "Editorial Notes," *HMM* 35 (December 1920): 92. Observations from New Mexico are found in Sue M. Zuver, "Plaza of Penasco," *HMM* 22 (November 1907): 16; Elizabeth Craig, "Passing of Old Customs," *HMM* 24 (November 1909): 2; Report of Superintendent of School Work to Board of Home Missions, 1913, 54; Elizabeth Craig, "Thirty Years in New Mexico," *HMM* 38 (November 1913): 11. Comments on Presbyterian impacts on southwestern Indians are found in Florence Dilley, "The Home-Making of Tucson Pupils," *HMM* 26 (February 1912): 86; 41st Annual Report, Woman's Board of Home Missions, 1920, 36.

23. During an eleven-year residence in New Mexico, the author became acquainted with many graduates of Presbyterian mission schools and discussed their school experiences and subsequent careers. While completing research for this study, I also had an opportunity to visit with graduates of several Indian schools and schools in Utah. These personal experiences confirm the conclusions about the internal divisions that Presbyterianism helped foster in the native southwestern societies. They also make even more clear the many positive contributions Presbyterians made to the region, which are described in the next paragraph.

24. For evidence of a commitment to ethnicity and pluralism in the existing schools, see, for example, Menaul School's *Enduring Heritages: A Guide to Multicultural Education in the Secondary School* (Albuquerque: Menaul School, 1976) and Dr. Cecil Corbett, "Goals for Indian Education," an address by the president

of Cook Christian Training School, January 1974, copy in Cook School library. John Hyson School in Chimayo, New Mexico (which as the only remaining elementary school operates under the Menaul School Board of Trustees), has made an outstanding record in the field of bilingual, multicultural education.

25. *The Constitution of the Presbyterian Church (U.S.A.), Part I: Book of Confessions* (New York: Office of the General Assembly, 1983), 9.42; Minutes of the 189th General Assembly of the UPUSA, 1977, 623; "Life and Mission Statement of the Presbyterian Church (U.S.A.) to the 197th General Assembly," Minutes of the 197th General Assembly of the Presbyterian Church (U.S.A.), 1985, 240–49. *A Present Day Look at the Latter-day Saints* (report prepared by Special Task Force of the Presbytery of Utah, Presbyterian Church [U.S.A.]) (Louisville: Office of the General Assembly, 1990).

Bibliography

Manuscript and Archival Material

Arizona Historical Society. Records of Tucson Indian Training School.
Arizona State University Library. Richard K. Smith Collection. Arizona Room.
Cook Theological School. Historical File. Library
Menaul Historical Library of the Southwest (Albuquerque, New Mexico)
    Albuquerque Indian School File
    Gilchrist Papers
    Menaul School Collection
    Presbytery of Santa Fe. Minutes, 1868–1928.
    Presbytery of Utah. Minutes, 1871–1908.
    General Assemblies of Presbyterian Church, U.S.A. Minutes, 1870–1925.
    Synod of New Mexico. Minutes, 1889–1925.
    Synod of Utah. Minutes, 1912–25.
    Vertical File
National Archives. Bureau of Indian Affairs. Record Group 75.
    Special Cases/SC 143, N.M.
    Education Division. Letters Sent.
    Reports of Inspections of the Field Jurisdictions, 1873–1890. Microcopy M-1070,
        Roll 41.
Pierce Historical Hall. Wasatch Academy, Mt. Pleasant, Utah. Vertical File.
Presbyterian Historical Society. Philadelphia, Pennsylvania.
    Board of Christian Education. Record Group 32. Records of Board of Aid to
        Colleges and Academies, 1883–1958.
    Board of Home Missions
        Annual Reports, 1870–1923
        Reports of Superintendent of School Work, 1895–1915
    Board of National Missions
        Record Groups 51 and 105. Records of Woman's Board of Home Missions,
            1879–1925, 1878–1948.

Record Groups 101 and 103. Records of Divison of Schools and Hospitals, 1878–1966, 1892–1960.

Record Group 104. Records of Department of Spanish-Speaking Work, 1890–1915.

Selected Correspondence and Reports of the Spanish Southwest Women's Board of Home Missions. Annual Reports, 1879–1921.

Sheldon Jackson Correspondence Collection

Sheldon Jackson Scrapbooks.Westminster College Archives. Salt Lake City, Utah.

William Mitchell Paden Collection

Books

Agnew, Edith. *Hand on My Shoulder.* New York: Board of National Missions, 1953.

Ahlstrom, Sidney. *A Religious History of the American People.* 2 vols. Garden City, N.Y.: Image Books, 1975.

Alexander, Thomas G. *Mormonism in Transition: A History of the Latter-day Saints, 1890–1930.* Urbana: University of Illinois Press, 1986.

Allen, T. D. *Not Ordered by Men.* Santa Fe: Rydal Press, 1967.

Allport, Gordon. *The Nature of Prejudice.* 25th anniversary edition. Reading, Mass.: Addison-Wesley Publishing Co., 1979.

Among the Pimas. Albany, N.Y.: privately published, 1893.

Aragon, Ray John de. *Padre Martinez and Bishop Lamy.* Las Vegas, N.M.: Pan American Press, 1978.

Arrington, Leonard. *Brigham Young: American Moses.* New York: Alfred A. Knopf, 1985.

—————. *Great Basin Kingdom: History of the Latter-day Saints.* Cambridge: Harvard University Press, 1956.

Arrington, Leonard, and Davis Bitton. *The Mormon Experience: A History of the Latter-day Saints.* New York: Alfred A. Knopf, 1979.

Barber, Ruth K., and Edith Agnew. *Sowers Went Forth: The Story of Presbyterian Missions in New Mexico and Colorado.* Albuquerque: Menaul Historical Library, 1981.

Beaver, R. Pierce. *American Protestant Women in World Missions: History of the First Feminist Movement in North America.* Grand Rapids, Mich.: Eerdman's Publishing Co., 1984.

Bender, Norman J., ed. *Missionaries, Outlaws, and Indians: Taylor F. Ealy at Lincoln and Zuni, 1878–1881.* Albuquerque: University of New Mexico Press, 1984.

Berkhoffer, Robert, Jr. *Salvation and the Savage: An Analysis of Protestant Missions and American Indian Response, 1787–1860.* Lexington: University of Kentucky Press, 1965.

—————. *The White Man's Indian: Images of the American Indian from Columbus to the Present.* New York: Vintage Books, 1979.

Billington, Ray A. *The Protestant Crusade, 1800–1860: A Study of the Origins of American Nativism.* Chicago: Quadrangle Books, 1964.

Bingham, Edwin. *Charles F. Lummis: Career in the Southwest.* San Marino, Calif.: Huntington Library, 1955.

Bitton, Davis, and Gary L. Bunker. *The Mormon Graphic Image, 1834–1914: Cartoons, Caricatures, and Illustrations.* Salt Lake City: University of Utah Press, 1983.

Bowden, Henry W. *American Indians and Christian Missions.* Chicago: University of Chicago Press, 1981.

Boyd, Lois, and Douglas Brackenridge. *Presbyterian Women in America: Two Centuries of a Quest for Status.* Presbyterian Historical Society Publications Series, 9. Westport, Conn.: Greenwood Press, 1983.

Boylan, Anne M. *Sunday School: The Formation of an American Tradition, 1790–1880.* New Haven: Yale University Press, 1988.

Brackenridge, Douglas, and Francisco Garcia-Treto. *Iglesia Presbyteriana: A History of Presbyterians and Mexican Americans in the Southwest.* San Antonio: Trinity University Press, 1974.

Brodie, Fawn. *No Man Knows My History: The Life of Joseph Smith.* New York: Alfred A. Knopf, 1946.

Bushman, Claudia, ed. *Mormon Sisters: Women in Early Utah.* Cambridge, Mass.: Emmeline Press, 1966.

Bushman, Richard. *Joseph Smith and the Beginnings of Mormonism.* Urbana: University of Illinois Press, 1984.

Carlson, Robert. *The Quest for Conformity: Americanization through Education.* New York: John Wiley and Sons, 1975.

Chavez, Fray Angelico. *But Time and Chance: The Story of Padre Martinez of Taos.* Santa Fe: Sunstone Press, 1981.

————. *My Penitente Land: Reflections on Spanish New Mexico.* Albuquerque: University of New Mexico Press, 1974.

Clark, Ira G. *Then Came the Railroads: The Century from Steam to Diesel in the Southwest.* Norman: University of Oklahoma Press, 1958.

Coleman, Michael. *Presbyterian Missionary Attitudes toward American Indians, 1837–1892.* Jackson: University of Mississippi Press, 1985.

Cook, Minnie. *Apostle to the Pimas.* Tiburon, Calif.: Omega Books, 1976.

Cott, Nancy. *The Bonds of Womanhood: "Woman's Sphere" in New England, 1780–1835.* New Haven: Yale University Press, 1977.

Craig, Robert. *Our Mexicans.* New York: Board of Home Missions, Presbyterian Church, U.S.A., 1904.

Cremin, Lawrence. *The Transformation of the School: Progressivism and American Education, 1876–1957.* New York: Alfred A. Knopf, 1961.

Cross, Whitney. *Burned-over District.* Ithaca, N.Y.: Colgate University Press, 1950.

Davis, Allen F. *American Heroine: The Life and Legend of Jane Addams.* New York: Oxford University Press, 1973.

Degler, Carl. *The Age of the Economic Revolution.* Glenview, Ill.: Scott, Foresman, 1977.

Deutsch, Sarah. *Culture, Class, and Gender on an Anglo-Hispanic Frontier in the American Southwest.* New York: Oxford University Press, 1987.

Downs, James. The Navajo. New York: Holt, Rinehart and Winston, 1972.

Dozier, Edward. The Pueblo Indians of New Mexico. New York: Holt, Rinehart and Winston, 1970.

Drury, Clifford M. Presbyterian Panorama: 150 Years of National Missions History. Philadelphia: Board of Christian Education, Presbyterian Church, U.S.A., 1952.

Dwyer, Robert J. The Gentile Comes to Utah. Salt Lake City: Western Epics, 1971.

Forbes, Jack D. Apache, Navajo, and Spaniard. Norman: University of Oklahoma Press, 1960.

Foster, Lawrence. Religion and Sexuality: Three American Communal Experiences of the Nineteenth Century. New York: Oxford University Press, 1981.

Garraty, John A. The New Commonwealth. New York: Harper and Row, 1968.

Gonzalez, Nancy. The Spanish Americans of New Mexico: A Heritage of Pride. Albuquerque: University of New Mexico Press, 1969.

Goodykoontz, Colin B. Home Missions on the American Frontier. Caldwell, Idaho: Caxton Printers, 1939.

Handy, Robert. A Christian America: Protestant Hopes and Historical Realities. 2d ed. New York: Oxford University Press, 1984.

————. We Witness Together: A History of Cooperative Home Missions. New York: Friendship Press, 1956.

————, ed. The Social Gospel in America. New York: Oxford University Press, 1966.

Hansen, Klaus. Mormonism and the American Experience. Chicago: University of Chicago Press, 1981.

Hayes, Florence. Daughters of Dorcas: The Story of the Work of Women for Home Missions since 1802. New York: Presbyterian Board of National Missions, 1952.

Hinsley, Curtis. Savages and Scientists: The Smithsonian Institution and the Development of American Anthropology, 1846–1910. Washington, D.C.: Smithsonian Institution Press, 1981.

Hopkins, Charles H. The Rise of the Social Gospel in American Protestantism, 1865–1915. New Haven: Yale University Press, 1940.

Horgan, Paul. Lamy of Santa Fe. New York: Farrar, Straus and Giroux, 1975.

Hyatt, Irwin T. Our Ordered Lives Confess: Three Nineteenth-Century American Missionaries in East Shantung. Cambridge: Harvard University Press, 1976.

Jensen, Joan, and Darlis Miller, eds. New Mexico Women: An Intercultural Perspective. Albuquerque: University of New Mexico Press, 1986.

Kaestle, Carl F. Pillars of the Republic: Common Schools and the American Society, 1780–1860. New York: Hill and Wang, 1983.

Keller, Robert H., Jr. American Protestantism and U.S. Indian Policy, 1869–1882. Lincoln: University of Nebraska Press, 1983.

Kelly, Robert. Cooperation in Education in Utah: Report on Westminster College in Salt Lake City. New York: Home Missions Council, 1922.

Kennedy, William B. The Shaping of Protestant Education: An Interpretation of the Sunday School and the Development of Protestant Educational Strategy in the United States, 1789–1860. New York: Association Press, 1966.

Kluckhohn, Clyde, and Dorothea Leighton. The Navajo. Cambridge: Harvard University Press, 1946.

Kroeber, A. L., and Clyde Kluckhohn. *Culture: A Critical Review of Concepts and Definitions.* New York: Vintage Books, 1963.

Lamar, Howard. *The Far Southwest, 1846–1912: A Territorial History.* New York: W. W. Norton, 1970.

Larson, Gustive. *The "Americanization" of Utah for Statehood.* San Marino, Calif.: Huntington Library, 1971.

Larson, Robert. *New Mexico's Quest for Statehood.* Albuquerque: University of New Mexico Press, 1968.

Lingle, Walter L., and John W. Kuykendall. *Presbyterians: Their History and Beliefs.* 4th rev. ed. Atlanta: John Knox Press, 1978.

Lippman, Walter. *Public Opinion.* New York: Macmillan Co., 1927.

Loetscher, Loefferts. *A Brief History of the Presbyterians.* 3d ed. Philadelphia: Westminster Press, 1974.

—————. *The Broadening Church: A Study of Theological Issues in the Presbyterian Church since 1869.* Philadelphia: Westminster Press, 1957.

McAfee, George. *Home Missions among the Mexicans.* New York: Woman's Board of Home Missions, 1912.

McLouglin, William G. *Champions of the Cherokees: Evan and John B. Jones.* Princeton, N.J.: Princeton University Press, 1990.

Mardock, Robert. *The Reformers and the American Indian.* Columbia: University of Missouri Press, 1971.

Marsden, George. *The Evangelical Mind and the New School Presbyterian Experience: A Case Study of Thought and Theology in Nineteenth-Century America.* New Haven: Yale University Press, 1970.

—————. *Fundamentalism and American Culture: The Shaping of Twentieth Century Evangelicalism.* New York: Oxford University Press, 1980.

Marty, Martin. *Righteous Empire: The Protestant Experience in America.* New York: Dial Press, 1970.

May, Henry F. *Protestant Churches and Industrial America.* New York: Harper and Brothers, 1949.

Means, Florence C. *Sagebrush Surgeon.* New York: Friendship Press, 1967.

Miller, Howard. *The Revolutionary College: American Presbyterian Higher Education, 1707–1837.* New York: New York University Press, 1976.

Miller, Lee Clark. *Witness to a Vanishing America: The Nineteenth-Century Response.* Princeton, N.J.: Princeton University Press, 1981.

Miyakawa, T. Scott. *Pioneers and Protestants: Individualism and Conformity on the American Frontier.* Chicago: University of Chicago Press, 1964.

Moorehead, James. *American Apocalypse: Yankee Protestants and the Civil War.* New Haven: Yale University Press, 1978.

Morse, Herman. *One Hundred and Twenty-Five Years of National Missions.* New York: Board of National Missions, 1927.

Murray, Andrew. *Presbyterians and the Negro: A History.* Presbyterian Historical Society Publications Series, 7. Philadelphia: Presbyterian Historical Society, 1966.

Nash, Gerald D. *The American West in the Twentieth Century: A Short History of an Urban Oasis.* Albuquerque: University of New Mexico Press, 1977.

Nyman, Emil. *A Short History of Westminster College*. Salt Lake City: Westminster College, 1975.

O'Dea, Thomas. *The Mormons*. Chicago: University of Chicago Press, 1957.

Ortiz, Alfonso. *The Tewa World: Space, Time, and Becoming in a Pueblo Society*. Chicago: University of Chicago Press, 1969.

————, ed. *New Perspectives on the Pueblos*. Albuquerque: University of New Mexico Press, 1972.

Parker, Inez Moore. *The Rise and Decline of the Program for Education for Black Presbyterians of the United Presbyterian Church, U.S.A.*. Presbyterian Historical Society Publications Series, 16. San Antonio: Trinity University Press, 1977.

Perrigo, Lynn. *The American Southwest: Its Peoples and Cultures*. Albuquerque: University of New Mexico Press, 1979.

Phillips, Clifton Jackson. *Protestant America and the Pagan World: The First One-Half Century of the American Board of Commissioners of Foreign Missions, 1810–1860*. Harvard East Asian Mongraphs, 32. Cambridge: Harvard University Press, 1969.

Pomeroy, Earl. *In Search of the Golden West*. New York: Alfred A. Knopf, 1957.

Powell, Phillip W. *Tree of Hate: Propaganda and Prejudices Affecting U.S. Relations with the Hispanic World*. New York: Basic Books, 1971.

Presbyterian Reunion: A Memorial Volume, 1837–1870. New York, 1870.

Prucha, Francis Paul. *American Indian Policy in Crisis: Christian Reformers and the Indian, 1865–1900*. Norman: University of Oklahoma Press, 1976.

————. *The Churches and the Indian Schools, 1888–1912*. Lincoln: University of Nebraska Press, 1979.

————. *The Great Father: The U.S. Government and the American Indian*. 2 vols. Lincoln: University of Nebraska Press, 1984.

————, ed. *Americanizing the American Indians: Writings by the "Friends of the Indian," 1880–1900*. Lincoln: University of Nebraska Press, 1973.

Riegel, Robert. *The Story of the Western Railroads*. New York, 1926.

Robinson, Cecil. *Mexico and the Hispanic Southwest in American Literature*. Tucson: University of Arizona Press, 1977.

Russell, Frank. *The Pima Indians*. Tucson: University of Arizona Press, 1975.

Sanchez, George. *Forgotten People: A Study of New Mexicans*. Albuquerque: Calvin Horn Publishers, 1967.

Sando, Joe S. *The Pueblo Indians*. San Francisco: Indian Historian Press, 1976.

Sherrill, Lewis J. *Presbyterian Parochial Schools, 1846–70*. Yale Studies in Religious Education, 4. New Haven: Yale University Press, 1932.

Shipps, Jan. *Mormonism: The Story of a New Religious Tradition*. Urbana: University of Illinois Press, 1985.

Smith, Elwyn A. *The Presbyterian Ministry in American Culture*. Philadelphia: Westminster Press, 1962.

Smith, Gary Scott. *The Seeds of Secularization: Calvinism, Culture, and Pluralism*. Grand Rapids, Mich.: Christian University Press, 1985.

Smith, Richard K., and J. Melvin Nelson. *Datelines and By-Lines: A Sketchbook* of Presbyterian Beginnings and Growth in Arizona. Phoenix: Synod of Arizona, 1969.

Schufle, J. A. Preparing the Way: The History of the First 100 Years of Las Vegas Presbyterian Church. Las Vegas, N.M.: First Presbyterian Church, 1970.

Shaw, Anna. The Pima Past. Tucson: University of Arizona Press, 1974.

Smith, Anne M. Indian Education in New Mexico. Albuquerque: University of New Mexico Press, 1968.

Spicer, Edward. Cycles of Conquest: The Impact of Spain, Mexico, and the United States on the Indians of the Southwest, 1533–1960. Tucson: University of Arizona Press, 1981.

Spidle, Jake W., Jr. Doctors of Medicine in New Mexico. Albuquerque: University of New Mexico Press, 1986.

Stewart, Robert Laird. Sheldon Jackson. New York: Flemming H. Revell, 1908.

Szasz, Ferenc M. The Divided Mind of Protestant America, 1880–1930. Tuscaloosa: University of Alabama Press, 1982.

————. The Protestant Clergy in the Great Plains and Rocky Mountain West, 1865–1915. Albuquerque: University of New Mexico Press, 1988.

Szasz, Margaret Connell. Education and the American Indian: The Road to Self-Determination since 1928. Albuquerque: University of New Mexico Press, 1977.

Turner, Frederick J. The Significance of the Frontier in American History. New York: Ungar, 1920.

Tuveson, Ernest. Redeemer Nation: The Idea of America's Milennial Role. Chicago: University of Chicago Press, 1968.

Tyack, David. The One Best System. Cambridge: Harvard University Press, 1974.

Tyler, Alice Felt. Freedom's Ferment: Phases of American Social History from the Colonial Period to the Civil War. New York: Harper, 1944.

Verdesi, Elizabeth Howell. In But Still Out: Women in the Church. Philadelphia: Westminster Press, 1975.

Von Waggoner, Richard S. Mormon Polygamy: A History. Salt Lake City: Signature Press, 1986.

Wallace, Anthony F. C. Death and Rebirth of the Seneca. New York: Vintage Books, 1970.

————. Religion: An Anthropological View. New York: Random House, 1966.

Walters, Ronald. American Reformers, 1815–1860. New York: Hill and Wang, 1978.

Weber, David J. The Mexican Frontier, 1821–1846. Albuquerque: University of New Mexico Press, 1982.

————, ed. New Spain's Far Northern Frontier: Essays on Spain in the American West. Albuquerque: University of New Mexico Press, 1979.

Weigle, Marta. Brothers of Light, Brothers of Blood: The Penitentes of the Southwest. Albuquerque: University of New Mexico Press, 1976.

Wiebe, Robert. The Search for Order, 1877–1920. American Century Series. New York: Hill and Wang, 1967.

Wiley, Tom. *Politics and Purse Strings in New Mexico's Public Schools.* Albuquerque: University of New Mexico Press, 1965.

Wishard, Samuel. *The Mormons.* New York: Literary Department, Board of Home Missions, 1904.

Young, Kimball. *Isn't One Wife Enough?* New York: Henry Holt, 1954.

Articles

Arrington, Leonard J., and Jan Haupt. "Intolerable Zion: The Image of Mormonism in Nineteenth-Century American Literature." *Western Humanities Review* 22 (Summer 1968): 243–57.

Axtell, James. "Some Thoughts on the Ethnohistory of Missions." *Ethnohistory* 29 (1982): 35–41.

Banker, Mark T. "Missionary to His Own People: Jose Ynes Perea and Hispanic Presbyterianism in New Mexico." In *Religion and Society in the American West,* edited by Carl Guarneri. Lanham, Md.: University Press of America, 1987.

———. "Presbyterians and Pueblos: A Protestant Response to the Indian Question." *Journal of Presbyterian History* 60 (Spring 1982): 23–41.

———. "Presbyterian Missionary Activity in the Southwest: The Careers of John and James Menaul." *The Journal of the West* 23 (January 1984): 55–61.

———. "They Made Haste Slowly: Presbyterian Mission Schools and Southwestern Pluralism." *American Presbyterians* 69 (Summer 1991): 123–32.

Barber, Ruth K., and Edith Agnew. "The Unique Presbyterian School System of New Mexico." *Journal of Presbyterian History* 49 (Fall 1971): 197–221.

Bass, Dorothy C. "Gideon Blackburn's Mission to the Indians: Christianization and Civilization." *Journal of Presbyterian History* 52 (Fall 1974): 203–26.

Beaver, R. Pierce. "Missionary Motivation through Three Centuries." In *Reinterpretation of American Church History,* edited by Jerald C. Brauer, 113–51. Chicago: University of Chicago Press, 1968.

Bender, Norman J. "A College Where One Ought to Be." *Colorado Magazine* 49 (Summer 1972): 196–218.

———. "Sheldon Jackson's Crusade." *Midwest Review* 4 (Spring 1982): 1–12.

Benkhart, Paula. "Changing Attitudes of Presbyterians toward Southern and Eastern European Immigrants, 1880–1914." *Journal of Presbyterian History* 49 (Fall 1971): 222–45.

Berkhoffer, Robert F., Jr. "Model Zions for the American Indian." *American Quarterly* 15 (Summer 1963): 176–90.

Billington, Ray A. "Anti-Catholic Propaganda and the Home Missionary Movement." *Mississippi Valley Historical Review* 22 (December 1935): 361–84.

Bitton, Davis. "Mormon Polygamy: A Review Article." *Journal of Mormon History* 4 (1977): 101–18.

Bitton, Davis and Gary Bunker. "Double Jeopardy: Visual Images of Mormon Women to 1914." *Utah Historical Quarterly* 46 (Spring 1978): 184–202.

Bloom, John Porter. "New Mexico Viewed by Americans." *New Mexico Historical Review* 34 (July 1959): 165–98.

Bowden, Henry W. "An Overview of Cultural Factors in the American Protestant Missionary Enterprise." In *American Missions: A Bicentennial Perspective,* edited by R. Pierce Beaver, 40–62. South Pasadena, Calif.: William Carey Library, 1977.

Brugge, David M. "Navajo Pre-History and History to 1850." In *Handbook of North American Indians.* 20 vols., edited by Alfonso Ortiz, 10:489–501. Washington, D.C.: Smithsonian Institution, 1979.

Buchanan, Fred S. "Education among the Mormons: Brigham Young and the Schools of Utah." *History of Education Quarterly* 22 (Winter 1982): 435–59.

Carter, Paul A. "Out West." In *Writers of the Purple Sage: Origins of a National Myth.* Tucson: Tucson Public Library and Arizona Historical Society, 1983.

Coleman, Michael. "Motivations of Indian Children at Missionary and U.S. Government Schools, 1860–1918: A Study through Published Reminiscences." *Montana: The Magazine of History* (Winter 1990): 46–55.

—————. "Not Race But Grace: Presbyterian Missionaries and American Indians." *Journal of American History* 67 (June 1980): 41–60.

Davies, George K. "A History of the Presbyterian Church in Utah." *Journal of Presbyterian Historical Society* 23 (December 1945): 228–48, 24 (January 1946): 44–68, 24 (March 1946): 147–81, 25 (January 1947): 46–67.

Davis, David B. "Some Themes of Counter-Subversion: An Analysis of Anti-Masonic, Anti-Catholic, and Anti-Mormon Literature." *Mississippi Valley Historical Review* 47 (1960): 205–24.

Egan, Fred. "Pueblos: Introduction." In *Handbook of North American Indians,* edited by Alfonso Ortiz, 9:224–35. Washington, D.C.: Smithsonian Institution, 1979.

Ellis, Florence H. "An Outline of Laguna Pueblo History and Social Organization." *Southwestern Journal of Anthropology* 15 (1959): 325–47.

Everett, Dianna. "The Public School Debate in New Mexico." *Arizona and the West* 26 (Summer 1984): 107–34.

Ezell, Paul. "History of the Pima." In *Handbook of North American Indians,* edited by Alfonso Ortiz, 10:149–60. Washington, D.C.: Smithsonian Institution, 1979.

Fisher, John H. "Primary and Secondary Education in the Presbyterian Church, U.S.A." *Journal of Presbyterian Historical Society* 24 (January 1946): 13–43.

Fontana, Bernard. "A Dedication to the Memory of Adolf A. F. Bandelier, 1840–1914." *Arizona and the West* 2 (1960): 1–5.

—————. "Pima and Papago: An Introduction." In *Handbook of North American Indians,* edited by Alfonso Ortiz, 10:125–36. Washington, D.C.: Smithsonian Institution, 1979.

Foote, Cheryl. "Alice Blake of Trementina: Mission Teacher in the Southwest." *Journal of Presbyterian History* 60 (Fall 1982): 228–43.

Forbes, Bruce David. "William Henry Roberts: Resistance to Change and Bureaucratic Adaptation." *Journal of Presbyterian History* 54 (Winter 1976): 405–21.

Forman, Charles W. "A History of Foreign Mission Theory in America." In *American Missions in Bicentennial Perspective,* edited by R. Pierce Beaver, 69–95. South Pasadena, Calif.: William Carey Library, 1977.

Goslin, Thomas S., Jr. "Henry Kendall: Missionaary Statesman." *Journal of Presbyterian Historical Society* 17 (June 1949): 69–87, 17 (September 1949): 161–78.

Handy, Robert. "American Religious Depression, 1925–1935." *Church History* 29 (1960): 3–16.

—————. "Charles L. Thompson: Presbyterian Architect of Cooperative Protestantism." *Journal of Presbyterian Historical Society* 33 (December 1955): 205–28.

Herberg, Will. "Religion and Education in America." In *Religious Perspectives in American Culture,* edited by James W. Smith and Leland Jamison, 11–51. Princeton: Princeton University Press, 1961.

Higham, John. "The Reorientation of American Culture in the 1880s. In John Higham, *Writing American History: Essays on Modern Scholarship,* 73–102. Bloomington: Indiana University Press, 1970.

Hinckley, Ted C. "The Presbyterian Leadership in Pioneer Alaska." *Journal of American History* 52 (1966): 742–56.

—————. "Sheldon Jackson and Benjamin Harrison: Presbyterians and the Administration of Alaska." *Pacific Northwest Quarterly* 54 (1963): 66–74.

—————. "Sheldon Jackson as Preserver of Alaska's Native Culture." *Pacific Historical Review* 33 (November 1964): 411–24.

—————. "Sheldon Jackson College: Historic Nucleus of the Presbyterian Enterprise in Alaska." *Journal of Presbyterian History* 49 (1971): 59–79.

—————. "Sheldon Jackson: Gilded Age Apostle." *Journal of the West* 23 (January 1984): 16–25.

Hough, Merrill. "Two School Systems in Conflict, 1867–1890." *Utah Historical Quarterly* 28 (April 1960): 112–28.

Hutchison, William R. "Modernism and Missions: The Liberal Search for an Exportable Christianity, 1875–1930." In *The Missionary Enterprise in China and America,* edited by John K. Fairbank, 110–31. Cambridge: Harvard University Press, 1974.

Ivins, Stanley. "Free Schools Come to Utah." *Utah Historical Quarterly* 22 (July 1954): 321–42.

—————. "Notes on Mormon Polygamy." *Western Humanities Review* 10 (Summer 1956): 309–21.

Johnson, Judith R. "An History of Embudo Hospital." *Menaul Historical Review* 10 (June 1983) 2–3.

—————. "A Mission to the Navajos." *Menaul Historical Review* 10 (October 1983): 2–3.

Keller, Rosemary Skinner. "Lay Women in the Protestant Tradition." In *Women and Religion in America.* Vol. 1, *The Nineteenth Century,* edited by Rosemary Radford Ruether and Rosemary Skinner Keller, 242–53. San Francisco: Harper and Row, 1981.

Lacy, James M. "New Mexican Women in Early American Writings." *New Mexico Historical Review* 34 (January 1959): 41–51.

Lankford, John. "The Impact of the Religious Depression on Protestant Benevolence." *Journal of Presbyterian History* 42 (June 1964): 104–23.

Logue, Larry M. "A Time of Marriage: Monogamy and Polygamy in a Utah Town." *Journal of Mormon History* 11 (1984).

Luzbetak, Louis J. "Two Centuries of Cultural Adaptation in American Church Action." In *American Missions: A Bicentennial Perspective,* edited by R. Pierce Beaver, 332–53. South Pasadena, Calif.: William Carey Library, 1977.

Lyon, Thomas E. "Religious Activities and Development in Utah, 1847–1910." *Utah Historical Quarterly* 35 (Fall 1967): 292–306.

McCutcheon, James M. "The Missionary and Diplomat in China." *Journal of Presbyterian History* 41 (December 1963): 224–36.

Madison, James. "Reformers and the Rural Church." *Journal of American History* 73 (December 1986): 645–68.

Matthews, F. H. "The Revolt against Americanism: Cultural Pluralism and Cultural Relativism as an Ideology of Liberation." *Canadian Review of American Studies* 1 (Spring 1970): 4–31.

Mead, Sidney. "Denominationalism: The Shape of Protestant America." *Church History* 23 (December 1954): 291–320.

Moore, Edgar. "The Bierkempers, Navajos, and the Ganado Presbyterian Mission." *American Presbyterians* 64 (Summer 1986): 125–36.

Noggle, Burl. "Anglo Observers of the Southwest Borderlands, 1825–1900: The Rise of a Concept." *Arizona and the West* 1 (Summer 1959): 105–31.

Parry, John H. "Plural Society in the Southwest: A Historical Comment." In *Plural Society in the Southwest,* edited by Edward Spicer and R. H. Thompson, 299–320. Tucson: University of Arizona Press, 1972.

Penfield, Janet Harbison. "Women in the Presbyterian Church: An Historical Overview." *Journal of Presbyterian History* 55 (Summer 1977): 107–24.

Pool, Ithiel de Sola. "Scratches on Social Science: Images, Symbols, and Stereotypes." In *the Mixing of Peoples: Problems of Identity and Ethnicity,* edited by Robert Rothberg, 27–36. N.p.: Greylock, Inc., 1978.

Reherd, Herbert. "An Outline History of the Protestant Churches of Utah." In *Utah Centennial History,* edited by Wain Sutton. Chicago: Lewis Historical Publications, 1949.

Reifsnyder, Richard W. "Presbyterian Reunion: Reorganization and Expansion in the Late-Nineteenth Century." *American Presbyterians* 64 (Spring 1986): 27–38.

Scholes, France V. "Troublous Times in New Mexico, 1659–1670." *New Mexico Historical Review* 12 (April, October 1937), 16 (January, April, July 1941).

Scott, Anne Firor. "What, Then, Is the American: This New Woman." *Journal of American History* 65 (December 1978): 679–703.

"Sheldon Jackson Invades the Rocky Mountains." *Journal of Presbyterian History* 37 (June 1959): 122–28.

Shipps, Jan. "Brigham Young and His Times: A Continuing Force in Mormonism." *Journal of the West* 23 (January 1984): 48–54.

——. "The Principle Revoked: A Look at the Demise of Plural Marriage." *Journal of Mormon History* 11 (1984): 65–77.

Simmons, Marc. "History of Pueblo-Spanish Relations to 1821." In *Handbook of*

North American Indians, edited by Alfonso Ortiz, 9:178–93. Washington, D.C.: Smithsonian Institution, 1979.

————. "History of the Pueblos since 1821." In *Handbook of North American Indians,* edited by Alfonso Ortiz, 9:206–23. Washington, D.C.: Smithsonian Institution, 1979.

Smith, Timothy L. "Progressivism and Education, 1880–1900." *Harvard Educational Review* 31 (Summer 1961): 168–93.

Stahler, Michael L. "William Speer: Champion of California's Chinese." *Journal of Presbyterian History* 48 (Summer 1970): 113–29.

Thompkins, Robert. "Presbyterian Religious Education among Negroes, 1864–1891." *Journal of Presbyterian Historical Society* 29 (September 1951): 145–71.

Topping, Gary. "The Ogden Academy: A Gentile Assault on Mormon Country." *Journal of the West* 23 (January 1984): 37–47.

Trennert, Robert. "Peacefully If They Will, Forcibly If They Must: The Phoenix Indian School." *Journal of Arizona History* 20 (Autumn 1979): 297–322.

Trulio, Beverly. "Anglo-American Attitudes toward New Mexican Women." *Journal of the West* 12 (April 1973): 229–39.

Tyack, David. "The Kingdom of God and the Common School: Protestant Ministers and the Educational Awakening of the West." *Harvard Educational Review* 36 (Fall 1966): 447–469.

————. "Onward Christian Soldiers: Religion in the American Common School." In *History of Education,* edited by Paul Nash, 212–55. New York: Random House, 1970.

Underwood, Grant. "Revisioning Mormon History." *Pacific Historical Review* 55 (August 1986): 403–26.

Varg, Paul A. "Motives in Protestant Missions, 1890–1917." *Church History* 23 (March 1954): 68–82.

Webster, John C. B. "Introduction to American Presbyterians in India and Pakistan." *Journal of Presbyterian History* 62 (Fall 1984): 193–94.

Welter, Barbara. "The Cult of True Womanhood: 1820–1860." *American Quarterly* 18 (1966): 151–75.

————. " 'She Hath Done What She Could': Protestant Women's Missionary Careers in Nineteenth-Century America." In *Women in American Religion,* edited by Janet Wilson Jones, 111–25. Philadelphia: University of Pennsylvania Press, 1980.

Papers, Theses, and Dissertations

Atkins, Jane. "Who Will Educate? The Schooling Question in Territorial New Mexico." Ph.D. diss., University of New Mexico, 1982.

Bailey, Alvin K. "The Strategy of Sheldon Jackson in Opening the West for National Missions." Ph.D. diss., Yale University, 1948.

Bender, Norman J. "Crusade of the Blue Banner: Rocky Mountain Presbyterianism, 1870–1900." Ph.D. diss., University of Colorado, 1971.

Benge, Reba. "Benjamin M. Thomas: Career in the Southwest, 1870–1892." Ph.D. diss., University of New Mexico, 1979.

Buchanan, Fred S. "Religion and Secular Challenge in Utah Schools." Paper presented at Annual Meeting of Western History Association, Sacramento, Calif., October 1985.

Buck, Lucius E. "An Inquiry into the History of Presbyterian Educational Missions in New Mexico." M.A. thesis, University of Southern California, 1949.

Foote, Cheryl. "'Let Her Works Praise Her': Women's Experiences in the Southwest, 1846–1912." Ph.D. diss., University of New Mexico, 1985.

Hagan, Maxine W. "An Educational History of the Pima and Papago Indians." Ed.D. dissertation, University of Arizona, 1949.

Hamilton, John M. "A History of Presbyterian Work among the Pima and Papago Indians of Arizona." M.A. thesis, University of Arizona, 1948.

Hessel, Deiter. "The Social Gospel in the Presbyterian Church." 1959. Presbyterian Historical Society. Typescript.

Huebert, Lois. "A History of Presbyterian Church Schools in New Mexico." M.A. thesis, University of New Mexico, 1962.

Loo, Harold Y. S. "The History of New Jersey–Logan Academy, 1878–1934." M.S. thesis, Utah State Agricultural College, 1954.

Lyon, Thomas E. "Evangelical Protestant Mission Activities in Mormon-dominated Areas, 1865–1900." Ph.D. diss., University of Utah, 1962.

McKinney, Lillie. "A History of Albuquerque Indian School." M.A. thesis, University of New Mexico, 1943.

Rathjen, Milton R. "The Distribution of Major Non-Mormon Denominations in Utah." M.S. thesis, University of Utah, 1966.

Shipps, Jan. "From Sartyr to Saint: American Attitudes toward the Mormons, 1860–1960." Paper presented at 1973 Annual Meeting of Organization of American Historians. Copy in L.D.S. Archives, Salt Lake City.

Stapleton, Ernest. "The History of Baptist Missions in New Mexico, 1846–1860." M.A. thesis, University of New Mexico, 1954.

Taylor, Bruce L. "Presbyterians and 'the People': A History of Presbyterian Missions and Ministries to the Navajos." Ph.D. diss., Union Theological Seminary, 1988.

Walker, Randi. "Protestantism in the Sangre de Cristos: Factors in the Growth and Decline of Hipsanic Protestant Churches in Northern New Mexico and Southern Colorado, 1850–1920." Ph.D. diss., Claremont Graduate School, 1983.

Wankier, Carl. "History of Presbyterian Schools in Utah." M.A. thesis, University of Utah, 1968.

Warner, Michael. "Protestant Missionary Work with the Navajo Indians, 1846–1912." Ph.D. diss., University of New Mexico, 1977.

Weatherby, Lela. "A Study of the Early Years of the Presbyterian Work with the Spanish-speaking People of New Mexico and Colorado and Its Development from 1850–1920." M.A. thesis, Presbyterian College of Christian Education, 1942.

Newspapers and Periodicals

Home Mission Monthly, 1886–1923.
La Aurora, 1900–1915.

Presbyterian Home Missions, 1882–83.
Presbyterian Home Missionary, 1883–86.
Rocky Mountain Presbyterian, 1872–82.

Interviews

Rev. Roe B. Lewis, interview with author, May 27, 1985.
Rev. Jaime O. Quinones, interview with author, June 22, 1987.

Index

Presbyterian Historical Society Publications

1. *The Presbyterian Enterprise* by M. W. Armstrong, L. A. Loetscher and C. A. Anderson (Westminster Press, 1956. Paperback reprinted for P.H.S., 1963 & 1976)
*2. *Presbyterian Ministry in American Culture* by E. A. Smith (Westminster Press, 1962)
3. *Journals of Charles Beatty, 1762-1769* edited by Guy S. Klett (Pennsylvania State University Press, 1962)
*4. *Hoosier Zion: The Presbyterians in Early Indiana* by L. C. Rudolph (Yale University Press, 1963)
*5. *Presbyterianism in New York State* by Robert Hastings Nichols, edited and completed by James Hastings Nichols (Westminster Press, 1963)
6. *Scots Breed and Susquehanna* by Hubertis M. Cummings (University of Pittsburgh Press, 1964)
*7. *Presbyterians and the Negro:a History* by Andrew E. Murray (Presbyterian Historical Society, 1966)
*8. *A Bibliography of American Presbyterianism during the Colonial Period* by Leonard J. Trinterud (Presbyterian Historical Society, 1968)
9. *George Bourne and "The Book and Slavery Irreconcilable"* by John W. Christie and Dwight L. Dumond (Historical Society of Delaware and Presbyterian Historical Society, 1969)
10. *The Skyline Synod: Presbyterianism in Colorado and Utah* by Andrew E. Murray (Synod of Colorado/Utah, 1971)
*11. *The Life and Writings of Francis Makemie* edited by Boyd S. Schlenther (Presbyterian Historical Society, 1971)
12. *A Younger Church in Search of Maturity: Presbyterianism in Brazil from 1910 to 1959* by Paul Pierson (Trinity University Press, 1974)
*13. *Presbyterians in the South,* vols. 2 and 3, by Ernest Trice Thompson (John Knox Press, 1973)
*14. *Ecumenical Testimony* by John McNeill and James H. Nichols (Westminster Press, 1974)
15. *Iglesia Presbiteriana: A History of Presbyterians and Mexican Americans in the Southwest* by R. Douglas Brackenridge and Francisco O. Garcia-Treto (Trinity University Press, rev. 1987)
16. *The Rise and Decline of Education for Black Presbyterians* by Inex M. Parker (Trinity University Press, 1977)
17. *Minutes of the Presbyterian Church in America, 1706-1788* edited by Guy S. Klett (Presbyterian Historical Society, 1977)
*18. *Eugene Carson Blake: Prophet with Portfolio* by R. Douglas Brackenridge (Seabury Press, 1978)
19. *Prisoners of Hope: A Search for Mission, 1815-1822* by Marjorie Barnhart (Presbyterian Historical Society, 1980)
20. *From Colonialism to World Community: The Church's Pilgrimage* by John Coventry Smith (Geneva Press, 1982)
21. *Facing the Enlightenment and Pietism: Archibald Alexander and the Founding of Princeton Theological Seminary* by Lefferts A. Loetscher (Greenwood Press, 1983)
22. *Presbyterian Women in America: Two Centuries of a Quest for Status* by Lois A. Boyd and R. Douglas Brackenridge (Greenwood Press, 1983)
23. *Kentucky Presbyterians* by Louis B. Weeks (John Knox Press, 1983)
24. *Merging Mission and Unity* by Donald Black (Geneva Press, 1986)
25. *Gilbert Tennent, Son of Thunder* by Milton J. Coalter, Jr. (Greenwood Press, 1986)
26. *A Guide to Foreign Missionary Manuscripts in the Presbyterian Historical Society* by Frederick J. Heuser, Jr. (Greenwood Press, 1988)
27. *The United Synod of the South: The Southern New School Presbyterian Church* by Harold M. Parker, Jr. (Greenwood Press, 1988)
28. *Presbyterians and Pensions: The Roots and Growth of Pensions in the Presbyterian Church (U.S.A.)* by R. Douglas Brackenridge and Lois A. Boyd (John Knox Press, 1988)
29. *Guide to the Manuscript Collection of the Presbyterian Church, U.S.* by Robert Benedetto (Greenwood Press, 1990)
30. *Historians' Handbook of the Presbyterian Church (U.S.A.)* edited by Carolyn Atkins (Presbyterian Historical Society, second edition, 1992)
31. *Presbyterian Missions and Cultural Interaction in the Far Southwest, 1850-1950* by Mark T. Banker (University of Illinois Press, 1993)

*Out of print.